Dave Says, 'Don't Worry!'

A Practical and Prayerful Guide

David Albans

Broad Place
publishing
broadplacepublishing.co.uk

First published in Great Britain in 2025

Broad Place Publishing

https://broadplacepublishing.co.uk

email: admin@broadplacepublishing.co.uk

Paperback ISBN 9781915034700
Ebook ISBN 9781915034717

A catalogue record for this book is available from the British Library.

Contents

Introduction 1
What is worry? 6
Facts about Worry 13
A Six-Point Strategy 26
- Personal 27
- People 46
- Praise 55
- Pay Attention 65
- Pray 74
- Practice 83

The Concluding Result: Peace 93

Introduction

> 'Happiness is as a butterfly, which, when pursued is beyond our grasp but which, if you sit down quietly, may alight upon you.'
>
> Nathaniel Hawthorne

I used to be a worrier.

If God hadn't intervened in my life, I would have qualified for an honour's degree in worry.

One of my earliest memories in life (perhaps as a six-year-old) is lying awake in bed worrying and crying about the thought of dying. Not something most children of that age worry about.

I recall considering what it might be like to become

Nothing*

*to not exist any longer

because that's what I thought 'being dead' might be like.

This idea scared me.

All through my early and teenage years, I worried frequently:

about being 'on time' for things,

making mistakes,

getting good school results,

not being allowed home after a minor operation,

and much more besides.

Worry still comes knocking at the door of my mind, but I have found a way to deal with it.

I want you to know that I come with some experience. But the truth is: we are all experienced in worry.

It affects all of us at some point or other.

For some, it can seem like a constant frame of mind, overpowering and debilitating.

Worry can

- Make us ill
- Affect our relationships
- Prevent us from sensing any joy or peace in life.

Although worries can feel isolating, we are far from being alone in our worries.

Even ancient King Solomon wrote:

> 'What do people get for all their toil and anxious striving with which they labour under the sun? All their days their work is grief and pain; even at night their minds do not rest.'
>
> Ecclesiastes 2:22–23

It is my prayer that as you read this book, you will start walking the path towards happiness or, better still, find the peace that will replace any worries you have.

This little book is not about transferring information (as if knowledge alone will solve our issues). It is designed to be a guide. As you explore this book and reflect, I hope you will find it is **personal, practical and prayerful.**

I'm going to share with you a spiritual strategy for alleviating worry.

The solution is not easy.

It will take effort because it involves *trust*.

For many of us, trust does not come easily. I'm not asking you to trust ***me!*** No. I hope that as you read this guide, you will be able to place trust in a ***God*** who loves you and cares for you.

God wants to free ***you*** from the burden of worry, as He did for me.

A tiny grain of trust will do.

If even this seems too big a leap for you at this moment, can I encourage you to read on anyway?

I think you'll discover that the suggestions made remain reasonable, practical and (most of all) helpful.

I am an ordinary person who's been in your shoes. However, I'm not a healthcare professional.

If worrying is affecting your daily life or causing you distress, please see your doctor. The advice given in this book can be used at any time, but it is not a replacement for professional medical assistance.

What is Worry?

Let's start by understanding what worry is. Most dictionaries come up with words like

They explain that worrying is thinking about problems (or potential problems) in a way that makes you unhappy or frightened.

But being worried about something is not the same as being concerned. Being concerned is not usually a negative thing. Here are some differences between worry and concern that I've found helpful:

Concern is born out of LOVE

It is right and proper to be concerned about
some things. For example, when my mum
was ill, it was a loving thing to be
concerned for her well-being
and care. To have had no
concern at all would
have been, by anyone's
standards,
rather cold
and insensitive.

Worry is born out of FEAR

Worry is driven by fear.
It is like the time I worried
that my boss would misrepresent
me to management in such a way that
my professionally integrity and reputation
would be seriously damaged. It was all about
my fears.

Concern is focused on OTHERS

Concern is driven by and directed
towards the benefit of others.
Like my care for my mum.

Worry is focused on OURSELVES

Worry is all about
us and our feelings.
My worries about my boss
really arose from my own vulnerabilities
and my mistrust of others.

Concern is CONSTRUCTIVE

It seeks a solution.

In the case of my mum, the concern for her health prompted research. How best could I care for her, and what support could I call upon?

Worry is DESTRUCTIVE

It will eat us up inside.

Worry is like a cancer; the more we entertain it, the greater it grows. It sits in our stomachs and won't let us forget it's there. What if we act upon our worry, only to find that our worry was unfounded in the first place?

Concern will PROMPT ACTION

When we are concerned enough about something, we want to do something about it. If there's injustice, we search for a way to put things right. If we are concerned about someone's health or a relationship, we might seek help or act ourselves to bring relief.

Worry leaves us feeling POWERLESS

We feel we can't change things and yet the issues remain, whether or not they are real or imagined. We can't control all things and therefore we imagine the worst.

Concern is based on what is REAL

Someone's diagnosis, or their bank balance.
Redundancy, separation, bereavement...
A real situation is being presented;
not simply the fear
of a situation.

Worry is based on IFS and MAYBES

Worry thrives on fear:
on the potential for something
to go badly. What if the doctor starts
his sentence with 'I'm very sorry to say...'
or the next round of redundancies affects me?

Is worry helpful?

The simple answer is ***NO.***
It has little or no value.

Yet, we worry about so many things, don't we?

Money

relationships

FAMILY

Jobs

possessions

HEALTH

But when worries are not fact-based, then they should be **resisted**.

We will look at six steps to help us do this later in the book. Meanwhile, I think it's useful to learn more about worry.

Facts About Worry

When we **recognise** what worry is, we can put it into its proper **perspective** and take away some, or all, of its power.

It's like the times when we receive a scam phone call; as soon as we recognise it for what it is, we find it easy to end the call.

So, let's dig deeper and note what worry is. These facts will help us shut down worries before they take hold.

1. Worry accomplishes nothing

Ex-Cricketer Glenn Turner once said,

> 'Worry is like a rocking chair. It gives you something to do but gets you nowhere.'

When it comes to situations that we face, there are two types:

Those we have some control over	**Those we have no control over**
We don't need to worry about these, because we have control over them.	It is futile to worry about these, because we have no control over them.
We have the power to change things.	Worrying is not going to make any difference to the outcome.

Jesus Christ said,

> 'Can any one of you by worrying add a single hour to your life?'
>
> Matthew 6:27

Some matters (and certainly some big matters) are outside of our control and worry achieves nothing.

In fact, the worrying itself could be detrimental to us in terms of mental and physical health.

2. Worry exaggerates a problem

It is said that worry gives a small thing a big shadow. The shadow of a hand (configured in the right way) can appear like a monster on a big screen.

Worries have the ability to project matters bigger than they really are.

Sometimes, what we worry about isn't as big as we think. As George Eliot said,

> **Rule #1: Don't sweat the small stuff.**
> **Rule #2: It's all small stuff.**

It's important that we put our worries into ***perspective***.

It may help to consider our worries in the context of our whole lives.

When we look at the bigger picture, the **small stuff** becomes more evident. We can then see how important, or rather unimportant, our worries are.

THINK: When I'm old, and I look back on my life, how significant will my current worry be?

Will it even be remembered?

If someone were to make a film of my life *(Could they get Ryan Gosling to play me, please?)* how much screen time would this worry take up?

I suspect, for most of us, the most severe times of worry would only be glimpsed for a moment, if at all.

3. Things we worry about often don't happen

Mark Twain said,

> 'I am an old man and have known a great many troubles, but most of them never happened.'

In a similar vein, U.S. President Coolidge said,

> 'If you see ten troubles coming down the road, you can be sure that nine will run into the ditch before they reach you.'

We tend to focus our worries on the ***potential*** for something to go badly, but rarely take account of the ***likelihood*** of it happening or its probability.

For example, we might worry about missing a train connection when statistics tell us that 92% of trains are punctual. We tend to fear the worst rather than consider the more likely alternatives.

4. Worries are temporary and fleeting

Nearly everything we worry about is temporary and forgettable.

We worry, the bad thing happens (or generally does not) and then we move on.

There are exceptions, of course, and it is right to acknowledge that major incidents in life, such as a terminal diagnosis or long-term unemployment, can cause worries of a more enduring nature.

However, it is more common that the everyday worries we face are here today and gone tomorrow. If you want to test this theory, try to recall what you were worried about a year ago, or perhaps even a month ago?

Worries tend to come and go with some frequency. So perhaps we should not pay so much attention to them?

5. Worry is Driven by Fear

We've already mentioned this, but it's worth spending a bit more time on. We fear all sorts of things: wrong decisions, taking risks, damaged relationships, mistakes and possible bad consequences.

What do you fear?

French philosopher, Montaigne, said,

> 'He who fears he shall suffer, already suffers what he fears.'

Like worry itself, fears are often based on possibilities rather than probabilities. Worry and fear do not help us in our situation. If anything, they make us suffer longer or unnecessarily.

In the Bible, God repeatedly says,

It is one of the most repeated messages.

God is aware that we can be fearful, but encourages us to trust in Him. He reassures us that we need not fear.

Why?

Because God is for us*

*He is on our side.

When our son, Graham, was about 4 years old, I remember walking down a footpath with him.

Beside the footpath was a low wall which he wanted to walk along. He climbed up and we continued our walk, his hand in mine.

The footpath started to dip away in a decline while the top of the wall remained at the same level.

The further we went, the higher Graham became in relation to me, until I was reaching above my head just to hold his hand.

At the end of the wall, his feet were level with the top of my head. Either we could walk all the way back for him to dismount the wall (which neither of us were inclined to do) or he could trust me and jump into my arms.

There was no hesitation in Graham's decision, and he duly leaped into my receiving arms, trusting me to catch him even though we had never practiced this.

He knew Dad was there to keep him safe and could be relied on.

God is our **perfect** and **heavenly** Father who loves us more than we can ever grasp.

Are you willing to trust a God like this? Are you willing to trust yourself into His safe and protective arms?

The book of Romans tells us,

> 'Neither death nor life, neither angels nor demons, neither the present nor the future, nor any powers, neither height nor depth, nor anything else in all creation, will be able to separate us from the love of God that is in Christ Jesus our Lord.'
>
> Romans 8:38-39

God demonstrated his love for us fully through the life, death and resurrection of His only Son, Jesus. If you want to know more about this, you can find Jesus' story by picking up a Bible and flicking to the books of Matthew, Mark, Luke or John.

Maybe ask a Christian that you know to read it with you?

6. Worry is a choice

In the 1994 film, *Marvellous*, Toby Jones plays Neil Baldwin in a true story about a man with learning difficulties who lived life to the full.

At different times, he became a circus clown, a lay preacher, a university welfare officer and manager to the 'Neil Baldwin Football Club'. When he decided to do something, he made it happen, even making links with Gary Lineker and Labour MP Tony Benn along the way.

Eventually he fulfilled a life-long dream of working for his beloved Stoke City Football Club as a kit man under manager Lou Macari. His positive outlook on everything endeared him to everyone he met.

In the film, there is a scene when Lou Macari asks Neil why he is always so happy. Neil answers,

> 'I always wanted to be happy, so I decided to be.'

Neil made the link that many of us miss: the connection between our wills and our emotions. He made the decision to be happy and let that drive his emotions.

Like happiness was Neil's choice, worry is also a choice. Worry can be a mindset: a way of thinking that can become established and hard to budge.

But it is possible to change. In his letter to the Church in Rome, St. Paul wrote,

> 'Do not conform to the pattern of this world but be transformed by the renewing of your mind.'
>
> Romans 12:2

But how can this transformation and renewal take place? If we need strength of mind to make the right choices, how do we get that strength? The Bible points us to the answer.

The Lord is near. Do not be anxious about anything, but in every situation, by prayer and petition, with thanksgiving, present your requests to God. And the peace of God, which transcends all understanding, will guard your hearts and your minds in Christ Jesus.

Finally, brothers and sisters, whatever is true, whatever is noble, whatever is right, whatever is pure, whatever is lovely, whatever is admirable – if anything is excellent or praiseworthy think about such things. Whatever you have learned or received or heard from me, or seen in me – put it into practice. And the God of peace will be with you.

Philippians 4:5-9

A Six-Point Strategy

When I look closely at the verses we just read from the Bible, I see within them an approach to worry and a strategy for overcoming it.*

It's this strategy I have used (and recognised in others) that has been so valuable and freeing.

Realising we need a strategy, and having one in place, is important in helping us form new ways of thinking and behaviour.

It sets us up nicely to begin taking charge of our worries instead of letting them control us.

So, pat yourself on the back for reaching this point. Now let's build on this and take a look at this strategy.

* If you skipped over them, why not flick the page back and read them again? They're going to be important...

Personal
People
Praise
Pay Attention
Pray
Practice

Personal

The first part of the strategy is recognising that God is a personal God. When I mention God, you may think of Him as some old man sitting on the clouds, or a Marvel superhero. Or maybe my earlier talk of Him being like a parent brought up bad memories, bad connotations?

Perhaps you haven't thought about God much at all. If any of these things are true, you probably don't believe the statement that God is a personal God. But I do, and this belief is an essential part of my strategy for defeating worry.

I'll aim to demonstrate it with four truths about God: He is **near**, He is **powerful**, He **cares** and He **loves**.

1. God is Near

'The Lord is near.'[1]

The Bible passage on which this strategy is built begins with a short but powerful statement: The Lord [God] is near.

It's an amazing thought, that the Creator of the universe, and the whole of mankind, should be close to you and me. You may not feel it, nor maybe believe it, but it is still true.

God is near and loves us, deeply.

It's personal.

There is a well-known story about a man walking along a beach with God; both leaving footprints.

In the story, they watch scenes from the man's life projected onto the sky. The man looks back and notices footprints in the sand for each scene. At the end, he questions God about something he noticed and found troubling. At

---

1 Philippians 4:5

the lowest and saddest times in his life, the man saw only one set of footprints.

Why had God abandoned him, when he needed Him most?

God responds by reassuring the man of His never-ending, unbreakable love, and explains that there were only one set of footprints because, in those times of suffering, God had carried him.

❊ Take time to pause and reflect on this story. ❊

2. God is Powerful

A repeated promise of God in the Bible is, 'Do not be afraid; I am with you'.[2] Most famously, we read in Matthew 28:20 of Jesus telling His disciples,

> 'I am with you always, to the very end of the age.'

[2] See Genesis 26:24; Isaiah 43:5; Jeremiah 1:8. There are more!

Christians believe that Jesus is God, so if this is true, **God is with us always**.

If God is with us, this leads us to the question: Is He big enough to deal with our worries? I've found out through personal experience that He is, and I hope you will discover this too.

God's story, told in the Bible, demonstrates that God is big enough to deal with rebellion, famine, tyrannical governments, slavery, suicidal thoughts, ill-health, miscarriages of justice, betrayal, all kinds of wrongdoing and death itself.

It is both reasonable and safe to believe that God is big enough to deal with our worries.

Jesus said,

> 'Come to me, all you who are weary and burdened, and I will give you rest.'
>
> Matthew 11:28

It's a simple offer, but one we may find hard to accept, however amazing it seems.

We are so used to looking with suspicion on offers that appear to be too good to be true. But this offer is both good and true.

In fact, Jesus longs for us to put our trust in Him; not just with our worries but with everything else in our lives too: our relationships, our possessions, our work.

What's more, He has the power to give us rest!

By now, I hope you are getting the message. We are not alone. A powerful God is on our side.

3. God Cares

In Matthew's gospel, we find Jesus giving important time to the issue of worry. He said,

> Therefore, I tell you, do not worry about your life, what you will eat or drink; or about your body, what you will wear. Is not life more than food, and the body more than clothes?

Look at the birds of the air; they do not sow or reap or store away in barns, and yet your heavenly Father [God] feeds them. Are you not much more valuable than they?

Can any one of you by worrying add a single hour to your life?... Therefore, do not worry about tomorrow, for tomorrow will worry about itself. Each day has enough trouble of its own.'

Matthew 6:25-34, 34

Pause to reflect on those words.

- Can you identify with any of the examples of worry Jesus talked about?
- What does God do for the birds?
- How do you compare to the birds?
- So, what do you think God will do for you?
- How does this make you feel?

Did you notice that Jesus doesn't deny we'll have troubles? He knows we will!

But Jesus' strategy for not worrying is remembering what we are in God's sight:

Valuable

Peter reaffirms this:

> 'Cast all your anxiety on him [God] because he cares for you.'
>
> 1 Peter 5:7

In the original language, the word **care** signifies care with deepest affection, and a watching over us.

God's love for us is deep and amazing.

It is also worth noting that we are not encouraged to tell our worries to God or show them to Him. We are encouraged to **cast** them:

Throw them off,
Get rid,
Shed,
Hurl,
Eject.

This suggests we should not, in any fashion, seek to keep hold of these worries. We will need to put our minds and wills into operation; make a conscious decision to let go and leave the worries behind.

With God's help, it is possible to do this. Can I encourage you to seek His help in prayer?

Here's a prayer that you might use:

Father God,

I believe that You care for me.
I want to throw off my worry, but I need Your help to let go of it. Please give me Your strength. *(Pause, taking a moment to receive this.)*

I now release into Your hands my worries concerning *(freely share your thoughts and feelings with God).*

Please free me from these things in Jesus' name.

Thank You for Your love.

If we dare to trust God, we will find that He does care and does not abandon us. He is on our side.

God is **for us** and **with us**.

The testimony of those who have trusted Jesus is that He does not let us down. His promises are trustworthy and true.

4. God Loves

Jesus tells a story to help illustrate how strong God's love is for us. It is often referred to as the story of the prodigal son, but it could equally refer to a prodigal daughter:

(From Luke 15)

A son asked for his inheritance from his father early. His dad wasn't even ill, let alone dead! The son's request was deeply dishonouring and extremely hurtful to the father.

It would be same today, wouldn't it? What reaction do you think there would be if a son asked his parents for half the sale price of the family home and wanted it there and then?

Despite this, the father granted the request and the son left the family home with money in his pocket.

The son then went to a far-away place where he squandered his wealth in wild behaviour. Like many young people, one can imagine him spending it on 'wine, women and song' or 'sex, drugs and rock'n'roll.'

After a time, the money ran out and a famine hit. He managed to find work feeding pigs. By this stage, he was so desperate and hungry that he wanted to eat the pig food.

He came to his senses, and decided the only way out of his mess would be to return to his father.

Realising his unworthiness to be called a son, he would seek to be a servant. Then the most moving thing happens...

'While the son was still a long way off, his father saw him and was filled with compassion for him; he ran to his son, threw his arms round him and kissed him.'

Despite the hurt the father had experienced, he had been looking out for the possible return of his son. I can imagine him peering into the distance as often as he could, hoping to see his son approaching on the horizon. Then one day, he returned!

Instead of being angry and bitter, the father was full of love and joy. So much so, that he sprinted out to meet his boy.

The humbled son sought to return as his father's servant, but the father would have none of that. The father didn't want a new servant, he wanted to celebrate the return of his son, who he thought he had lost forever. The love and forgiveness were complete, and then, the party began.

This story illustrates our relationship with God. It reflects the fact that all of us have to some degree or other gone our own way: lived as if our Father God either didn't exist or didn't matter.

If we are honest with ourselves, we also mess up. We find that we have either damaged someone else, or at least damaged ourselves

by some of the choices we have made. The Bible calls this 'sin'.
But the good news is that God, like the father in the story, waits and longs for us to return to Him, and there is no sin He won't forgive.

Nothing can separate us from God's love. Remember that verse?

> 'Neither death nor life, neither angels nor demons, neither the present nor the future, nor any powers, neither height nor depth, nor anything else in all creation, will be able to separate us from the love of God that is in Christ Jesus our Lord.'
>
> Romans 8:38-39

As you reflect on the above, perhaps you have felt stirred inside, perhaps moved emotionally and prompted to respond? If so, that's probably God's Holy Spirit speaking to you.

Jesus calls the Holy Spirit, 'The Comforter,'[3] which is great description! He's the one who comes to comfort you when you are worried and you ask for God's help.

Perhaps you feel it is time to admit to God that you have lived like the prodigal child and need to return to a loving and perfect heavenly Father?

You can seek His forgiveness and ask for a fresh start. And you don't need any special equipment, or to be in a church. You can do it right now, because He is with you!

If that's you, here is a short prayer you may like to use:

---

[3] John 14:26 (KJV)

Dear God,

Thank You that You love me and have always loved me. Thank You that You sent Jesus.

Thank You that after He died, You raised Jesus back to life. This shows that the promise of eternal life is true.

I am sorry for all the things I have said and thought and done that have hurt others, myself and You. Please forgive me.

I want to know You better and live Your way. Please fill me now with Your Holy Spirit.

I pray this in the name of Jesus.

Something Practical

Get hold of a pebble or two to represent your worries. If you have access to the sea, a lake, a river or pond (or even a bucket of water or bath), drop or throw them in. As you do, be prayerful and offer those worries to God.

You may find that, as you contemplate a particular worry, you find it difficult to let go of the pebble. Take your time and seek the strength of the Holy Spirit. Be aware of that inner struggle but, when you are ready, make the choice that will help bring freedom. Be mindful that as you 'cast your worries,' God cares for you.

Margaret's Story

I learned about trusting God in a situation when I was leaving Canada after nearly 20 years to return to the UK.

My house had been on the market for 3 months and although there had been a lot of interest, there had been no offers. Time was getting short.

I was planning to visit friends in Australia and New Zealand before coming home. Flights were booked. Furniture ready to be sold. Trunks ready and labelled. But still no buyer for the house.

I went to see a good and trusted Christian friend who asked, 'What do you want us to pray for?'

'Well, to sell the house, of course,' I replied.

'What do you think God wants for you?'

'I know He wants me to go back to England. I'm sure about that,' I insisted.

'Then, don't you think He knows about selling the house?'

'Well, yes, I suppose so. But does He understand that I'm really worried about this? What shall I do if it doesn't sell?'

'Can you trust Him to find the right buyer for your house in his timing?'

'But there's only 2 weeks before I leave! Maybe God's timing and mine are different.'

'God knows your needs,' my friend reassured me. 'Trust Him. Present your request to Him. Cast all anxiety on Him.'

I promised to try, and we prayed together.

One week to go, and I'm trying to trust God. A phone call comes from the estate agent:

> We have a buyer for your house. They came to see it 2 months ago but something happened which meant they were unable to make an offer at that time. They really like it and are offering more if they can have some of the furniture as well!

Thank you, dear Lord!

'Cast all your anxiety on him because he cares for you...'

Prayer, petition, thanksgiving: yes, God had it all in hand. I just had to learn to trust Him.

People

Naomi had good reason to worry. She was living in a foreign land amongst a people who had traditionally been hostile to her race.

Forced there by famine, she had lost her husband and both her sons. In a time and culture where men were viewed as the family providers, this put her in great difficulty. All she had for comfort were her two daughters-in-law, both foreigners.

The uncertainties, fears and worries must have been overwhelming. Naomi even wanted to be known as *Mara*: a name meaning bitter. She felt that God had made her life a misery.

Hearing that the famine was over in her own land, Naomi decided to go back there. Her worries would have mounted up: What would it be like after her time away? Where would she live? Would she find work or a way to survive? Who would care for her as she got older?

You may have faced, or be facing, similar issues.

So, what got Naomi through her worries?

It was her daughter-in-law, Ruth. Ruth listened, cared and showed great kindness to Naomi, even to the point of saying,

> 'Where you go I will go, and where you stay I will stay. Your people will be my people and your God my God.'
>
> Ruth 1:16

That was enough to spur Naomi on.

Worry can isolate us. It can make us introspective. We can exclude others from our thoughts and feelings, hide our worries and shut down.

What Naomi needed was someone who would journey alongside her, someone who would **listen** and **not judge**, someone she could **trust** and **respect**, who would encourage her and offer a new perspective.

Can you think of someone in your life who could be that type of person?

Do you want to know how Naomi's story ends? The two ladies returned to Naomi's hometown of Bethlehem. Thanks to the help of Ruth, Naomi's fears and worries never came to fruition.

They found a home, food and family security from an unexpected source. The name Mara didn't stick. You can read the story in the Old Testament book of Ruth.

Naomi thought that God had stopped caring for her. But

- It was God who gifted Ruth with a kind, compassionate and loyal heart.
- It was God who inspired Ruth to say and do those things that made such a difference in Naomi's life.

If you ever feel that God is distant, see if you can discern His presence in unexpected places, people or circumstances, or hear His voice from an unexpected source.

Sometimes God will be working through other people in surprising ways that we are unaware of, and yet, could be profoundly affecting our lives. (Like in Sandy's story at the end of this chapter.)

How does God show us His care and help us overcome our worries?

Often it is through **others**.

That's one of the reasons He formed the Church.

This community of people is called to offer support and care for those who need it:

the poor,
the sick,
the stranger,
the widow,
the orphan...

I feel this list could include:

the worrier.

In the book of Romans, Christians are called to,

> 'Be devoted to one another in love... Be joyful in hope, patient in affliction, faithful in prayer. Share with the Lord's people who are in need. Practice hospitality... Rejoice with those who rejoice; mourn with those who mourn.'
>
> Romans 12:10, 12-13, 15

Your experience of Christians may not match these ideals.

I'm sorry if that's the case, but there are faithful people in the Church who are obedient to be good listeners and carers. Ask around, and you will find them.

But, of course, you could find support from any friend, whether they have faith or not.

In our passage from Philippians, the author, Paul, is addressing his spiritual **'brothers and sisters'.**

He acknowledges the importance of community.

We are meant to tackle our way of thinking together, with the support of those around us who have similar problems, values and aims.

People are important; we are not designed to struggle alone. We've already described worry as a cancer that eats us up inside. Can you imagine trying to remove a real cancer from your body by yourself?

No, you would need a surgeon at least and, in reality, a group of medics.

So, don't resist seeking the help of another person. The very act of verbalising your worry will lessen its hold over you. Let someone help you bear the burden you carry.

Something Practical

Choose a friend, or someone you respect and trust, and ask if you could share your worries with them over a coffee (a coffee shop might not be appropriate if there's a possibility you might be emotional).

It's not even necessary for that confidant to offer good advice; it's more important that they are a good listener. In the sharing, we hear ourselves verbalise our worries. As we hear our own voice, we take onboard how those worries may sound and be perceived by our listener.

At such times we may realise which worries are trivial. We may think to ourselves, 'This worry is unjustified and sounds unimportant.' Try it and see.

Sandy's Story

One Sunday afternoon, my husband died suddenly in a road accident. I had two small children at the time and the pain, grief, and shock were immense.

On the following Sunday, a week later, I decided to go to the place where he died. While I was there, I suddenly felt a sense of complete peace, like something I had never experienced before.

I can only say that it was a peace that was tangible: I could reach out and touch it. I was surrounded by it. I didn't understand it and it only lasted for an hour or so.

I still had a lot of pain to go through.

In the many cards and letters I received the following week, some people were saying, 'Our church prayed for you on Sunday.'

Slowly it dawned on me that this was the day when that deep peace had come over me and I began to see that prayer had something to do with it.

This was when my journey with Jesus began, and I also started a prayer adventure that continues today.

I know from that experience that there is a centre of peace inside me which is always there, no matter what storms are raging.

I have a place in my spirit where I can always go, where the Holy Spirit meets me in peace.

Personal
People
Praise
Pay Attention
Pray
Practice

Praise

Do not be anxious about anything, but in every situation, by prayer and petition, with thanksgiving, present your requests to God.'

Philippians 4:6

Being thankful in every situation may seem like a very odd suggestion, especially when our circumstances seem really dark, but it appears in a slightly different form in Paul's letter to the church in Thessalonica too:

> 'Rejoice always, pray continually, give thanks in all circumstances; for this is God's will for you in Christ Jesus.'
>
> 1 Thessalonians 5:16-18

Please note, we are not being encouraged to be thankful *for* all circumstances; but in them.

Paul knew the power of giving thanks in this way. In the book of Acts, we read of a time when Paul and his friend Silas were unjustly put in a Roman colony prison.

They were in an inner cell (presumably without windows) and their feet were in stocks. This was a first century jail, so you might imagine how grim Paul's situation was.

Not only was he unfairly locked up, he was in a dark hole, being treated as if he were some violent criminal. *How would you feel?*

And yet, we find Paul

praying and

singing hymns

to ***God!***[4]

Singing hymns to God is not the first thing that would have sprung to mind if I were in Paul's sandals!

---

[4] Acts 16:25

Yet we find Paul and Silas still praising and thanking God in very dire circumstances. As they are doing this (at midnight by the way) a violent earthquake occurs that shakes the prison's foundations.

Miraculously, the prison doors fly open, and their chains are loosed. There is more to this story, but the point is, they are **freed**.

Is there a lesson here for us today? Worry can be a chain that binds us. Is it possible that as we turn to God in thanksgiving, a miracle might happen for us, that we might also be set free?

At the time Paul wrote to the Church in Philippi, encouraging them to give thanks in every situation, he was in prison (again)!

He exhorted them to 'rejoice in the Lord always' (Philippians 4:4). Clearly Paul had reason to believe how important this activity was.

Putting aside the miraculous for a moment, being thankful in this way may be likened to looking for the silver lining to a dark cloud.

It offers the light of hope and a new point of focus. Put another way, thanksgiving gives us a new horizon to concentrate on.

I recall going on a fishing trip off the north coast of Scotland. It was a beautiful sunny summer's day, and the boat had no waves to contend with. The 50ft vessel took eight of us out from the harbour on a three-hour trip. It turned out to be the longest three hours of my life!

We hadn't ventured far from land when the captain turned off the engine and encouraged people to cast their lines into the sea.

In very little time, shouts of 'I've got one!' started, and fish began to fill our buckets.

Even I caught one, and I had never fished before!

However, although there were no waves battering our boat, the sea was offering a significant swell. The roll of the boat soon took effect on my stomach.

It's not a pleasant experience when your breakfast returns, not once but twice! Apparently, my face had turned the stereotypical shade of green, and I was not interested in the onboard snacks on offer, nor the fishing itself.

I looked at my watch. There were still two hours of this trip to survive, when all I wanted to do was step ashore and lie down!

For the next 120 long minutes, the only strategy that offered any kind of relief was standing and focusing my eyes on the sea's horizon. Only then could I use my legs and body to compensate for the movement of the boat, minimising the effects of the swell.

The minutes ticked by very slowly. It seemed like forever, but eventually the hours passed, and we made it back to harbour where my sister was waiting. As only sisters can, she almost cried with laughter at the colour of my face, which she had spotted from afar. Needless to say, I didn't eat our catch that day!

Looking for the horizon helps us navigate the waves that may batter us, or the heavily disguised swell that builds up, generating disabling worries. We need to lift our eyes: our perspective. Finding things to be thankful for offers this new perspective.

Don't just take my word for it. Clinical psychologist, Lisa Firestone, says,

> 'Gratitude is perhaps the most important key to finding success and happiness... Research demonstrates that focusing on what we are grateful for is a universally rewarding way to feeling happier and more fulfilled.'

She goes on to say that, among other things, the benefits of gratitude are associated with better health [including mental health], more optimism and positive emotions.[5]

Try it for yourself when worry hits. Turn your thoughts to things you are grateful for:

What makes your heart sing?

What makes you feel energised?

What makes you rejoice?

What can you find that is praiseworthy?

---

5 https://www.psychologytoday.com/gb/blog/compassion-matters/201511/the-healing-power-of-gratitude (Accessed 16/09/2024)

Something Practical

Write down 3 things that make you thankful. They may be people in your life that bless you, hobbies or sports you enjoy, experiences you have treasured, pets that give you pleasure... anything really. You can add to them if you like.

Now, place that list in a prominent position in your home where you can read it often. Let it bring a smile to your face. If you are creative, perhaps use photos or your own illustrations. Perhaps make the list into an attractive fridge magnet that you will see every time you get the milk for a cup of tea?

Be as creative as you wish, but make sure the list can be seen and read often. Why not change the list from time to time to keep it fresh?

Margaret's Story

I thought I would continue work as an Occupational Therapist (the job that I loved in Lincoln) for as long as I could physically manage it.

But a change in management made it no longer possible for me to remain in the situation, and I retired earlier than expected. To 'rejoice and give thanks in all circumstances' proved to be a bit of a problem... I didn't like the circumstances!

I prayed for opportunities to use my experience; I gave thanks for the unknown future. What was God's plan?

Within weeks I had a phone call from Christian friends who were working on a project in Bangladesh. Could I come to help them? They hadn't asked before, because they thought I was still working. Perfect timing!

I was free to go to Bangladesh. It was a wonderful experience with young people who were training to work with disabled adults and children in rural villages.

A year later, and my friends had been invited to start a similar project in Nepal. Could I spare some time to join them? Oh, yes. I love Nepal!

Some people have a definite and clear call from God to go to a specific country, but when people ask if I knew God was calling me to work in Canada in the 1960s, I have to say honestly that I didn't hear His voice.

I just believed that God's plan for me was to worship Him, to make Jesus known wherever I went and to honour His name.

God's will for me? To rejoice, to pray, and to give thanks... easy when you know how!

Personal
People
Praise
Pay Attention
Pray
Practice

Pay Attention

'Whatever is true, whatever is noble, whatever is right, whatever is pure, whatever is lovely, whatever is admirable – if anything is excellent or praiseworthy – think about such things.'

Philippians 4:8-9

Read these words again slowly, words that will add themes to our thoughts and put our minds to better work:

True Noble *(decent, honourable, good)*

Right ***Pure***

Lovely Admirable

Excellent

Praiseworthy

These themes are great, aren't they? Much better than their antonyms: things that are false, bad, wrong, spoiled, repulsive, deplorable, poor, disgraceful.

It is worth noting, I think, that the list here starts with

'Whatever is true'

Worry loves to feed off things that are without foundation, exaggerated or false.

We are often advised not to feed ducks with bread - it's not good for them - yet many of us still do. Similarly, it's unhelpful to feed our minds with lies and falsehood - anything that is not true - it's not good for us!

So, it is no wonder that the Bible encourages us to think about truth instead.

As stated in an earlier chapter, worries are based on ifs and maybes, not facts. Therefore, we can never hold those things to be true or reliable.

On the other hand, Jesus says in John 8:32,

'The truth will set you free.'

This phrase has several deep meanings (too many to go into detail here) but, in the context of our worries, focusing our minds on what is true will certainly set us on the road to being free.

When the temptation is to sit in our bubble of worry, it may not be easy to think of good things.

But here again, God comes to our rescue. In Paul's letter to the church in Rome, he encourages us to be *transformed by the renewing of our minds.*[6] This transformation is another work of God's Holy Spirit, who we mentioned earlier.

A renewed mind is a key part of the new life offered by God. Paul encourages us to ***'take captive every thought to make it obedient to Christ.'***[7] Somebody summarised it this way,

> When a thought comes knocking at the door of your mind, see what it is before letting it in.

---

[6] Romans 12:2

[7] 2 Corinthians 10:5

Choosing whether or not to let a thought come and stay right at the start is important. Making the right choice to keep worries out,

not letting them get through the front door of your mind,

is so much easier than trying to evict them once they have made themselves at home.

At this point, it's worth taking the time to understand something about our souls. The word 'soul' can conjure up all sorts of ideas and can be quite vague. So, let's add some clarity. Our souls are the non-physical part of us that makes us, ***us***.

The soul is made up of the mind, the will and the emotions. In terms of what happens when thoughts come knocking at our door, it works like this:

1. Our minds are put to work. This is where we process the thought. What is the thought? What is being presented? Is it true or false? Can I trust the source? And more questions besides.

2. The emotions come into play. Here is where the reaction takes place. How do I feel about this thought? What does it invoke within me: anger, compassion, sadness?

3. The will is awakened. How am I going to respond? What am I going to do?

We need to put our wills to helpful use,
deciding to condition our circumstances
instead of
being conditioned by them.

Remember Neil Baldwin? His approach to life and his choice to be happy? He was putting his will into action.

So, the lesson here is to pay attention. What am I choosing to think about? What thoughts am I going to engage with or evict?

How can I put my mind to better work?

Something Practical

Every morning as you wake, and before anything else, say these words from ancient scripture. They were written by someone who knew affliction, weeping over the destruction of his home city and the capture of his people by an enemy force. Let them become part of your daily routine; perhaps memorise them. They are a reminder of God's love and presence: things that are true, good, pure, lovely and praiseworthy:

Because of the Lord's great love
I am not consumed,
for His compassion never fails.
It is new every morning;
Great is His faithfulness.*

*Adapted from Lamentations 3:22-23

Dave's Story

I found a lump where a man should not find a lump. I'd had a suspicion something was wrong for a few days but on this discovery, a whole host of thoughts and questions came flooding into my mind:

Why had I not regularly checked?

How long had the lump been there before I discovered it?

Had I discovered it too late for successful treatment?

Then the big thought entered without invitation:

I've got cancer and it's terminal.

The emotions kicked in:

fear,

regret,

sadness,

and a sense of deep loss for those I would leave behind.

I had only one option: to get a GP appointment as soon as possible.

The next day I contacted the surgery. The best they could offer was an appointment in six days' time. Would the delay make a difference to the cancer being curable or terminal, I worried? But that same day, I recalled that worry was a choice and that I had to capture the thoughts entering my mind.

The truth was that I didn't know what the perceived lump might be. It might not be cancer, and even if it were, it might be easily treated. My mind had let in all sorts of fearful and worrying thoughts unchallenged and (potentially) untrue.

I decided to put my will into action. I decided that until I knew some facts, I would not entertain the fearful, worrying thoughts.

So, when those thoughts came calling, I put my mind to work on something else, giving even a trivial subject my full concentration.

For instance, I once diverted my attention to thinking up a list in my mind of my top favourite films. It worked, and the more often I did this, the easier it became and the less often, it seemed, the worrying thoughts stepped forward.

It was as if they started to give up, knowing that they would not gain a foothold in my mind.

Six days later, I was reassured by my doctor but sent for a scan anyway. The scan confirmed that there was no cancer, just some harmless cysts. For two weeks I could have been in the depths of worry and fear. I'm glad I didn't waste that time!

Personal
People
Praise
Pay Attention
Pray
Practice

Pray

Prayer is something lots of us do, whether we consider ourselves religious or not.

Christian prayer is simply talking and listening to the God revealed through the Bible. I called it 'Christian prayer' because, whilst many people pray, it is important to direct our prayers to the right place.

The world has many 'gods' and beliefs. However, this book is a guide to overcoming worry by the best means possible – through the intervention of the God I introduced you to earlier: the personal God who has demonstrated His love for us through Jesus Christ.

And **that God** has the power to change lives.

If He is powerful enough to create the universe and raise dead people to life, I think it's safe to say, He has the power to unburden us from our worries!

But He does ask for a response: our cooperation and commitment to follow His instructions. After all, you wouldn't visit a doctor, then ignore their diagnosis and prescription.

God has so much more for us than dealing with our worries. God wants us to trust Him, not just with our worries, but with our whole lives. He invites us into a relationship with Him where the highs and lows of life can be walked through together.

In Mark 11:22-24, Jesus encouraged His disciples to pray like this:

> 'Have faith in God... Truly I tell you, if anyone says to this mountain, "Go, throw yourself into the sea," and does not doubt in their heart but believes that what they say will happen, it will be done for them.
>
> Therefore, I tell you, whatever you ask for in prayer, believe that you have received it, and it will be yours.'

We have discussed before about worry exaggerating our problems, or making mountains out of molehills. Whether they are molehills that we've made into mountains, or humongous peaks, what 'mountains' are you facing?

The good news is, mountains can be moved!

But only with the power and authority of Jesus. When you pray, sometimes Jesus will move the mountain. Other times, the mountain won't move, but He will either show you it's just a molehill, or He will give you the strength to climb it.

Returning to our main scripture:

> The Lord is near. Do not be anxious about anything, but in every situation, by prayer and petition, with thanksgiving, present your requests to God.
>
> Philippians 4:5-6

We might find these words overwhelming, but I like to think of God like a perfect parent. He loves to hear from His children, and when we pray, He is more interested in *what* we say than *how* we say it.

For some of us, our concept of a parent has been damaged by the parenting we received. Some people have suffered badly at the hands of their parents.

That is extremely sad, and I don't wish to underestimate the harm caused. I find it helpful to consider those qualities we want to see in a parent: those characteristics we would like to see in our own parenting, whether we are parents now, or might be in the future.
Qualities like:

love,

patience,

kindness,

goodness,

gentleness,

faithfulness,

self-control,

forgiveness.

God displays these qualities perfectly; they are characteristics of Him.

So, let's direct our prayers to this loving and healing God. **Let's make prayer our first resort rather than our last.**

You can use whatever words you like, but here's a prayer you could use if you're not sure where to start:

Dear God,

I need Your help to stop worrying about *(name the person(s) or situation).* Help me to know Your strengthening and comforting presence with me, by Your Holy Spirit.

Thank You that You care for me and those I love, and I am grateful for *(think of someone or something to be thankful for).*

Please help me with my thoughts and emotions, so that I may know and experience Your peace in my life.

Thank You.

Something Practical

Make time, maybe just a few minutes each day, to reach out to God in prayer. If you can, find a quiet moment and place to tell God how you're feeling, and listen out for His response. It's often described as an 'inner voice'. Perhaps you could use the prayer above again, as a way to get started?

And remember, it's always good to give thanks as well as pouring out our worries. However short or long, make prayer part of your daily routine. If a quiet place/time is out of your reach, then don't be discouraged from praying whilst doing the washing up, for example, or while driving (Note: you don't need to close your eyes to pray)!

Mary's Story

With the breakdown of my marriage in the year 2000, I was left facing the financial dilemma of having to provide for myself and our two young teenagers. At the time, I was working part-time as an administrator for a charity.

I was trained and had worked as a teacher previously and knew I needed to get a full-time teaching post. Everything felt overwhelming, life was difficult and the future seemed uncertain. I had (and have) very supportive family and friends, but most importantly, a heavenly Father who has faithfully loved and provided for me.

During this time, as I was looking for work, there were two things in particular that encouraged and helped me.

One was a picture given to me by a praying friend. She said she saw me as an owl who was watching over her young.

An owl has binocular vision and can see things clearly at a distance. She felt that God was saying I would be able to see clearly which work to go for and know it was the right thing, being able to see in the dark when things appeared 'murky'.

The second was an unusual scripture that the Holy Spirit highlighted to me in my daily reading of the Bible.

It was Isaiah 37:30. The context was very different to the situation I was in!

The King of Assyria was threatening to attack Jerusalem and overthrow King Hezekiah. Hezekiah had prayed, and Isaiah delivered this message to him from God:

'This year you will eat what grows by itself, and the second year what springs from that. But in the third year, sow and reap, plant vineyards and eat their fruit.'

It was a promise of protection and provision.

I knew this was God speaking directly to me. It was so helpful to be able to remind myself of these two things at times when I was struggling to remain peaceful.

Over the following three years, I experienced the fulfilment of this scripture. The first year, I worked in a part-time teaching post alongside my part-time admin role. As a result of this job, I was offered a full-time maternity leave teaching post in another school.

The third year, I was approached by a teacher-friend who was deputy head in a special school, to see if I would be interested in teaching there as another maternity vacancy became available. I had never worked in special education before but had always been interested.

I found that I loved working there! One day during that time, the Head approached me to ask if I would be interested in a permanent full-time post! This was to be my 'vineyard' for the next 15 years.

God is faithful and He is good!

Practice

'Whatever you have learned or received or heard from me, or seen in me – put it into practice.'

Philippians 4:9

Paul, the author of this Bible passage, encourages those reading his God-inspired advice to 'put it into practice'.

We need to practise these things –

- Believing that God is near,
- Being thankful in all circumstances,
- Praying,
- Thinking about good and positive things.

If we are to overcome our worries, it will take wise choices, but it is likely to also involve practice:

Repeated effort.

Repeating a new behaviour will start as an effort but will turn into a habit if we persist.

Much depends on the depth of motivation, but one of the influences that will hasten the process is using a strategy that replaces a **bad** habit with a **good** one.

For example, putting our minds to better work, by regularly and repeatedly thinking of whatever is ***true, noble, right, pure, lovely, admirable, excellent or praiseworthy,*** is a good, practical strategy.

It is important to practise. Overcoming months, years, perhaps a lifetime of worrying is unlikely to happen overnight.

Repeat the steps in the strategy. Repeat again. If it takes you two months (or longer) to overcome worry, won't that still be time well spent in the context of your life?

I became a marathon runner in my 60s. Overcoming years of inactivity and weight gain started with one very short, lung-squeezing run (I still remember it)!

But one, or even a few, similar training sessions were never going to be enough to put right my flabby tummy and give me a healthier heart, let alone get me around a 26-mile road race.

No.

It took **repeated effort**, but after a few weeks, I was running a 5km park-run with comparative ease. The practice had given me a level of fitness that meant I could, amazingly, both run and breathe!

The Bible tells the story of Joshua. Moses had just died, and God gave Joshua the task of leading the Israelites into the Promised Land following their escape from Egyptian slavery. God gave Joshua some instructions:

> Make sure you carry out The Revelation that Moses commanded you, every bit of it. Don't get off track, either left or right, so as to make sure you get to where you're going.

> And don't for a minute let this Book of The Revelation be out of mind.
>
> Ponder and meditate on it day and night, making sure you practice everything written in it. Then you'll get where you're going; then you'll succeed. Haven't I commanded you? Strength! Courage! Don't be timid; don't get discouraged.
>
> God, your God, is with you every step you take.
>
> Joshua 1:7-9, The Message

God wanted Joshua to succeed, but in order to do so, it would take 'day and night' effort and practice.

The good news is that Joshua listened and carried out the instructions, and as a result, the Promised Land was reached and entered. He followed the book's guidance on how to live. I'm not asking you to 'ponder on it day and night'(!) but, perhaps you could practise the strategy in this book as a way to reach your goal?

If you went to see your GP, their advice would be well and good, but it is following that advice that is crucial. If they said, 'Take this medicine every day for 9 weeks,' you would probably do it.

The same principle applies here. Don't just read the strategy to overcome worry; follow it and practise it.

Something Practical

Think of this as a 'repeat prescription'. The steps outlined in this strategy need to be followed and repeated as often as worries arise (or the same worry crops up). So, the next time a worry comes calling, go through the steps:

1. Remember that God cares deeply about you and is on your side.
2. Let people help you.
3. Bring to mind people or things you are grateful for, and offer thanks to God.
4. Put your will into action, and decide to shut the worry out by thinking of better things.

5. Offer to God your thoughts, and seek His help and strength.
6. Repeat as necessary!

If it helps, write out this list on your phone or in a handy notebook so that you can refer to it quickly in times of need.

Perhaps a shortened bullet point approach may help you to memorise the steps, using the chapter headings and letter 'P' as a prompt:

Personal

People

Praise

Pay Attention

Pray

Practice

Ness' Story

I think, like many people, I have battled with worry over the years. The last ten years I have struggled with Chronic Fatigue Syndrome, which means I have very limited energy and must pace myself extremely carefully.

I've had to give up work completely and I am often unable to leave the home. Simple everyday tasks like getting dressed, hanging out the washing or preparing a sandwich, can seem impossible.

It's easy to allow worrying thoughts in: 'Will I be able to manage this? Will this be too overwhelming? What if I can't do it?'

This 'weakness' has required me to lean totally on God for help, especially when no one else is around.

I've come to see that this is an amazing way to live in many ways.

Simple prayers like, 'Help me, Jesus' and, 'Thank You, Jesus!' when I see another time God has miraculously answered my prayers, have now developed into, 'Thank You Jesus that You're going to help me. I know You'll help me to do all that You want me to do.'

I'm more and more convinced He's going to give me that extra strength I need, or send someone – just at the right time – to help me. Also, He enables me to help others, and He has never failed me. What amazing love!

I have found that it is possible to keep myself busy, thanking Him continually through the day for the things I CAN do, and also for His countless blessings: these comfy clothes, this hot cup of coffee, the sunlight in the trees, the supermarket food delivery, a smile, keeping my husband safe on his bike, that lovely hug from my son or daughter.

No wonder God commands us to be thankful: it keeps us full of peace and joy and in deep appreciation of our wonderful God!

I've been learning through this how very deeply God loves me. His 'anticipatory love' is amazing! He always has everything planned in advance, and if I can but simply trust Him in childlike delight, there is no room for worry.

Jesus said, 'Do not worry... Your heavenly Father knows what you need (Matthew 6:25,32).'

God gives me the choice, moment by moment, either to allow worry to creep in, sitting myself on the throne of my heart, rather than allowing God to be in control (all of which inevitably rob me of God's peace and grace) OR to live in trusting thankfulness and dependence on God's love, which has never failed me.

The Concluding Result:

Peace

'The peace of God, which transcends all understanding, will guard your hearts and your minds in Christ Jesus... The God of peace will be with you.'

Philippians 4: 7,9

Peace - **God's extraordinary peace** - is the consequence of taking the actions laid out for us in our main scripture from Philippians.

If we know God is with us, lean into the people around us, realise how dependable God is and how much He loves us, be thankful in all circumstances, put our minds to better work, *and* pray, then we can expect God's peace.

Some of us might rile against this notion. Some of us want God to wave His 'magic wand' and take all our worries away.

But that was never God's way.

If it was, perhaps...

- Adam and Eve wouldn't have been expelled from the garden of Eden,
- Joseph wouldn't have found himself in prison on his route to the palace,
- the Egyptians would have released Israel from slavery,
- Israel wouldn't have been taken into Babylonian exile...

Perhaps a man named Jesus would not have died on a cross.

No, as hard as it might be to understand, God has always chosen to work ***with people***, in relationship, in cooperation, rather than just making everything ok again by imposing His power.

After all, what would you think of a human parent that, every time a child

broke something,
made a mistake,
upset someone,
failed in their work responsibilities or
frittered money away,

just came along and made everything ok again?

Wouldn't it be right and just for the parent to expect their child to take some **responsibility** and action themselves?

He is not a 'Father Christmas' God that accedes to every request presented to Him. If that were the case, I'm not sure what would happen when a farmer prayed for rain in the same area as a holiday-maker was praying for sunny, dry weather!

In the film *Bruce Almighty*, God allows Bruce to take on His role. When all the millions of prayer requests come rolling in (many at conflict with one another), Bruce grants them all and chaos ensues.

It's a film worth watching to get a perspective on God.

Peace is a gift of God that is not earned, as if God owed us anything in the first place!

It is a gift that comes through following the Maker's instructions.

God doesn't give us rules and guidance to spoil our lives. He gives them in the knowledge that, if lived by, they will offer us the best life possible: a life filled with

love, **peace** and **hope**.

If you have a car, you will know that following the car manufacturer's instructions will mean you get the best from that car:

- Putting the correct fuel in,
- Having it serviced on time,
- Using the correct oil,
- Having the tyres at the right pressure, etc.

The same principle applies with following God's instructions for our lives. He made humankind, and He knows what's best for us.

Note what that peace does. It will

'guard your hearts and minds'.

The description of *guard* in the original language and context is not one we might associate with a security guard in a shopping mall, whom a nimble shoplifter might avoid.

The picture intended here is one with the strength of a garrison. 'Like a squadron of soldiers looking after a treasure chest'[8] as former Bishop of Durham, Tom Wright, put it.

Nothing is going to get past this armed guard to disturb, damage or steal!

Church Leader, Woodrow Kroll, said,

> 'If our minds are stayed on God, His peace will rule the affairs entertained by our minds. If, on the other hand, we allow our minds to dwell on the cares of this world, God's peace will be far from our thoughts.'[9]

---

[8] Tom Wright, Paul for Everyone – The Prison Letters, SPCK, 2004, P.131
[9] God's priorities for your life for men, Hendrickson Publishers, 2006, P.275

We have a choice to make: to look to and follow God, or settle back into old habits that we know are damaging to our physical, mental and spiritual health.

But there is some really good news! When we choose the God-way, we are promised the power of His Holy Spirit and His reassuring presence.

We are not left alone.

He comes alongside us to help and guide. Without the power of the Spirit we may struggle, but with Him, anything is possible.

Jesus said in Mark 10:27,

> 'All things are possible with God.'

Church Leader, Pete Greig, very helpfully comments on how God works with us in our struggles.

He reminds us that when we are suffering 'instead of airlifting us to safety, God parachutes down to join us in the muck and chaos of our situation.'[10] He comes alongside us and helps us.

So, in the knowledge that God is near, that He cares for you and will send His Holy Spirit to help you in your struggle, are you ready to jump off the wall of worry into the arms of a loving and trustworthy Father God?

Can I encourage you to do so? Let go of those worries.

Cast them,
throw them,
fling,
hurl
and pitch them
onto Jesus.

[10] Pete Greig, God on Mute, Baker Publishing Group, 2011

Something Practical

How about writing a letter to God?

Write whatever you like to express what you are thinking and feeling at this moment.

Take the opportunity to pour out those worries on paper as a symbolic act of casting them on to Jesus.

Let this letter become your prayer.

Seek His help.

Seek His peace.

Richard's Story

My church had decided to offer a former school building we owned as a shelter for Asylum Seekers.

After several weeks of very vocal concerns from some members of the local community, we organised a public meeting.

The meeting was packed, not just with locals but also members of the English Defence League who had come to support the faction opposing the scheme.

The Police were waiting outside.

I won't say that I wasn't concerned, but I firmly believed in bringing these worries to God in a spirit of deep trust.

Part-way through the meeting things began to go badly; people were getting heated and the meeting seemed likely to get out of control.

In addition to all the prayer that had gone on beforehand, I (and I'm sure all the other church members there) began to pray very fervently.

We found the truth of this Philippians passage: God 'guarded my mind'. He kept me calm, gave me the words to say and the courage to say them.

I stood up and shared a solution that had literally only come to me at that moment. And what I said completely defused the meeting. No-one had anything further to say, and the meeting ended.

As I spoke, I felt an incredible sense of peace. A group of us continued to pray as people were leaving, and we all felt God's peace.

There was still much work to be done to bring about the solution I had proposed, but this work brought about much that was true and admirable.

It also brought many others in the village to work with us to bring about a new community initiative.

I won't say no-one was anxious, but at the end of that meeting, and through all the subsequent work, we felt a deep peace. The deep presence of God working in and through us.

One final thing...

This book is called *'Dave says, 'Don't Worry.'*

You will have read the same message from my friends, Margaret, Sandy, Mary, Ness and Richard.

But I hope that you've heard from my best friend:

Jesus says, 'Don't Worry!'

Acknowledgements

I want to thank my wife, Kathleen, for being my best friend and biggest supporter, often making sacrifices to enable me time to write this book. Thank you for being my companion on this adventure.

Thank you to our son, Graham, for your inspiration and encouragement. We've been so blessed to be writing and releasing Jesus-centred books at the same time.

My siblings and I were so blessed to have the parents we had. For Mum, who first introduced me to belief in God as a child, and Dad, who modelled what a good father looks like, thank you.

I am so grateful to Kirby and Kathy Haye. In my teenage years they introduced me to Jesus Christ. It was life-changing! Without their amazing and sacrificial input, my life would have been very different and spiritually poorer. Big thanks to Joy Vee and Natasha Woodcraft at Broad Place Publishing, for believing in me and this project. I am grateful for your enthusiasm, encouragement and editing skills (3 e's – you know how I like alliteration!)

I also owe great thanks to Margaret Inkpen, Sandy Brown, Mary Maguire, Ness Hodge and Richard Steel for contributing their stories to this book. You've brought the text alive! To other friends whose stories didn't make the edit, I really appreciate the time and trouble you took to write them.

To all my friends and family who have loved and encouraged me over the years – Thank you! Not least among these, Alan Hoare, for being a spiritual hero and pointing me in the right direction.

This is for Jesus Christ, who gave everything for me.

About the Author

David Albans lives in Lincoln with his wife, Kathleen, who describes him as the least annoying person she knows!

He loves being creative, whether that's through songwriting, authoring or preaching in Church. Playing one of his many guitars, going for long runs, watching football, bird-spotting, and eating pastries are some of his other interests.

Dave has a first-class honours degree in Theology and currently serves as a lay minister in his local parish church. He believes the Bible has some really helpful and practical advice for readers about dealing with life, whether they have faith or not.

Also from

BROAD PLACE
publishing
broadplacepublishing.co.uk

What do you do when your life's work lies in ashes at your feet? When your heart and body are broken and your faith is shattered?

Disillusioned, grief stricken and feeling abandoned by the God he once trusted, Brother Silas runs. He sets out on a lonely journey, not knowing where the path will take him, determined to distance himself from his painful past.

But Silas cannot escape the Love that will not let him go. Through the unexpected kindness of strangers, and a series of inexplicable events, Silas's heart begins to heal. Then an unlikely reunion puts him on the path to rediscovering who he really is.

Will Silas find somewhere he truly belongs or will he remain a stranger forever?

The Stranger is Christian Fiction set among the abbeys and landscapes of medieval Wales.

Who is Benny Wellander?

To his mother, he's her precious baby, forever in need of protection. To his sister, he's "Pestie", the kid who destroyed her happy childhood. To his classmates, he's the quiet loner plagued by seizures. To his father, he's barely visible; a constant disappointment.

Caught in a web of insecurity, Benny defines himself by his illness and the damage it's wrought on his mind. But is he truly rubbish at everything? Or could he be worth loving?

Join Benny on a poignant journey of self-discovery as he seeks to understand his own worth. What will it take for him to break free from his labels and embrace the person he truly is?

Just Benny is a beautiful, gentle piece of Contemporary Fiction, suitable for all. It is an excellent introduction to the Christian faith through subtle storytelling.

A tea tin. Owned by one girl, found by another over half a century later. What mysteries does it hide?

In 1960s Leningrad, Vera dreams of rising thorough the Kirov Ballet and becoming a People's Artist. Yet her family holds a secret that could change the course of her life.

In modern-day Lincoln, Fay is a pastor's kid, disillusioned with her parents' faith. While attending a theatre summer programme, Fay accidentally discovers an old tea tin.

The lives of two girls, half a century apart, are about to become curiously entwined.

They Whisper about Us is an intriguing split time-line story, with a dose of mystery and a subtle Christian message.

"Sin is crouching at the door, ready to pounce. You must master it before it masters you."

Kayin lives in the shadow of his parents' expulsion from Eden and its lingering cloud of shame. He believes in the Creator but struggles for affirmation. When suffering comes and sibling rivalry threatens, Kayin wrestles with doubt and fear, until his youthful hopes lie shattered, replaced by a twisted dance of pride and jealousy.

As Kayin spirals, misunderstandings within the family dominate, and whispers of temptation slither through the cracks. Then a chance at redemption presents itself. With flames of envy still raging hot, Kayin and his brother present their sacrifices...

No one foresees the resulting tragedy.

The Wanderer Scorned is the first book in Natasha Woodcraft's creative exploration of the Cain & Abel narrative.

Berlitz
CHINA
POCKET GUIDE

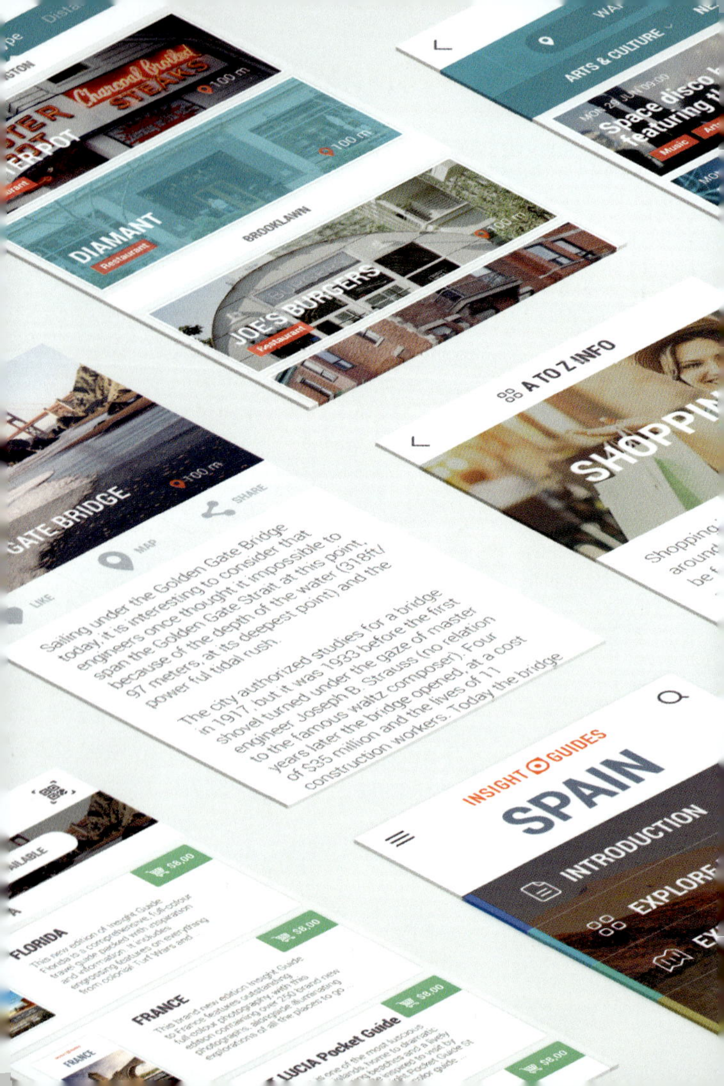
Charcoal Broiled STEAKS
100 m
100 m
DIAMANT
Restaurant
BROOKLAWN
JOE'S BURGERS
Restaurant
100 m
ARTS & CULTURE
Space disco featuring
Music
A TO Z INFO
SHOPPING
GATE BRIDGE
100 m
LIKE
MAP
SHARE
Sailing under the Golden Gate Bridge today, it is interesting to consider that engineers once thought it impossible to span the Golden Gate Strait at this point, because of the depth of the water (318ft/97 meters at its deepest point) and the power ful tidal rush.
The city authorized studies for a bridge in 1917, but it was 1933 before the first shovel turned under the gaze of master engineer Joseph B. Strauss (no relation to the famous waltz composer). Four years later the bridge opened, at a cost of $35 million and the lives of 11 construction workers. Today the bridge
INSIGHT GUIDES
SPAIN
INTRODUCTION
EXPLORE
$8,00
FLORIDA
$8,00
FRANCE
$8,00
LUCIA Pocket Guide
$8,00

TOP 10 ATTRACTIONS

LI RIVER

Take a boat trip to see river life against a stunning backdrop. See page 166.

THE GREAT WALL OF CHINA

It winds from the Yellow Sea to the Gobi Desert. See page 67.

THE FORBIDDEN CITY

This vast area was the Imperial Palace of the Ming dynasty. See page 55.

TERRACOTTA WARRIORS

An emperor's 2,000-year-old army, near Xi'an. See page 106.

LIJIANG
A lovely old village with a stunning mountain backdrop. See page 186.

LHASA
Centre for Tibetan culture. See page 202.

SUZHOU
Famous for its canals and gardens. See page 123.

SHAOLIN MONASTERY
The birthplace of martial arts. See page 97.

SHANGHAI
The colonial and modern coexist in this dynamic city. See page 110.

YANGZI RIVER
Cruise through the Three Gorges. See page 179.

A PERFECT TOUR

Days 1–2

Beijing

Spend an afternoon walking from Tiananmen Square through the Forbidden City to Beihai Park. After dusk, dine at one of the restaurants along the Shichahai Lakes or go for home-style food on the old Nan Luogu Xiang pedestrian alley nearby. The next day, take a coach to the Mutianyu Great Wall and hike up its steps through ancient guard towers.

Day 3

Pingyao

Take the overnight train to Taiyuan and proceed by coach to Pingyao. Pass through the gates of this Ming- and Qing-dynasty banking burgh's 6km (4-mile long) protective wall into a Unesco Heritage Site of old homes and shops.

Day 4

Xi'an

Xi'an is best known for the terracotta warriors, hundreds of lifelike statues buried over 2,000 years ago to guard the tomb of the first Qin emperor.

Days 5–6

Shanghai

Fly to China's biggest and richest city, Shanghai. Ascend the Oriental Pearl TV Tower for a magnificent panorama, then cross the Huangpu River for a walk through the Old Town (Nanshi). Hang out on the Bund at night for views of the active riverfront. On the second day, explore the French Concession and Xintiandi.

OF CHINA

Day 8

Hangzhou

Travel by train or coach to nearby Hangzhou for a walk around the wooded West Lake. Stop for pavilion-gazing and cups of locally grown Longjing green tea.

Day 7

Suzhou

Travel by train to Suzhou for a tour of its numerous historic, immaculately landscaped gardens, such as Forest of Lions and Master of the Nets. Between gardens, peek down into canals where locals still commute by boat.

Days 9–10

Guilin

Fly to Guilin. Hike to Catch-Cloud Pavilion for 360-degree views of the city known for its limestone peaks. Walk into the mountains at Reed Flute Cave, where the largest chamber can hold 1,000 people. Next day, take the 4–5-hour trip along the Li River to see the amazing scenery and visit the riverside town of Yangshuo.

Day 11

Chengdu

Board a train to the Sichuan provincial capital, Chengdu. See the pandas at Chengdu Zoo and take in the city's relaxed temples, leaving time to sip tea outdoors as per local tradition. Eat the spiced yet fragrant food that has put Sichuan province on the world culinary map.

Days 12–14

Yangzi River

From Chengdu, take a day trip to Leshan for views of the world's largest seated Buddha. Then embark on a two-day Yangzi River cruise from Chongqing through the magnificent Three Gorges and the new dam to Yichang.

CONTENTS

INTRODUCTION 10

HISTORY 24

WHERE TO GO 49

Beijing 49
Beijing in History 50, Sightseeing 51, Tiananmen Square 52, Forbidden City (Gu Gong) 55, Parks and Pavilions 58, Temple of Heaven Park 59, Top Temples 60, An Ancient Observatory, Zoo and Aquarium 61, Hutong and Courtyards 62, Shopping Districts 64, The Summer Palace 65, The 2008 Olympics 66, Excursions from Beijing 67

The Northeast and Inner Mongolia 74
Dalian 74, Shenyang 75, Harbin 75, Hohhot 79, The Grasslands 81

Northern Heartlands 82
Datong 83, Shijiazhuang 85, Taiyuan 86, Pingyao 86, Jinan and Taishan 87, Qufu 90, Qingdao 90, Yantai 93, Kaifeng 94, Zhengzhou 96, Luoyang 96, Xi'an 100, Excursions from Xi'an 106, Yan'an 110

Shanghai 110
Shanghai in History 112, The Port and Bund 114, Around Nanjing Road 115, The Old City 116, The French Quarter 118, 'New' Shanghai: Pudong 120, Outlying Sights 121, Entertainment and Cuisine 122

The Lower Yangzi 123
Suzhou 123, Wuxi 127, Lake Tai 130, Hangzhou 131, Ningbo 135, Nanjing 135, Huangshan 140, Wuhan 142

Southern China 145
Guangzhou 145, Shenzhen 152, Hainan 153, Hunan Province 154, Shaoshan 156, Jingdezhen, Jiangxi Province 158, Mt Lushan 158, Xiamen 158, Fuzhou 161

Southwest China 161
Guilin 162, Yangshuo 168, Huangguoshu Falls, Guizhou Province 169, Chengdu 170, Leshan 173, Mt Emei 174, Chongqing 175, Excursions from Chongqing 179, Kunming 180, The Stone Forest 183, Dali 184, Around Dali 185, Lijiang 186, Shangri-la 187, Xishuangbanna 188

Northwest China 189
Lanzhou 189, Dunhuang 191, Jiayuguan 194, Turpan 194, Urumqi 198, Kashgar 200, Lhasa 202

WHAT TO DO 205

Shopping 205
Entertainment 212

EATING OUT 218

A–Z TRAVEL TIPS 226

DICTIONARY 252

INDEX 276

INTRODUCTION

Ancient, vast, evolving and exciting, China is the trip of a lifetime. It also happens to be a place that almost everyone in the world is talking about. Economists, historians, filmmakers, heads of state and business executives are among those watching closely as the country changes at a lightning pace.

China's beauties – both natural and man-made – vie for attention. Imagine mist-muffled hills silhouetted behind sampans on a winding river; proud pavilions of brilliant red and gold; the Great Wall undulating over ridges and mountains receding far into the distance; an elegant porcelain vase that has survived for centuries. In China all the senses are engaged. Touch a 2,000-year-old inscription in stone or a bolt of newly woven silk. Taste the food once served to emperors. Listen to children singing. Smell the temple incense or the scent of a fresh melon in the marketplace.

Traditional pavilion in Changsha, Hunan

Getting to China means crossing more than mere oceans and time zones. It's another world, culturally, linguistically and ideologically.

It's a first world and a third world. Ten minutes from your modern hotel, you'll find water buffalo toiling in rice fields or a farmer and his son, pulling a primitive wagon, loaded with cabbage for market. Villagers might share a public outhouse, while city dwellers have enough money to build mini mansions. This is China today.

LANGUAGE AND 'CHINESENESS'

The most obvious source of dislocation for the newly arrived traveller is the language. More people can read Chinese than any other language on earth, but the visitor, bewildered by the elegant characters, finds this no consolation. Spoken Chinese is tonal, making it challenging for Westerners. But knowing a few phrases will go a long way to earning you appreciation from locals. The Chinese themselves speak more than 150 regional dialects – some of them almost separate languages. Someone from the north can scarcely understand a word of the Cantonese spoken in the south. To help everyone communicate, the government encourages the use of an official spoken language, Putonghua (known abroad as 'Mandarin'), based on the Beijing dialect. Happily, no matter what dialect a Chinese person uses in speech, the written language is universal. In addition, there are China's ethnic minorities, making up about 8.5 percent of the population, who speak tongues as diverse as Mongolian and Miao, Thai and Tibetan. In parts of the sparsely settled western deserts and mountains, the minorities are the majority.

English spoken

English is the most widely spoken foreign language in China. Millions of Chinese study English in college or school (starting at the age of six), and through television programmes. However, for many, English is just a tool to pass tests, long forgotten after studies have ended. A few words of Chinese therefore will greatly enhance any tourist's visit to China.

Language aside, the visitor also must figure out the timeless 'Chineseness' and the modern overlay of communism. Is the proliferation of bureaucrats a Marxist or a Mandarin touch? Do families live three generations to an apartment because of tradition or because of the housing shortage? Why do Chinese infants almost

What to talk about

You should feel free to discuss politics, religion or social problems with Chinese people, but refrain from argument or disrespect towards the country or its leaders. Also keep in mind that many Chinese associate individuals with their governments, and may therefore link travellers to their homeland's foreign policies, including those disputed by Beijing.

never cry? Do they feel thoroughly loved or are they conditioned to be docile?

China is the most populous of all countries. This well-known fact comes to life when visitors set foot in the People's Republic. Around 350,000 babies are born each day, which means that about every eighth child born in the world is Chinese. China (including Taiwan) has more than 150 cities of more than a million inhabitants, and in any of them the rush hour is as hair-raising as a traffic jam in New York or London. In one of the most crowded provinces, Sichuan (Szechuan), you can journey for hours and never lose sight of people or houses, even in the most remote rural areas.

As you travel the country by rail or air, you cannot fail to be impressed by the work-intensive (that is, *human* work-intensive) agriculture. In the paddy fields you'll see hundreds of barefoot men and women collecting rice for processing by means of a single, hand-operated threshing machine. Farmers work every inch of ground that isn't rock or sand or nearly vertical. When you subtract the mountains, deserts and other totally inhospitable terrain, only a small fraction – around 10 percent – of China's great landmass is under cultivation, and problems are exacerbated by frequent floods, drought and fast-growing urban sprawl.

GEOGRAPHY AND CLIMATE

China is the world's third-largest country by area, covering nearly 9.6 million sq km (3.7 million sq miles). Only Russia and Canada are larger. China is bordered (clockwise from the north) by Mongolia, Russia, North Korea, Vietnam, Laos, Myanmar, India, Bhutan, Nepal, Pakistan, Afghanistan, Tajikistan, Kyrgyzstan and Kazakhstan.

As you might expect over such a huge area, the weather blows hot and cold. It's about 5,800km (more than 3,600 miles) from northernmost China to the southern extremity, so while northerners are shovelling snow, southerners are sowing rice or vacationing on tropical Hainan island. Most of the rain falls in summer, largely in southern and central China.

The most mountainous part of the country is the west, where the Himalayas reach their apogee with Mt Everest (8,850m/29,035ft), on the China–Nepal border. On the Chinese side, Everest is known as 'Qomolangma'. It is also in the west that the desert descends to about 150m (nearly 500ft) below sea level, so there's a vast topographic range. China's great rivers – the Yangzi, the Yellow and several other less legendary ones – originate in the west, and their waters are put to effective use in irrigation and hydroelectricity projects, irking downstream neighbours in Southeast Asia who get only the dregs. The rivers also electrify Chinese life with the periodic drama of floods, some of which have figured among mankind's great natural disasters.

TEEMING CITIES

Since the end of World War II, China's population has doubled to more than 1.34 billion. It is the most populous nation on earth, with

China's budding gymnasts

more than one-fifth of all of the world's people. There are 56 ethnic groups in China, of which the Han are by far the largest. Most others are East Asian in appearance and live in the west or the far north-east. Religious beliefs include Buddhism, Daoism, Confucianism, Islam and (for a very small minority) Christianity. Few Chinese devoutly follow any organised religion, due largely to the Communist government's opposition to it, though ancestor worship and a strikingly profound patriotism permeate much of the nation.

The bulk of China's vast population is concentrated in the country's east and south, where even a provincial town might have hundreds of thousands of inhabitants. China has 134 cities with populations of at least half a million. Combining family-planning measures with restrictions on internal migration, the authorities once tried to maintain a constant balance of urban and rural populations by keeping the great majority in the countryside (around 60 percent). Despite these efforts, millions of surplus farm labourers pour into the cities in search of work. As a result, China's big cities are immense.

Riding a bicycle to work across any of these cities can be a daily chore taking one or two hours. The number of cars in China's cities has exploded since the turn of the century, making cycling more

BABY RATIONING

Chinese toddlers are among the cutest in the world, but between 1979 and 2015, official policy stated families were only permitted to have one child. However, the policy was gradually relaxed in 2013, when offspring from one-child families who married a partner who was also an only child were allowed to have two children. The policy finally ended in 2015 when it was declared that all couples were free to have two children, but many young urban families still opt for a single child, citing reasons such as economic pressures and busy lifestyles.

hazardous. It has also deepened the pollution problem caused by exhaust fumes spewed out from heavy trucks and buses. Rush-hour traffic jams are so severe in Beijing that even commuter rail lines opened over the past decade can't ease what people in the capital call a 'paralysis' in the streets.

Early-morning taijiquan (t'ai chi) in a Shanghai park

The prospect of a long trek to the factory is only one of the disadvantages of big-city life. The housing is cramped and usually drab (though the fast-growing middle class has remodelled many of those units, while developers carve out swathes of older cities for ornate high-rises). Shopping can be time-consuming and inconvenient due to crowds and traffic jams. But life in town is generally much more comfortable than in the countryside with facilities available from hospitals to schools.

Wages range from a dollar per day in the countryside to thousands of *yuan* per month for urban white-collar workers. Costs of living in China are a fraction of those in the West, though Beijing and Shanghai are quickly losing their bargain status to inflation. Still, rent might run to only 100 *yuan* per month in rural areas, and basic foods are cheap.

The 'iron ricebowl' concept of assured income regardless of productivity was once as firm a tradition as the daily siesta. For hundreds of millions of peasants, poverty was shared equally. Then, to the consternation of hard-line Communist theoreticians the post-Mao leadership decided to reward extra effort and good ideas with old-fashioned money.

Modern China: A light show in Qingdao

EXPLOITING THE LAND

China's soil is often unproductive, the climate is capricious, and the enormous population is constantly increasing. A drought or typhoon can still upset the balance between the supply of food and the demand, however modest each individual's requirements.

Every available scrap of usable land, including plots that seem impossibly arid or inaccessible, has to be exploited to the very limit, regardless of the scarcity of tractors, trucks, pumps, pipes and other equipment. The problem is certainly not new, but the solutions adopted are. When the Communists came to power in 1949, about 10 percent of the population owned 70 percent of the land. The ideological breakthrough began on the farm, where reformers took aim at decades of lacklustre agricultural production; high costs, low yields and mismanagement had made farming uneconomical.

Realising that the people and the land were the country's most vital assets, the new regime set out to reorganise agriculture along more profitable lines. While allowing peasant smallholders to retain their property, the authorities confiscated land from wealthy landlords and redistributed the bulk of it to the previously landless masses. Slowly a new agricultural order evolved.

THE GREAT LEAP FORWARD

To start with, mutual aid teams were formed in which labour, draught animals and implements were pooled. The next step was the development of cooperatives, in which land, animals and tools were held in common and income was shared. Sometimes as many as 200 families from one or more villages would join forces. Revenue would be collectively owned and invested for the welfare of all.

Mao Zedong believed that China could be industrialised as rapidly as possible, fuelled by ideological motivation and the reorganisation of production. Not only the cities but also rural communities were encouraged to use their surplus labour and resources for heavy industries, especially steel production. Cooperatives were merged into an even larger unit – the commune – a group of villages and outlying hamlets responsible for local agricultural and industrial enterprises, commerce, education and home defence. By the end of 1958, virtually every peasant family was part of a people's commune.

'Backyard furnaces', as they were known, were built to produce steel, but because of a lack of expertise, most of the steel produced was unusable. Agricultural production was expected to increase, and so local leaders falsely reported astronomical growth to advance their careers and avoid being called politically uncommitted. Between 1959 and 1961, the failure of the Great Leap Forward policies, combined with three years of bad weather, led to the 20th century's greatest famine.

THE 'SECOND REVOLUTION'

After the death of Mao Zedong in 1976, a gradual rehabilitation of individual initiative and the profit motive spread across the countryside. Farmers were first allowed, then encouraged, to devote themselves to their private plots. Incentives were phased in so that peasants were allowed to sell their surplus production and the yield of their private gardens for whatever the market would bear.

With a green light for cottage industries, rural profits snowballed. The new approach to agriculture soon filled the markets with an abundance of produce and improved the living standards of enterprising farmers.

The success of the new agricultural policy was so striking that the authorities turned to the industrial field. To the dismay of traditional ideologues, Beijing called for a decentralised economy. Factory managers were instructed to adapt to market pressures, although the method of doing so often defied solution. At the same time, private entrepreneurs were allowed to open their own restaurants, shops and service industries. The infallibility of Marx and Lenin was officially questioned: the *People's Daily* conceded that the prophets of Communism could not solve all modern-day problems. These trends exploded after 2000, prompting jokes that

Rice terraces in Guangxi

Communism is just a name in China, no longer an ideological directive. Today, China is the world's second-largest economy.

LIFE ON THE FARM

If you have a chance to visit a rural community, don't miss it. From all you've heard about communes, you might imagine barracks for living quarters and a mess hall for dinner. Instead you'll find a collection of villages, each a cluster of single-storey brick or cement-block houses or, in poorer regions, a scattering of mud huts with thatched roofs. In the main street of each village (which probably isn't paved) a shop sells everything from cotton rations to pots and pans. Bicycle repairmen hammer and clang, old men play cards and apple-cheeked children peer curiously at foreigners. In richer villages, it's a different story. You'll find houses that resemble modern villas. Inside, the amenities can rival those of China's most prosperous cities.

Many of China's most prosperous farmers are concentrating less on farming than on profitable sideline industries. Hancunhe, one of 11 villages in a commune near Beijing, for example, formed a construction company of local bricklayers in 1978 to build homes and offices for urban Beijing's rising middle class. Incomes shot up from destitution to millions of US dollars for the village. Since 2000, numerous Chinese villages have shunned farming for theme tourism or redevelopment into bedroom communities for big cities.

Life on many farms, of course, continues to be harsh, with back-breaking work, long hours, low returns and little public health care. Increased mechanisation is beginning to ease the farmers' burden in more remote areas. With bureaucratic constraints relaxed and grassroots initiative rewarded, peasants with imagination and energy are earning money – sometimes small fortunes – in the free markets of nearby villages and towns, selling surplus produce and the yield of their private plots and whatever they can manufacture. The official policy now smiles on enthusiastic peasants who 'get

The bicycle is still a popular means of transport across much of China

rich first', because unless those in the countryside prosper, those in the cities can hardly rest easy.

TOURIST EXCURSIONS

For the tourist, seeking to unveil the workings of agriculture and industry adds much to the fascination of China, and tourism authorities routinely arrange excursions to factories and farms. Originally a propaganda exercise, these tours proved a great success. There is no longer any attempt to deny evident shortcomings. Nor do official guides disguise the fact that they are showing off model institutions of which the nation is proud, and not necessarily typical establishments. If your tour group happens to be served a nine-course banquet at a collective farm's canteen, no one will try to convince you that this is the way ordinary farmers really live.

Such excursions are among the advantages of package tours to China. You might not know in advance (even up to the day before) what's on the agenda but the local tourism authorities try hard to organise varied and fulfilling programmes.

Self-guided travel has become increasingly convenient over the past decade. Many Westerners without language skills wing it on their own over railway lines, on bumpy public buses and through flashy new airports. They must occasionally forage for English-speakers, but those are seldom too far off. Hotel clerks and some foreign service desks in railway stations can almost always help.

China's formal tourist attractions are so varied and dispersed that a first trip can be little more than a preview. Even if time and money permit more than three weeks, you will probably have to choose between a Yangzi River voyage and the Mogao Caves, or between Lijiang and the Silk Road.

EATING AND SHOPPING

Most tourists would agree that the food in China is an attraction in itself. Whether you're attending an official banquet or trying your luck at a noodle stall, now is the time to sample classic recipes prepared with genuine ingredients in time-honoured manners (see page 218).

Souvenir-shopping is on almost every visitor's must-do list. Tourist areas are packed with local-themed stalls and markets. Typically on offer are ceramics, jade, silk, paintings, traditional clothes and a wealth of other mementoes. Some are what they claim to be, others are fake. Just be sure to bargain.

You can also find heaps of bargains in neighbourhood department stores. Shopping malls in larger cities, such as Beijing and Shanghai, sell genuine Western-branded goods, as well as the pirated versions. You will also find

Visiting a farm

If you are visiting Beijing, you can take city buses from Dongzhimen or Dawanglu to farming villages 10 to 50km (6 to 31 miles) outside the urban sprawl, spend a day there and return by nightfall.

familiar names such as Carrefour and Wal-Mart. In smaller towns or remote areas where minorities live you may find local products unique to that area.

EXOTIC ENTERTAINMENT

After a long day of sightseeing, you might be tempted to pass on the 'nightlife' – don't. This could be your only chance to see an authentic opera, Chinese acrobats or comics you will laugh at without understanding a single word. Note that people tend to be miserly when it comes to applause, but don't let that take away from the fun.

Even after you've seen China's treasures, you can still find reasons to keep coming back. Language classes lasting days to years are available at many universities while acupuncture, opera,

THE ART OF LACQUER

Since the feudal Zhou dynasty some 2,500 years ago, works of art in lacquer, a resinous varnish, have been a Chinese speciality. The lacquer and the dyes used are of a particular type, and applying the various layers of this fragile material is a time-consuming exercise. Sometimes, as in the Song style, layers of different colours are applied, each highly polished, then the finished object is engraved to reveal its multiple nuances. In the sumptuous Tang pieces, the shimmering surface is painted or inlaid with mother-of-pearl.

Lacquer is used to decorate boxes, fans, plates, musical instruments, furniture and the pillars of temples and palaces. Examples from the Ming and Qing dynasties, delicately engraved and painted in red, are still copied today.

Many Chinese towns and villages have at least one lacquer factory where tourists can watch the manufacturing process, which is still largely carried out by hand.

cooking and martial arts appeal to many. But the most unforgettable experience of China is simply being among the people. Wade into the sea of China's billion people to see mobs of angrily honking cars, anxious throngs at bus stops, and groups doing slow-motion callisthenics. See a pensioner take his canary out for an airing or stumble upon a busy market stall preparing snacks. The tourist draws attention: there'll be stares and occasions when you may even feel uncomfortable, but this is all part of the unique experience.

Dim sum in a Guangzhou restaurant

NOTES ABOUT SPELLING

For the past century, the commonest way to spell Chinese words in roman letters was the Wade-Giles method. However, *pinyin* (literally 'phonetic sound') is the modern standard, and is the official system used inside the People's Republic.

This book uses *pinyin*. Travellers will encounter both forms of spelling in Asia, so must sometimes make certain linguistic leaps of recognition. The capital was spelt Peking in the Wade-Giles method, and is Beijing in *pinyin*. The founder of the Communist Party used to be Mao Tse-tung; now he's Mao Zedong.

The only *pinyin* transliterations that are not fairly obvious as regards pronunciation are *qi*, which is pronounced *chee*, and xi, pronounced *shee*. Thus, the Ch'ing dynasty is now the Qing dynasty, and the ancient capital Sian is now Xi'an.

A BRIEF HISTORY

Hundreds of thousands of years ago, the prologue to Chinese civilisation was enacted by means of the flicker of a carefully tended fire. 'Peking Man' – *Homo erectus*, a forebear of *Homo sapiens* – achieved a mastery of fire. We might call it the first Chinese invention. Not that he devised any way of creating fire. Peking Man simply learnt how to capture flame, perhaps from a forest fire, and keep it alight. He thus enjoyed two revolutionary luxuries: light and heat.

Technologically and sociologically, it was a phenomenal breakthrough: with fire, communities could live year-round in one cave, in which cooking and even smelting could be pursued. And so, by 600,000 BC, about 50km (31 miles) southwest of present-day Beijing, the ancestors of mankind were ready to settle down. Several hundred thousand years later, when Marco Polo reached the capital of China, he was astonished by a further development in fire technology. The Chinese, he announced, used black stones dug out of mountains as fuel. Europeans did not yet have a word for 'coal', nor had they discovered a use for it.

THE FIRST DYNASTIES

The confluence of mythology and history in China took place around 4,000 years ago during what is referred to as the Xia (Hsia) dynasty. This was still the Stone Age, but the people are thought to have mastered the art of making silk (see box), and written language was already in use, originally by oracles and then by official scribes – China's first scholars.

The secret of silk

From as early as the Neolithic period, the Chinese people made silk from thread produced by the caterpillars they cultivated on the leaves of mulberry trees. It remained a closely guarded Chinese secret until the 6th century AD, when silkworms were smuggled to the West.

Chinese writing has an unbroken history of over 4,000 years

During the second of the quasi-legendary dynasties, the Shang (from about the 16th to 11th centuries BC), the Chinese developed an interest in art. Careful geometric designs as well as dragon and bird motifs adorned bowls and implements. And with the arrival of the Bronze Age, the Chinese created bronze vessels of such beauty and originality that, until recently, Western archaeologists refused to believe they were cast 3,000 years ago.

The Shang gave rise to the concept of one Chinese nation under one government. Among the advances of the era were the introduction of astronomical calculations, the use of cowrie shells as a unit of exchange, the construction of palaces and temples, and the refinement of table manners through the introduction of chopsticks.

The Zhou (Chou) clan had long been vassals of the Shang, but eventually grew strong enough to defeat them in warfare in the 11th century. They continued to hold sway until the 5th century BC. They built a capital at Chang'an (now called Xi'an), and the sons of Zhou rulers were dispatched to preside over vassal states in a feudal-like system. Chinese boundaries were expanded, land reform was instituted and towns were built. But perhaps more significantly, the declining years of the Zhou era produced two of China's most influential thinkers.

In the rest of the world, China's supreme sage, Kongfuzi (K'ung Fu-tzu), is better known by the romanised name 'Confucius'. He was born in 551 BC in what is now Shandong province in eastern China. So profound was his influence that 11 Chinese emperors made pilgrimages to the birthplace of the Great Teacher. You, too, can pay your respects at the vast temple raised on the site of his home in the small town of Qufu, and at his tomb in the woods just to the north.

The classics of Confucius, while seldom addressing spiritual and metaphysical matters, set standards for social and political conduct that still underlie many of the Chinese ways of doing and perceiving. Confucius laid great stress on the proper and harmonious relationships between ruler and subject, parent and child, teacher and student, the individual and the state. These relationships were deemed to be hierarchical and dictatorial. If the order was disturbed, dire consequences inevitably resulted. The son who disobeyed the father would bring disaster upon himself and his family, just as the emperor who defied the 'mandate of heaven' or ignored the good of the empire brought ruin upon the nation.

Over the centuries Confucius has suffered more changes of fortune than probably any other philosopher. Honoured soon after his death as the greatest of scholars, he was later revered as semi-divine; you can still visit temples to Confucius in many cities. But during the Cultural Revolution (1966–76) he was denounced as a counter-revolutionary force. It was only after the

Shang bronzes

Chinese craftsmen of the Shang dynasty mastered the art of bronze casting. First a wax model was coated with clay and fired. This melted the wax and hardened the clay into a mould, into which molten bronze was poured. More elaborate Shang bronzes were moulded in several sections then assembled.

death of Chairman Mao (1976) and the opening of China to the outside world under more progressive reformers that Confucius, too, was 'rehabilitated'.

Statue of Confucius in his Beijing temple

Unlike Confucius, about whose life many specific details are known, the philosopher Laozi (Lao Tse or Lao-Tzu) is something of an enigma. Estimates of his date of birth vary by well over a century. One legend even says he taught the young Confucius. Laozi is immortalised by his book of thoughts on man, nature and the universe, *Daodejing* ('The Way and Its Power'), which became the major text of China's greatest indigenous religion, Daoism (Taoism). With its emphasis on nature, intuition, the individual, paradox ('the knowledge which is not knowledge') and the cosmic flow known as 'the Way', Daoism became the religion of artists and philosophers.

After the death of Confucius, the Zhou dynasty entered a time of upheaval known as the 'Warring States' period (475–221 BC). Despite political strife, social and economic advances included the introduction of iron, the development of infantry armies, the circulation of currency, the beginning of private land ownership, the expansion of cities and the breakdown of class barriers. This era would give birth to the first emperor to unify China.

THE CHINESE EMPIRE

The word *China* is a relatively recent innovation, believed to be derived by foreigners from the name Qin (Ch'in), the first dynasty to unify China

Qinshi Huangdi persecuted Confucian scholars

after the Warring States period. 'China', of course, is a non-Chinese term. Even today, the Chinese still call their nation *Zhongguo* (literally 'Middle Kingdom'), referring to its position at the centre of the universe in respect to heaven and earth.

Under the first emperor, Qinshi Huangdi (221–206 BC), the empire was organised along strict lines. Land was divided into provinces and prefectures, with power vested in a central government staffed by highly educated bureaucrats. Disapproved books were burnt and dissidents were either executed or exiled. Canals, roads and the Great Wall were built under the auspices of an extensive public works programme staffed mostly by conscripts. Official decrees standardised weights and measures and even the axle dimensions of all wagons (the latter edict kept transport in the same ruts for countless years). You can visit a site of the Qin dynasty today at Xi'an, where the first emperor's terracotta army was unearthed in 1974 (see page 106).

The Han dynasty (206 BC–AD 220), which followed the Qin, consolidated the imperialistic order. Civil servants were selected by exams, the centralised government standardised currency, and the 'Silk Road' across Central Asia opened up global trade. On the military front, the Han triumphed over the marauding Huns and the Central Asian nomads, and Chinese sovereignty was extended almost to today's frontiers.

A golden age began, and a university was established in the capital city, Chang'an (now Xi'an). Intellectuals, who had been harried by the Qin, were now encouraged in their creative endeavours, and with the invention of paper, the influence of their writings became more widespread. Trade and industry developed and communication systems improved. Sculpture, ceramics and silk manufacture flourished. And the arrival of Buddhism, which came to China from India via Tibet, was to have an enduring effect on Chinese life and art.

THE THREE KINGDOMS

Like many dynasties before and after, the Han succession ended around AD 220 in a new struggle for power and anarchy. As a result, the nation was split into three competing kingdoms. The era of the Three Kingdoms lasted only about half a century, but it had as a legacy some thrilling tales of derring-do that later inspired various plays and a classic Ming-dynasty novel. And the first mention of tea-drinking in China occurs in the 3rd century, a footnote of fascination for social historians.

Over the next several hundred years a series of dynasties, some led by foreign rulers, held power under almost constant threat from usurpers at home and abroad. Regionalism and class distinction re-emerged, and strong national government was set back by division and conflict. During this period many people moved to the south, and the Yangzi (Yangtze) valley became the leading centre of Chinese culture. As for foreign invaders, they brought new ideas but, as often happened in China, they were assimilated into the more advanced society of the Middle Kingdom.

National unity and strength were renewed under the Sui dynasty (AD 581–618), a brief prelude to the highest achievements of Chinese art. The Sui built a stately new metropolis at Chang'an, near the site of the old Han capital (present-day Xi'an, in Shaanxi province). They also began work on the Grand Canal, which was to link the rice-growing areas of the Yangzi valley with Beijing, an engineering achievement comparable to the building of the Great Wall.

THE GLORY OF THE TANG

In the realm of culture, no era of Chinese history has surpassed the Tang (T'ang) dynasty (618–907), during which poetry and art reached a brilliant apex. China's Imperial Academy of Letters was founded, about 900 years before any such institution was established in Europe. The first-known printed book, a Buddhist scripture, was published in China in 868.

The capital city, Chang'an, had a population of more than a million, which was far more people than European cities had at the time. In Chang'an, extravagant palaces and temples were interspersed with markets stocked with exotica from as far away as Byzantium. Foreign traders journeyed here to purchase silk, porcelain and spices.

BUDDHISM IN CHINA

Founded in India in the 6th century BC, Buddhism is believed to have reached China about 500 years later. It was brought by merchants who arrived in caravans via the Silk Road, the trade routes that were later travelled by Marco Polo. Monumental artworks in the caves at Dunhuang, created in the 4th and 5th centuries AD, reveal that Buddhism had long been flourishing in western China. By the time of the Tang dynasty, Buddhist temples and pagodas were a prominent feature of the Chinese landscape, and Buddhist monks, pilgrims and worshippers numbered in the hundreds of thousands. Several Tang emperors officially supported the religion; the empress Wu Zetian, in particular, surrounded herself with Buddhist advisers.

Buddhism reached its zenith in China in the 9th century, but it has continued to shape Chinese culture to the present day, especially in its Chan (Zen) school. The temples and sculptures that survive are among China's leading tourist attractions. Today more than 294 million Chinese (about 21 percent of the population) are Buddhists, and the temples are active places of worship.

Scholars, poets and artists all achieved prominence. Encyclopaedias were compiled, and poetry evolved a metrical system and lines that rhymed. As Buddhism gained strength and took on a Chinese character, it inspired the construction of great temples and pagodas adorned with frescoes and statues. Artists painted sensitive landscapes and perfected the subtle brushwork of calligraphy. Sculptors excelled in portraying lifelike human, animal and religious figures.

With the invention of paper came a flowering of calligraphy

However, by the beginning of the 10th century, the Tang rulers had lost their control of the country. Revenues from tax collection dwindled, ambitious palace eunuchs plotted, reform schemes failed and rebellious forces threatened. By 907 the people could see, through all the turmoil and confusion, that the Tang dynasty had lost the 'mandate of heaven', and so it was that the last of the Tang monarchs abdicated.

THE SONG DYNASTY

The next half-century is known as the era of 'The Five Dynasties and the Ten Kingdoms'. This transitional period was marred by political and military infighting, and by rivalry, intrigue and cruelty. Then, a general named Zhaokuangyin (Chao K'uang-yin) came onto the scene and founded the Song (Sung) dynasty (960–1280), which ensured Chinese cultural supremacy for the next three centuries.

The number of cities in China increased dramatically under the Song, mostly in the Yangzi valley and in the southeast. Where there were

Sculpture from the Tang dynasty is both lifelike and lively

cities, there were scholars, artists and artisans. Movable type revolutionised printing, books became more common and literacy increased; Chinese scientists published works on botany, astronomy, mathematics and geography. Emperors appointed court painters, and glazed porcelain was received abroad with admiration and awe.

But while art and scholarship continued to thrive, the political and military situation deteriorated under the Song. Foreign invaders chipped away at the empire. Taxpayers groaned under the burden of the army and the tribute paid to foreign rivals, and complained about the luxuries of palace life. Disaster was inevitable: invaders from Manchuria forced the Song to retreat to the south. And the Mongol invaders, headed by Genghis Khan, swept across China, bringing the country under foreign rule for the first time.

UNDER MONGOL RULE

A poignant drama signalled the Mongol conquest of China (1279–1368). After 20 years of resistance, the Song armies were finally ready to capitulate. The boy emperor was hidden aboard a ship, but when it was surrounded by enemy craft, the last of the loyal commanders seized the eight-year-old monarch in his arms and leapt with him to his death in the sea.

The new era, known as the Yuan dynasty, lasted less than a century. Creativity declined, but the new ruler of China, Kublai Khan (grandson of the great Genghis Khan), had an open mind and a generally humane attitude. He appointed Chinese bureaucrats and scholars to help rule the country. Historians generally conclude that Kublai Khan became an 'almost authentic' Chinese emperor, that the conquerors changed more profoundly than the conquered.

The capital of the new empire was built on the site of present-day Beijing and was called 'Dadu' or, in Mongolian, 'Cambaluc' – spelled Kanbalu by that most renowned of medieval travellers, Marco Polo. His account of the vast new capital throbs with admiration for the palaces and bazaars and the profusion of shade trees. He regards with wonder the Great Khan's religious tolerance, generosity and admirable taste in wives. He reports all manner of innovations, not least the invention of paper money. (Counterfeiting, he reports, had also been discovered.)

With the death of Kublai Khan in 1294, the Mongols started to lose their grip. The emperor's successors lacked his vision and vigour. Insurrection was in the air, met by oppression and resulting in ever more sustained resistance. Finally, an uprising led by a peasant general, Zhuyuanzhang (Chu Yüan-chang), routed the Yuan rulers. In 1368 Zhuyuanzhang assumed the throne of the Middle Kingdom, founding yet another dynasty – the Ming.

THE BRILLIANCE OF MING

In Chinese, the word Ming is written as a composite of the characters for 'sun' and 'moon', which are combined to mean 'brilliant' or 'glorious'. In fact, the dynasty (1368–1644) didn't quite live up to its name. Beauty was achieved in architecture, sculpture and the decorative arts. But literature, now serving a wider audience, produced few masterworks, and philosophy saw no new developments. Science, which had been far more advanced than in Europe, was so gravely neglected that China became a technological backwater.

Perhaps to compensate for the Mongol interlude, the Ming emperors opted for traditional Chinese values.

Conservatism and hostility to foreign ideas, however, could not be absolutely maintained. During the Ming era, China imported

A 16th century illustration

tobacco, pineapples and peanuts. The first Christian missionaries came to China with the arrival at Guangzhou, in 1516, of Portuguese ships. Thanks to the emancipated Confucian tradition, they were usually welcomed, although they hardly achieved mass conversions. From the Jesuits the Chinese learnt mathematics and astronomy.

At first the Ming headquarters were moved south to the Yangzi River port of Nanjing ('Southern Capital'), but at the beginning of the 15th century the capital returned to what was now renamed Beijing ('Northern Capital'). Here Ming architects and artisans produced some of China's most elegant palaces, temples and parks, including the Forbidden City and Temple of Heaven, masterpieces that survive today.

The move northwards made the supervision of defence efforts on the ever-sensitive borders of the empire easier. The Ming rulers oversaw the construction and renovation of the sections of the Great Wall that millions of tourists visit today, but even this eventually proved incapable of keeping out enemies. By the 17th century, after repeated forays, infiltrations and invasions, forces from Manchuria capitalised on domestic upheavals in China to take power in Beijing, almost by default. But consolidating control over the rest of the country was a long and brutal business. The Manchu invaders called their new dynasty the Qing (Ch'ing). It held power until modern times (1644–1911).

PIGTAILS AND PROSPERITY

The Manchu adopted all the refinements of Chinese civilisation, and installed a regime so conservative that it began to hold back progress. But for all their Confucian outlook and traditionalism, the Manchu imposed one singular feature of their own culture: the wearing of pigtails.

One of the most dynamic emperors was Kangxi (K'ang-hsi), who reigned at almost the same time as Louis XIV of France. He presided over an era of prosperity and positive achievement, rebuilding Beijing, encouraging scholarship and expanding the empire to its greatest area. By his predecessors' standards, Kangxi lived modestly; his concubines numbered no more than 300.

A GALAXY OF FIRSTS

Many inventions first saw the light in China, often centuries before they reached the West. The Chinese produced cast iron from the 4th century BC, 1,800 years before Europe discovered the technique. From the 1st century AD – 1,000 years before Europe – paper was made by pulping rags and wood fibre. Block printing was known in China in the 9th century, and movable type came into use a couple of hundred years later. Printing was not invented in Europe until 1440.

The Chinese made mechanical clocks, powered by a waterwheel, from the 8th century. Water was also used to drive early textile and winnowing machinery. They were the first to build suspension bridges, combining bamboo and cast-iron chains. They invented the foot-stirrup, which revolutionised cavalry warfare, and gunpowder, which was used to propel arrows from bamboo tubes – the first rockets.

The magnetic compass was another Chinese first, and at least 200 years before vaccination was developed in Europe, Chinese doctors were practising immunisation by placing pus from a smallpox pustule in a patient's nostril.

Under Emperor Qianlong (Ch'ien Lung), Kangxi's grandson, conflict arose between Europe's empires and the Middle Kingdom. King George III of Britain sent an emissary to negotiate diplomatic and trade relations. The emperor flatly turned him down but thanked him for showing such 'submissive loyalty in sending this tribute mission'.

China believed itself to be the centre of the world: it had nothing to learn or gain from so-called foreign devils. But such sublime self-assurance was to be short-lived.

The soaring demand in Europe for Chinese tea, silk and porcelain brought increasing pressure for freer trade. However, the Chinese were stubborn. Needing no commodities, they would accept only silver bullion in exchange for goods, thus undermining Britain's balance of payments. Then, at about the turn of the 19th century, wily foreign traders thought of an alternative medium of payment – opium. Tons of the drug were brought into China from India.

In 1839 the Chinese government finally cracked down on this drain on the treasury, which was also causing mass addiction among the Chinese. Some 20,000 chests of opium were confiscated from British merchants in Guangzhou (Canton), and a Qing imperial edict was issued that terminated trade between China and Britain.

Retaliation came a year later in the first of the Opium Wars, which culminated in a series of 'unequal treaties' forced on an increasingly weak Manchu regime. Under the 1842 Treaty of Nanjing, China was obliged to pay an indemnity to Britain, to open major ports to foreign political and economic penetration, and to surrender Hong Kong to Britain.

The Jesuits

In addition to Christian texts, Jesuit missionaries published more than 100 treatises in Chinese on Western science and technology. Outstanding among the Jesuits was Matteo Ricci, who mastered Chinese, devised his own system of transliteration and compiled a dictionary.

A Guangzhou opium den in the 19th century

Infinitely more costly in human terms was the Taiping Rebellion, which began in 1850 as a peasant revolt. There was a struggle between the Qing dynasty and rebels determined to overthrow such traditional values as respect for religion, private property and male supremacy. The revolt lasted 14 years and cost more lives than World War I. The Qing finally won, but the regime and the nation would never be the same again.

WAR WITH JAPAN

This became patently clear during the Sino-Japanese War of 1894–5, in which the inadequacy of the Chinese army was starkly displayed. Japan and Western powers were dismantling the Chinese Empire. Demands for reform won the support of the emperor, but his notoriously scheming aunt, the Empress Dowager Cixi (Tz'u Hsi), edged him off the throne. Soon after, Cixi had the chance to exploit the Boxer Rebellion (1900), a revolt against foreign influence. It was finally put down by the intervention of all the great powers, which joined together in an unprecedented alliance. China was saddled with the payment of

The Nine Dragon Screen in Beihai Park

a humiliating indemnity and a further loss of respect.

The elderly empress died in 1908, one day after the mysterious death of her nephew, the unseated emperor. The heir apparent was a two-year-old prince, Puyi – hardly the leader the dynasty and the nation needed in the face of civil disorder and foreign threats. Less than three years later, an army uprising took place in Wuhan and quickly won widespread support. The success of the revolution surprised many observers. It came so suddenly that Dr Sun Yat-sen, the inveterate revolutionary who had led several earlier insurrections, was still abroad at the time. He returned in triumph to accept the presidency of the Chinese Republic. The Manchu dynasty and its child-emperor surrendered in 1911. Puyi continued to live in the Imperial Palace (Forbidden City) in Beijing until 1924, but the rule of the Sons of Heaven on the Dragon Throne, which had begun 4,000 years earlier, had come to an end.

But the path of the new republic was strewn with dangers. A warlord seized power in Beijing, hoping to restore the monarchy. A harried Sun Yat-sen then moved his new Guomindang (Nationalist Party) south to Guangzhou. Towards the end of hostilities, China entered World War I on the side of the Allies. But the 1919 Versailles Peace conference proved a bitter disappointment when Japan, and not China, won control over Germany's former holdings in Shandong province. Frustration inspired protest demonstrations. The targets of increasingly widespread bitterness were the foreign powers and the regime in Beijing, as agitation for drastic social reforms caught the imagination of students and factory workers.

In 1921, the Communist Party of China (with a total membership of 53) held its first national congress, in secret, in Shanghai. A cautious Communist alliance was arranged with the Guomindang in 1924. Disappointed with the Western powers, Sun Yat-sen turned for support to the leaders of the young Soviet regime. The Kremlin obliged by sending political and military advisers. In turn, Dr Sun dispatched his 37-year-old follower, Chiang Kai-shek, as head of a mission to Moscow. Dr Sun, who rallied the Chinese with his Three Principles – Nationalism, Democracy and the People's Livelihood – died in 1925. His successor, Chiang Kai-shek, took over the campaign, moving the capital to Nanjing.

In 1927 Chiang turned on the Communists as well as on leftists within his own party, unleashing a vehement, bloody purge. The Communists, who had already organised the support of millions of peasants, gathered strength in the south. But, facing increasing military pressure, they set forth on the epic Long March to northwest China, a distance of some 10,000 perilous kilometres (over 6,200 miles). During one of history's greatest strategic retreats, one of the founders of the Chinese Communist Party, Mao Zedong (Mao Tse-tung), was chosen as party leader. It was a mandate he was to retain for the rest of his life.

THE BITTER YEARS OF WAR

In 1931 Manchuria was seized by Japan and then proclaimed as the 'independent' state of Manchukuo. This was to be a fatal prologue to World War II. Over the next few years Japanese troops advanced into several other areas of northern China. The government of Chiang Kai-shek was so busy tracking Communists that the Japanese foe merited only casual attention. At one point Chiang himself was kidnapped by some of his own officers, a sensational interlude known as the Sian (Xi'an) Incident. Its aim was to convince him to unite with the Communists.

But by the time concerted action could be planned, the invaders had moved on to a broad offensive. The Japanese juggernaut crushed all resistance in the big coastal cities as well as in Beijing and Nanjing. The retreat ended in 1938 with the Nationalist government dug in behind the gorges of the Yangzi River, in the last-ditch capital of Chongqing.

Even before entering World War II, the US was supporting the armies of Chiang Kai-shek with food, fuel and transport. However, once in the field, the Americans soon became disheartened with the confusion, corruption and stalling. Chiang, they believed, was hoarding everything from rice to aircraft in the struggle against the Chinese Communists and leaving the Allies to worry about the Japanese.

When Japan surrendered in 1945, Chiang Kai-shek could share the victory toasts as one of the Allies. But he was already losing the battle of his lifetime – for China. By V-J Day (15 August), when Japan officially surrendered, the Chinese Communists controlled

HISTORICAL FOOTPRINTS

Even today, you occasionally see old Chinese women hobbling along on deformed feet – living relics of the feudal practice of foot-binding. As early as the Song dynasty, nearly 1,000 years ago, the preference for women with small feet took a sinister turn. Small girls had their feet broken, turned under, then bandaged to prevent them from growing. The fact that they were in excruciating pain and could never again walk normally seemed secondary to the potential appeal of 'three-inch feet'. It also kept the women effectively in their place, virtually house-bound. At first, it was practised by only the very rich, who regarded it as a status symbol. Over the years, the practice spread even to poor farming families. Foot-binding was outlawed from time to time, but generally remained a fact of Chinese life over the centuries. It began to die out only after the fall of the monarchy in 1911.

an area inhabited by nearly one-quarter of the nation's population. At first the Americans tried to mediate between the Communists and the Nationalists, even while continuing to supply the Nationalists. But any chances for post-war cooperation between right and left were wrecked in a matter of months. China was sinking into civil war.

Mao Zedong's famous Little Red Book

Despite early setbacks, the Communist armies became an overwhelming force. They were greeted as liberators by the peasants and met only desultory resistance in most cities. The Nationalists, in despair, fell back and finally fled, moving the government and countless national treasures to the island of Taiwan, pledging to return one day.

In Tiananmen Square in Beijing on 1 October 1949, Chairman Mao Zedong proclaimed Zhonghua Renmin Gongheguo – the People's Republic of China. After thousands of years of empire and a few decades of violent transition, the most populous country in the world was committed to Communism.

IMPOSING THE NEW ORDER

Before any grandiose plans could be implemented, China's fledgling rulers had to rebuild society and a crippled economy. Agrarian reform was the first revolutionary innovation, followed by organisation of the cities under Party control.

Hardly had the groundwork been laid than China entered the Korean War, sending 'volunteers' to fight against American-led United

Nations forces. Relations between the US and China suffered, but Beijing's ties with Moscow prospered in comradely harmony. The USSR shipped technical advisors and roubles to China, and many new institutions were set up along Soviet lines. As in Russia, the farms were collectivised and heavy industry took economic precedence.

Mao Zedong's 'Great Leap Forward' (1959) was designed as a crash programme of economic growth, but it kept the country in turmoil and brought unconvincing results. At about the time the Leap was suddenly reversed, relations between China and the Soviet Union plunged from polite to frosty to hostile because of differences in ideology and competing national interests.

From 1966 to 1976, China was convulsed by the Great Proletarian Cultural Revolution. This was Mao's attempt to put an end to bureaucratic stagnation and the degeneration of the Chinese Revolution. He saw students as his activists and encouraged them to turn on their teachers. The most chaotic phase lasted from May 1966 until late 1967. Students organised Red Guard units all over China. Mao's slogan that 'It is right to rebel' propelled their campaign to destroy remnants of the old society. Brandishing Mao's *Little Red Book* of quotations, they destroyed temples and historic sites, and broke into homes to burn books and art. Much of China's cultural heritage was lost. Party leaders and other 'counter-revolutionary' forces were denounced and put on trial.

Changes came in quick succession in the 1970s. In 1971 China was admitted to the United Nations. In 1972 the US president, Richard Nixon, visited China, thus paving the way to normalising relations between the two countries. And in September 1976 Chairman Mao Zedong died.

Women's progress?

Mao-era laws to bring equality for women and make divorce possible seemed, in theory, like true progress. In reality, women had to hold full-time jobs in addition to maintaining the home.

THE REPUBLIC AFTER MAO

Chairmain Mao gazes out towards Tiananmen Square

Mao's widow, Jiang Qing, and her close associates (the so-called 'Gang of Four') were arrested, tried and imprisoned. Accused of a wide variety of crimes, they served as convenient scapegoats for the havoc of the Cultural Revolution. Thousands who had suffered during the fervent 1960s and 1970s, including the forceful pragmatist Deng Xiaoping, were rehabilitated. In 1978 Deng became China's paramount leader and inaugurated what he called a 'second revolution'. Mao had considered politics the key to China's progress. Deng put his faith in economic advances.

Relations with the United States were normalised in 1979. Deng travelled to the US and met President Jimmy Carter and business leaders. Deng's policy of 'opening' China to the outside was a recognition that the country needed technological expertise and capital from elsewhere.

To modernise agriculture, Deng disbanded Mao's communes, which had proved over the decades to be a disaster. Farmers could now sell surplus vegetables, fruit, fish or poultry in private markets and keep the profits. As a result, rural agricultural production more than doubled in the 1980s. Deng began reforming industry in China by upgrading technology and managerial systems, implementing price reforms, promoting foreign trade and investment, revamping the banking system and encouraging private business. Later, he even introduced limited stock markets.

Chinese President Xi Jinping

But Deng may be remembered most for enforcing the one-child policy that kept the population in check – a stark contrast to Mao's wishes for a larger population to spur economic growth. Until 2015, parents could legally have only one child, although the original 1978 edict was softened in the 21st century, allowing ethnic minorities, those whose first-born was handicapped, rural inhabitants and parents who were only children to have more than one child. The one-child policy came to an end in 2015. Nowadays, each Chinese couple is permitted to have two children.

CONTEMPORARY CHINA

In April 1989, Tiananmen Square became the focus of the world's media, as students and workers aired their grievances against the government. Angered by widespread corruption, they demanded democratic reform. As the number of protesters swelled to a million, martial law was imposed, and, on the night of 3 June and early hours of 4 June, the army stormed Tiananmen Square. Although debate continues concerning bloodshed in the square itself, at least 300 people are believed to have died in surrounding streets. The incident provoked international outrage and also showed that China's leadership would not tolerate political challenge. To this day 4 June remains a quiet sticking point, with survivors and well-known political dissidents, though carefully watched by authorities, still wanting official acknowledgement of the army's actions.

Despite crushing the democracy movement, the government knew that its survival depended on both absolute power and the continuing success of its economic reform. The 1990s were a decade of high economic growth as well as tension between China and other nations, as Deng's successor, Jiang Zemin, grappled with China's new role in the international community.

US–China relations have improved since the terrorist attacks of September 11, 2001. In 2001 China joined the World Trade Organisation, and in 2003 Hu Jintao succeeded Jiang Zemin as president and Wen Jiabao replaced Zhu Rongji as premier, completing the shift to a younger leadership.

Since the millennium's turn, China has undergone amazing economic growth. In the first half of 2010 the mainland's GDP grew by 11.1 percent, consistent with much of the past decade, overtaking Japan to become the world's second-largest economy. Under its World Trade Organisation obligations, the government has slowly been opening the economy to foreign players and developing the stock markets. Friendship stores have been replaced by the likes of Wal-Mart, Carrefour and Ikea.

Many people in the cities of the eastern coastal regions and the south have become wealthy, but progress has been slow to reach the countryside, and the rich–poor divide has widened, sparking migration to already crowded cities and occasional riots against rural authorities. Farmers struggle with corrupt local government and loss of land, while many workers are left jobless from defunct state-owned enterprises. The nation's economic miracle is also taking a heavy toll on the environment (China is the world's biggest emitter of carbon) thanks to the uncontrolled expansion of industry, an explosion in car ownership and rising power consumption mostly fuelled by high-pollution coal-fired power stations. The spectre of corruption looms from the smallest village government to the nation's highest court. In the meantime, while life seems freer – you can discuss any issues with friends, travel abroad and watch once-banned movies – the government closely controls content in all mass media, including the proliferation of newspapers in big cities. It blocks sensitive content on the Internet as well as social networking sites such as Facebook and Twitter, as these could be used to organise mass protests.

CHINA'S CENTURY

Beijing's 2008 Olympics told the world China had arrived as a major power. The nearly flawless Games crowned more than a decade of scrambling for Olympics-related foreign investment that saw multinationals retool their world business plans to cash in on China's huge consumer market.

The Chinese have also gained two Nobel Prize laureates. In 2010, Liu Xiaobo was awarded the Peace Prize for his fight for human rights in China, (although he was imprisoned by an outraged government). In 2012, the Nobel Prize for Literature was awarded to novelist and short-story writer Mo Yan.

Political moves in Beijing grab the attention of Washington, Tokyo, Brussels and other world centres. Newly confident as a world economic power, China fears no dispute with other nations over the likes of currency valuation or territorial claims. One-time political rival Taiwan has also begun warming to Beijing since 2008, following the election of a conciliatory president of Taiwan.

But several battles at home keep the government – Communist only in name, but still authoritarian – on guard. Traffic congestion, pollution, lack of affordable housing and spiralling consumer prices are among the complex issues that must be resolved.

China has begun developing alternative energy sources to coal, including domestic solar panels and wind farms. However, economic growth in 2015 has slowed to its lowest level since 2009 and in mid-2015 the world looked on in horror as the Chinese stock market took a dive, halted only after some hefty government intervention. Since 2015, the country's GDP rate has remained stable. Undoubtedly, there is an emergence of a new political and economic order in China.

HISTORICAL HIGHLIGHTS

21st–16th century BC Xia dynasty: the first Chinese state.
16th–11th century BC Shang dynasty. Bronze casting.
11th–5th century BC Zhou dynasty. Capital established at Chang'an. 771 BC Zhou capital moved to Luoyang.
551 BC Birth of Confucius.
475–221 BC Conflict between the 'Warring States'.
221–206 BC Qin dynasty. Construction of the Great Wall.
206 BC–AD 220 Han dynasty. International trade along the Silk Road.
AD 220 Three Kingdoms. First mention of tea-drinking.
265–420 Jin dynasty. Luoyang's temples and palaces destroyed by invaders.
386–581 Northern dynasties. Construction of the Datong Buddhist caves.
420–589 Southern dynasties. China invaded by Huns and Turks.
581–618 Sui dynasty. Printing invented. Grand Canal construction begins.
618–907 Tang dynasty. Invention of gunpowder and porcelain.
907–60 'Five Dynasties and Ten Kingdoms'.
960–1280 Song dynasty. Movable-type printing and paper money.
1279–1368 Yuan (Mongol) dynasty. Beijing the capital. Marco Polo in China.
1368–1644 Ming dynasty. Imperial Palace built in Beijing.
1644–1911 Qing dynasty (Manchu). Rebellions and Opium Wars.
1911–49 Republic of China under Sun Yat-sen then Chiang Kai-shek.
1938–45 Japanese invasion and World War II.
1949 Revolution: Mao Zedong proclaims the People's Republic.
1966–76 Cultural Revolution.
1976 Mao dies, succeeded by Deng Xiaoping. Economic reforms instituted.
1989 Popular demonstration savagely crushed in Tiananmen Square.
1992 Deng restarts economic reforms.
1997 Deng Xiaoping dies. Hong Kong reverts from British to Chinese rule.
1999 Macau reverts from Portuguese to Chinese sovereignty.
2008 Beijing hosts the Olympic Games.
2013 Xi Jinping succeeds Hu Jintao as president.
2015 The one-child policy comes to an end and is replaced with a two-child policy.
2018 China's congress decides to remove a two-term limit for the president.

The Great Wall winds from the Yellow Sea to the Gobi Desert

WHERE TO GO

The most popular cities and sights in China, as well as a selection of less frequently visited ones, are described in detail in this chapter, arranged in eight sections, which encompass broad geographical regions, as well as China's two most important cities, Beijing and Shanghai. Hong Kong and Macau have been omitted, as they are fully explored in their own Berlitz Pocket Guide. The names of the cities and other attractions are given in official pinyin spelling. There is more on language and pronunciation on page 11 and in the Travel Tips section of this guide (see page 238).

PLANNING YOUR TRIP

Choosing an itinerary can be difficult. To see the country in any depth requires at least three weeks. A suggested two-week tour appears on page 6, taking in Shanghai and surroundings, the Yangzi Gorges, Lijiang, Beijing and Xi'an. Less taxing would be a week in and around Shanghai, focusing on the legendary charms of Suzhou and Hangzhou, or a week in and around Beijing. A visit to Yunnan province – the south-western region home to members of many of China's minority groups and some stupendous scenery – is recommended. It can easily be combined with a trip to Guilin and its magnificent landscapes.

BEIJING

A visit to **Beijing ❶**, the medieval and modern capital of China, is an exhausting though rewarding round of palaces and museums, temples and monuments, and streets and stores – a jolting juxtaposition of imperial pomp and contemporary energy.

Beijing has a permanent population of around 21 million, but it is spread over a huge area of 16,800 sq km (about 6,500 sq miles). Some neighbourhoods of the Old City are lined with old *hutong* (alleyways) between tracts of traditional one- and two-storey stone courtyard houses (called *siheyuan*), where life has been highly resilient to change. Around the corner from these fast-disappearing cosy alleys are new housing projects, offices, modern shopping plazas and open-air markets. Hosting the 2008 Olympics gave city authorities the opportunity to expand Beijing's subway system, construct new roads and add green spaces. The city's modernisation has also knocked out all but a few of the courtyard homes, most of which are now protected from further demolition.

Mostly the city is flat, a fact that displeased emperors in the Middle Ages, who ordered hills to be built just north of the Forbidden City (at Jingshan) so they could go up and, in total privacy, enjoy a summer breeze and a birds-eye view over the curved tile roofs of their imperial compound. Try it yourself, perhaps at dawn, when a thin haze drapes itself over the pavilions, redefining yet softening the features of this storybook skyline. You'll see why the emperors wanted it all for themselves.

BEIJING IN HISTORY

Not far from the present-day suburbs of Beijing was the habitat of 'Peking Man', discovered in the 1920s. A cave near the town of **Zhoukoudian** held the skull of a small-brained but upright ancestor of mankind who lived half a million years ago. Scientists are still sifting for the bones, and visitors can tour the site of the dig.

Excavations in downtown Beijing show that it was inhabited over 20,000 years ago, but the place made little stir until the Warring States period (5th–3rd century BC) when, known as Jicheng, it became the capital of the Kingdom of Yan. Renamed Yanjing, the town served as capital for the Liao dynasty in the 10th century ad. The 12th-century Jin (Chin) dynasty called it Zhongdu ('Central Capital') and built an imperial palace as well as the Lugou Bridge; known abroad as the 'Marco Polo Bridge', it is still in use.

The Mongol armies of Genghis Khan levelled Zhongdu in the 13th century, then rebuilt it under the name Dadu ('Great Capital'). By the

The Temple of Heaven

time Marco Polo arrived, the city outshone the capitals of Europe. The Ming dynasty transferred most of the imperial pomp south to Nanjing in the 14th century. Predictably, Dadu received yet another name, Beiping ('Northern Peace'), but had to wait more than 50 years to win back its imperial status and a fresh name. This one – Beijing ('Northern Capital') – is still around. So, happily, are the Ming palaces and temples.

At the beginning of the Qing dynasty, Beijing prospered. New palaces and gardens were laid out and scholarship flourished. It's no surprise that Beijing is still a hub for universities. A long, slow decline from c.1800 culminated in the Boxer Rebellion of 1900, when European armies wrought havoc in the city in retaliation for the siege of their embassies.

SIGHTSEEING

The historic heart of Beijing consisted of three concentric cities, rectangular and symmetrical, and a fourth – Outer City – to the south. Most of the miles of walls that protected each of the four cities

Monument to the People's Heroes

have been destroyed, but the innermost, Forbidden City, still stands high behind its original fortifications.

The elegance of this city plan, which is basically 700 years old, has never been surpassed. A precise north–south axis links the main elements, from the Bell Tower all the way to the gate of the Outer City, 8km (5 miles) to the south. On either side of the axis, important buildings were laid out as mirror images. Thus Ritan (Altar of the Sun) has its equivalent in Yuetan (Altar of the Moon). Similarly complementary were Xidan and Dongdan, the eastern and western business quarters. At the centre of it all is the Forbidden City, the imperial heart of the Middle Kingdom.

TIANANMEN SQUARE

The largest city square on earth, **Tiananmen Square** Ⓐ covers 40 hectares (100 acres) in the very centre of Beijing. The square was the focus of world attention during the student demonstrations of 1989 and their deadly aftermath. The square is breathtaking in its scale and, despite the brash Communist architecture, affords a pleasant panorama, filled by visitors from every corner of China and overflown by kites. At the time of the emperors, the square was only about a quarter its present size. It was expanded in the 1950s to hold up to a million people. In the old, less expansive incarnation Mao Zedong first raised the flag of the new nation on 1 October 1949. Rallies of Red Guards took place here during the Cultural

Revolution. On 1 October 1999, the People's Republic celebrated its golden anniversary here, each of the square's concrete blocks replaced by granite.

ARCHITECTURAL HEIGHTS

China's capital city has exploded in the past decades from a crumbling Soviet-style slum to a modern city of glass skyscrapers, steel shopping malls and curling expressways. In the process, Ming-dynasty maze-like alleyways, *hutongs* (see page 62) have been bulldozed to make way for carbon-copy high-rise housing estates, which are built so hastily that after a few years they already look bedraggled and in some cases themselves need to be replaced. But in the luxury residential and commercial sector, top architects have been inspired to leave their mark on the city. Some were brought out in the lead-up to the 2008 Olympics; others, such as I.M. Pei, had already played their part.

Some of the more ambitious projects include:

National Stadium: Designed by Swiss architects Herzog & de Meuron and nicknamed the Bird's Nest, this 250,000 sq m (2,700,000 sq ft) stadium is a theatre of latticework seating up to 100,000 people.

China Central Television Headquarters: Standing 230m (755ft) high, the headquarters for China Central Television is an Escher-like loop of crazy glass with a companion building shaped like a trapezoidal boot; it is brainchild of Dutch architect Rem Koolhaas. The project's contorted shape on an otherwise conventional skyline ignited quiet discontent in Beijing, but it won CTBUH's best tall building award in 2013.

China National Grand Theatre: This giant shiny spacepod, next to Tiananmen Square, has been dubbed 'The Egg'. Conceived by French architect Paul Andreu, the glass and titanium casing is semi-transparent, allowing passers-by to peep in at performances.

The Great Hall of the People

The low, squat building at the southern end of the square is the **Chairman Mao Zedong Memorial Hall** (Mao Zhuxi Jiniantang; July–Aug Tue–Sun 7–11am, Sept–June 8am–noon; free), which contains the embalmed body of the man who led the People's Republic for its first 27 years. The mausoleum, which is bigger than Lenin's tomb in Moscow's Red Square, is open to a procession of tourists, who are allowed only a few minutes inside.

Just to the north is the **Monument to the People's Heroes**, a granite obelisk unveiled in 1958, which is a perfect example of the Socialist Realist style. The democracy movement established its headquarters here in 1989.

On the western side of the square, the **Great Hall of the People** (Renmin Dahuitang), erected in 1959, is the grandiose meeting place of the National People's Congress, a rubber-stamp parliament. It's a conference centre for hire when the congress isn't meeting (tours available). Behind the Great Hall is the titanium and glass dome of the new **China National Grand Theatre** (http://en.chncpa.org/; see page 53).

Across the plaza to the east is the **National Museum of China** (Tue–Sun 9am–4.30pm; free; http://en.chnmuseum.cn/), which actually consists of two museums. The **Museum of Chinese History** (Zhongguo Lishi Bowuguan) holds about 9,000 items, ranging from prehistoric fossils to breathtaking pottery and bronzes. The **Museum of the Chinese Revolution** (Zhongguo Geming Bowuguan) houses photos, paintings, documents and relics from the period of the Communist revolution.

North across Chang'an Avenue from Tiananmen Square (and leading to the Forbidden City) is the **Gate of Heavenly Peace**, with its portrait of Chairman Mao. On top of this stone wall is a rostrum for reviewing parades, and behind it a huge wooden gate-tower with a double roof. The original 15th-century gate complex was rebuilt in 1651.

FORBIDDEN CITY (GU GONG)

Beijing is too sprawling for strolling around, or the sort of browsing that some European cities offer. Among several exceptions, though, is the **Forbidden City** B (Tue–Sun 8.30am–5pm summer, 8.30am–4.30pm winter; charge; www.dpm.org.cn). Here you will find more than 72 hectares (175 acres) of grandeur, with palaces, courtyards and gardens.

The Forbidden City, so described because it was off-limits to ordinary people for nearly 500 years, is now called the Palace Museum (Gu Gong). Designed to contain the auspicious number of 9,999 rooms, its scale is overwhelming and leaves many visitors bewildered. Built between 1406 and 1420, it was the residence of 24 emperors, their families and their enormous retinues for nearly seven centuries.

Most tourists enter the Forbidden City from the south, after a long walk along a cobbled roadway from the Gate of Heavenly Peace. The main entrance to the compound, **Meridian Gate** I (Wumen), was designed in the 15th century. Officials used the left portal, members of the imperial family the right. Next comes another ceremonial gate, the **Gate of Supreme Harmony** II (Taihemen), first erected in 1420. A pair of monumental bronze lions stand guard.

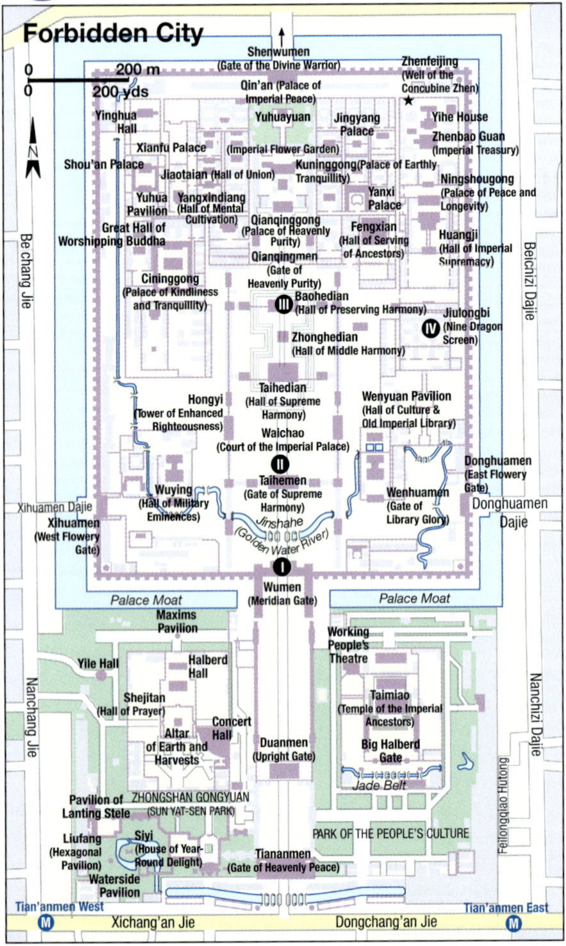
Forbidden City
0 200 m
0 200 yds
N
Shenwumen (Gate of the Divine Warrior)
Zhenfeijing (Well of the Concubine Zhen)
Qin'an (Palace of Imperial Peace)
Yinghua Hall
Yuhuayuan (Imperial Flower Garden)
Jingyang Palace
Yihe House
Zhenbao Guan (Imperial Treasury)
Xianfu Palace
Shou'an Palace
Jiaotaian (Hall of Union)
Kuninggong (Palace of Earthly Tranquillity)
Ningshougong (Palace of Peace and Longevity)
Yuhua Pavilion
Yangxindiang (Hall of Mental Cultivation)
Yanxi Palace
Great Hall of Worshipping Buddha
Qianqinggong (Palace of Heavenly Purity)
Fengxian (Hall of Serving of Ancestors)
Huangji (Hall of Imperial Supremacy)
Be chang Jie
Beichizi Dajie
Qianqingmen (Gate of Heavenly Purity)
Ciningong (Palace of Kindliness and Tranquillity)
Baohedian (Hall of Preserving Harmony)
Jiulongbi (Nine Dragon Screen)
Zhonghedian (Hall of Middle Harmony)
Hongyi (Tower of Enhanced Righteousness)
Taihedian (Hall of Supreme Harmony)
Wenyuan Pavilion (Hall of Culture & Old Imperial Library)
Waichao (Court of the Imperial Palace)
Donghuamen (East Flowery Gate)
Wuying (Hall of Military Eminences)
Taihemen (Gate of Supreme Harmony)
Wenhuamen (Gate of Library Glory)
Xihuamen Dajie
Xihuamen (West Flowery Gate)
Jinshahe (Golden Water River)
Donghuamen Dajie
Wumen (Meridian Gate)
Palace Moat
Palace Moat
Maxims Pavilion
Working People's Theatre
Yile Hall
Halberd Hall
Shejitan (Hall of Prayer)
Taimiao (Temple of the Imperial Ancestors)
Concert Hall
Altar of Earth and Harvests
Duanmen (Upright Gate)
Big Halberd Gate
Nanchang Jie
Nanchizi Dajie
Jade Belt
Pavilion of Lanting Stele
ZHONGSHAN GONGYUAN (SUN YAT-SEN PARK)
Feilongqiao Hutong
PARK OF THE PEOPLE'S CULTURE
Liufang (Hexagonal Pavilion)
Siyi (House of Year-Round Delight)
Tiananmen (Gate of Heavenly Peace)
Waterside Pavilion
Tian'anmen West
Tian'anmen East
Xichang'an Jie
Dongchang'an Jie

Beyond this line of defence stands China's supreme ensemble of ancient architecture, three great halls and courtyards that reflect the Three Buddhas and the Three Pure Ones of Daoism. First and foremost is the **Hall of Supreme Harmony** (Taihedian), popularly called the 'Hall of the Imperial Throne'. This is the biggest building in the Forbidden City and one of China's most beautiful wooden structures. For hundreds of years during the Ming and Qing dynasties this was the tallest building in all Beijing; by law no house could rise higher. (Counting the hall's upswept roof decorations, that meant the limit was about 37.5m, or 123ft.) Inside, on a raised platform, the 'Son of Heaven' sat on his Dragon Throne surrounded by symbols of longevity and power and cowering acolytes, all covered in a fog of incense. To the tune of gongs and chimes, visitors knelt to kowtow nine times. This is the place where the most solemn ceremonies, such as the New Year rites or the enthronement of a new emperor, were held.

The Front Gate

The 500-year-old Qianmen, one of the original nine gates of the city wall, still stands on a traffic island at the southern end of Tiananmen Square. Most of the other gates fell when the wall was demolished during the modernisation of Beijing in the late 1950s.

Less formal occasions took place in the smaller, golden-roofed **Hall of Middle Harmony** (Zhonghedian), behind the Hall of Great Harmony. A third hall, the **Hall of Preserving Harmony** (Baohedian), was used for, among other things, the palace examinations, which were the world's first civil-service tests. Behind this hall, in the centre of a stairway, is a ramp full of sculptured dragons carved from a single slab of marble weighing more than 200 tonnes. The stairway was reserved for the passage of the emperor's sedan chair.

From here to the north, the density of structures in the Forbidden City increases markedly as one passes from the Outer Court (where

One of the bronze lions that watch over the Forbidden City

of the Inner Court (where the emperor, the imperial family and court members lived). Many of the old palaces and halls are now used to display the artwork and more prosaic belongings of the emperors. The **Clock Museum and Imperial Treasury**, collections of gifts to the emperors, are worth a detour to the right, as is the detailed and ornate **Nine Dragon Screen** Ⓥ (Jiulongbi), carved in 1775.

The rear (northern) section ends at the **Imperial Flower Garden** (Yuhuayuan), with magnificent stone rockeries.

PARKS AND PAVILIONS

Just north of the Forbidden City complex, along the main imperial axis, is **Jingshan Park**, formerly known as Coal Hill (daily 6.30am–9pm; charge). The highest point of Old Beijing, the hill was created from earth that was originally removed to form the moat system around the Forbidden City. Each of the five artificial peaks was provided with a romantically designed pavilion. The three-tiered **Pavilion of Ten Thousand Springs** (Wanchunting), on the middle peak, offers an inspiring view over the rooftops of the Imperial City, with the high-rise office towers of the modern capital visible in the east.

Beihai Park Ⓒ (daily 6.30am– 8pm Nov–March, longer in summer; charge; www.beihaipark.com.cn), Beijing's favourite park, has been a beauty spot for many hundreds of years. Its lake, which young couples now explore in rented rowing boats, was created in the 12th century. The graceful Bridge of Eternal Peace (Yonganqiao) leads to an artificial island a mile in circumference, with a long covered corridor that sweeps along the northern shore. On a hill in the centre of the isle is situated a Tibetan-style stupa, the **White Dagoba** (Baita), at the back of Yongan Temple. It was built in 1651 to commemorate the first visit of the Dalai Lama to Beijing, and stands on the site of Kublai Khan's winter palace. During the spring, the dagoba seems to burst from waves of green leaves. In summer and autumn, this is the most beautiful and lively park to stroll through in the capital. Just ask the throngs of Beijing natives who pack the place.

TEMPLE OF HEAVEN PARK

Tiantan Park, known to foreigners as **Temple of Heaven Park** Ⓓ (daily 8am–5.30pm March–Jun, longer in summer; charge; http://en.tiantanpark.com), is the biggest of Beijing's parks, celebrated for its assembly of thrilling 15th-century architecture separated by vast lawns and hand-planted forests. The highlight is the circular, blue tile-roofed **Hall of Prayer for Good Harvests** (Qiniandian). This marvel of geometry, art and engineering, built of wood without a single nail, measures 37.5m (123ft) to the gilded orb on its topmost roof. In 1889 the masterpiece was struck by lightning and burnt almost to the ground. The ruin was quickly restored to its original, resplendent state.

At the winter solstice, the emperor expressed thanks here for the previous harvest, then, on the 15th day of the first lunar month of the year, was carried here in a procession to pray to the gods of the sun and moon, clouds and rain for a bountiful

Eunuchs

For nearly 2,000 years, the Chinese emperors required that their male servants be eunuchs, in order to protect their concubines. The Ming court would have contained up to 20,000. Even as late as 1911, the eunuch population in the Qing Forbidden City was as high as 1,000.

The White Dagoba, or Baita, in Beihai Park

harvest in the year to come. The floor plan of the hall provides the key to the building's function. The four central columns represent the seasons; then come two concentric rings of 12 columns each, representing the months and the dozen two-hour periods into which the day was divided; and 28 hardwood pillars symbolise the constellations.

Although tourists can no longer enter this monument, its colourful interiors can still be glimpsed from outside. Other attractions at the park include the **Round Altar** (Yuanqiu) – three tiers of balustrades with 360 pillars representing the days of the lunar year – and **Echo Wall**, where whispers ricochet and are mysteriously magnified, crossing an immense courtyard, without modern technology.

This park is the best place in Beijing to observe practitioners of t'ai chi at their morning exercise, or calligraphers at work, or people flying kites, playing badminton or traditional music, or even practising ballroom dancing.

TOP TEMPLES

Beijing's most popular temple is a 17th-century Lamasery, the **Palace of Harmony and Peace** (Yonghegong), popularly known as the **Lama Temple** **E** (daily 9am–4pm; charge). It was originally the palace of the prince who became the Emperor Yongzheng. The stately Buddhist complex of wooden buildings, with nearly 1,000 rooms, has been painstakingly restored. The temple recalls 18th-century efforts to unify China, Mongolia and Tibet.

Across the street and down a narrow lane from the Lama Temple is Beijing's most serene place of worship, the **Temple of Confucius and Imperial Academy** (Kong Miao Guozijian; daily 8.30am–5pm May–Oct, longer in summer; charge; www.kmgzj.com), with statues and stone tablets honouring the ancient sage. This was where emperors came to offer sacrifices to Confucius for guidance in ruling the empire. Built in 1306, it is the second-largest Confucian temple in China, after the one in Confucius' hometown, Qufu. The adjoining Imperial Academy, where Ming-dynasty scholars studied Confucian texts, is set in a pleasant campus, its Riyong Emperors' Lecture Hall fringed by a tranquil moat.

Other temples of significant interest and variety are the **Big Bell Temple** (Dazhongsi; Tue–Sun 9am–4.30pm; charge), with China's leading collection of antique bells; the **Temple of the White Pagoda** (Baitasi; daily 9am–4.30pm), with its 13th-century Tibetan stupa and excellent collection of Buddhist statues; the **Five Pagoda Temple** (Wutasi; daily 9am–5pm), decorated with Indian-influenced sculptures; and the **White Clouds Daoist Temple** (Baiyunguan; daily May–Sept 8.30am–4.30pm, winter until 4pm; charge), where Beijingers of all ages crowd in to pray for good fortune. Those who line up to touch a tiny monkey carved in stone near the entrance are supposed to walk out with especially good luck.

AN ANCIENT OBSERVATORY, ZOO AND AQUARIUM

The **Ancient Observatory** (Gu Guanxiangtai; Wed–Fri 9.30am–3.30pm, Sat–Sun until 4.30pm; closed on Mon and Tue; charge; http://eng.bjp.org.cn/) was built in 1442 and stands on top of a remnant of the old city wall near one of the busiest intersections in central Beijing (where Jianguomenwai Dajie meets the 2nd Ring Road). Many of the bronze instruments, sundials and sextants on display inside and on the roof of the observatory were gifts from Jesuit missionaries who lived in the capital during the 17th century.

Beijing Zoo (Beijing Dongwuyuan; summer 7.30am–6pm, winter 7.30am–5pm; charge), in the northwest of the city, is the largest in

The wooden Lama Temple

China. It now includes a separate indoor-outdoor pavilion for its lovable giant pandas. The older buildings house Manchurian tigers, Tibetan yaks, snow leopards and Père David's deer. The zoo is popular with local children, but most foreign visitors find the facilities antiquated and its conditions poor for the animals.

Rather than upgrade its aged facilities, Beijing Zoo opened the **Beijing Aquarium**, the largest of its kind in China, on adjacent property (summer 9am–5.30pm, winter 10am–4.30pm; charge). Home to whales, dolphins and 50,000 fish, the huge conch-shaped facility also features a Touch Tidepool, sea mammal shows and some of the world's largest viewing panels.

HUTONGS AND COURTYARDS

Growing in popularity in the face of extinction by bulldozer, the *hutong* (traditional alleyways) and courtyard houses of Beijing are worth a visit. Every year these old neighbourhoods are reduced as the capital relentlessly reconstructs itself, but you can still book a guided pedicab tour of the *hutongs* or walk along streets such as Nanchang just outside the Forbidden City. Traversing the backstreets in the old lake district north of Beihai Park, these pedicab caravans make stops at the ancient **Drum Tower** **F** (Gulou; daily 9am–5pm) for panoramic views over courtyard houses that remain nearby, at **Prince Gong's Palace** (Gongwangfu; summer 8am–5pm, winter 9am–5pm, closed on Mondays; charge; http://en.pgm.org.cn/) for tea and sometimes opera in a lavish Ming-dynasty estate, and at a typical courtyard home in a *hutong* neighbourhood for a chance to meet and talk with Beijing residents.

If you have time to explore these old neighbourhoods further, look around Qianhai and Houhai lakes for weekend street markets. Here you'll find **Songqingling Guju** (daily 9am–6pm summer, until 4pm winter; charge), the former home of Song Qing Ling (the second wife of modern China's founder, Dr Sun Yat-sen), who lived in this courtyard mansion after the revolution. The building is now a family museum.

LABYRINTH OF LANES

In Old Beijing, the principal streets divided the city into a grid, in which each square section was filled with a network of lanes, or *hutong* (from the Mongolian *hut* or horse trough). Between the lanes, square single-storey houses were built around a central courtyard, with few outward-facing windows and one wooden gate, which often had carved characters intended to bring good fortune to the house owner or his trade. The houses were built so close together that the lanes were just wide enough for a rider on horseback. The name of each *hutong* tells its story by describing the life it contained. Some indicate professions or crafts: Bowstring Makers' Lane, Cloth Lane, Hat Lane. Some lanes, if they were inhabited by a single family, carry the family name. The best areas to see *hutong* are around Shichahai Lakes, west of the Forbidden City, and around the Bell and Drum towers (north of Beihai Park).

Hutong transport

A number of the more elegant courtyard homes adjoin the Qianhai-Houhai-Shichahai (Back Lake) chain of human-made waterways. So popular are these three lakes that developers have built new homes designed to look like the old. By day, Beijing natives swim in the sometimes frozen lake, believing that cold (though brief) dips improve health. At night the lakesides sparkle with cafés and bars, some relaxed and some full of raging drunks. As Shichahai becomes commercialised with the influx of visitors, nearby Nan Luogu Xiang, a north–south lane between courtyard homes, is drawing travellers who prefer something quieter. Coffeehouses, bars and handicraft shops bring the lane *(xiang)* to life from early in the day to past midnight.

SHOPPING DISTRICTS

Some of Beijing's few walkable areas are its chief shopping streets and markets. **Wangfujing**, running north a few blocks east of the Forbidden City, is the capital's primary shopping street, lined with upmarket boutiques and glittering shopping plazas, although a few venerable arts and crafts shops, small galleries and old department stores still survive.

An excellent range of clothes can be found on the five floors of the **Sanlitun Yaxiu Clothing Market** (adjacent to a rebuilt bar district). The **Hongqiao Market**, just to the east of the Temple of Heaven, features clothing, crafts (including antique clocks) and freshwater pearls. For traditional Chinese paintings, calligraphy supplies and rare books, poke around **Liulichang**, a restored Ming-dynasty shopping street southwest of Tiananmen Square. The most colourful market is **Panjiayuan** (daily 8.30am–6pm, from 4.30am weekends; www.panjiayuan.com), which starts at sunrise every day and closes around 4pm, with its stalls of collectables, antiques, family treasures, tomb art, Tibetan rugs, furniture and Mao memorabilia. Prices can be low if you bargain.

Beijing's once-famous Old Beijing-style Dazhalan Street, in the Qianmen area just south of Tiananmen Square, has been largely demolished and rebuilt as a theme street reminiscent of its old self.

Factory 798 (aka Dashanzi; www.798district.com), a former munitions plant occupied in recent years by artists who held out against redevelopment plans, is an exhibit of Beijing's hipper side. Visitors can tour the vast complex's galleries, see concerts and stop for sandwiches or spicy Sichuan food. One of the bigger halls features modern art and sculptures commemorating the Chairman Mao days. It's open early to late, with no centralised admission charge.

Wangfujing street food

THE SUMMER PALACE

The Chinese name for this convergence of natural and man-made beauty is

Panjiayuan Market

Yiheyuan – the 'Park of Nurtured Harmony' (daily 6.30am–6pm summer, 7am–5pm winter; charge; www.summerpalace-china.com). Foreigners call this 280-hectare (700-acre) imperial estate the **Summer Palace** ❻. In actual fact, the 250-year-old palaces, pavilions, temples and halls occupy only a small part of the dreamily landscaped area. By far the largest feature of the park is man-made Kunming Lake.

Funds intended for the imperial navy were siphoned off to make Yiheyuan a luxurious private park. Perhaps the most astonishing item on which the Empress Dowager Cixi squandered the naval budget is a double-decker **Marble Boat** at the edge of the lake. You can view this monument to royal folly, but you can no longer board it.

A few kilometres from the Summer Palace is the **Old Summer Palace** (Yuanmingyuan; daily 7am–7pm, later in summer; charge; www.yuanmingyuanpark.cn/ymyen/), which was once the emperor's summer retreat. In 1860 British and French soldiers attacked and destroyed most of the grand buildings, including a complex modelled after Versailles. Lakes and forests beyond the ruins allow some of the few peaceful hikes in central Beijing.

THE 2008 OLYMPICS

Though the Beijing Olympics are long over, core venues such as the gargantuan 'Bird's Nest' **National Stadium** for track-and-field events and the 'Water Cube' **National Aquatics Centre** for swimming races periodically open to visitors. An Olympic fencing venue and the media centre, both near the Bird's Nest, have been remodelled into conference spaces, and flats in the Olympic Village have been sold to private owners. A walk along Beichen West Road offers glimpses of the latter as well as some other major venues.

EXCURSIONS FROM BEIJING

The area around Beijing has farming villages, artist colonies and wooded hiking trails, attracting visitors hoping to spend time away from the chaos of the capital. Transport by train or bus is readily available and convenient, though for half-day trips such as the Great Wall and the Ming Tombs, which are at least an hour from the city centre, a hired car may be easiest. Travel agents can also help to arrange such trips.

The Great Wall

It is about 80km (50 miles) from the centre of Beijing northwest to the most visited stretch of the **Great Wall of China**, at **Badaling**.

The first elements of the wall system were built more than 2,000 years ago, but the expansion and consolidation of the project, in the harsh mountainous country north of Beijing, began under the Ming dynasty in the 14th century. The serpentine stone bulwark and elevated highway became Wanlichangcheng – 'The Wall Ten Thousand Li Long' (about 6,000km/3,700 miles).

The restored section of the wall at Badaling, undulating up the unexpectedly steep hillsides, can be a test of endurance. It is steeper than it may look from a tourist brochure. Out of breath, many visitors exchange sympathetic smiles along the way as they ascend to one or another of

Six horses wide

The top of the Great Wall was designed so that five or six horsemen could ride side by side, between the crenellated walls. Fortified towers, signal beacon towers and garrisons completed the defences.

the towers. If you walk far enough west, you reach dilapidated and unrestored sections of the wall that trail off into the distance.

The Badaling section is often overcrowded these days, and there are countless stalls selling a range of tacky souvenirs. Two other sections now provide relatively easy access to tourists: the Great Wall at **Mutianyu**, as beautiful as the section at Badaling but a little less steep, and the Great Wall at **Simatai**, more distant from Beijing (100km/60 miles to the northeast) than other sections but virtually unrestored. Simatai is the least crowded and most original of the Great Wall sites. Although it too has a cable-car concession, Simatai bills itself as 'the most dangerous section of the Great Wall'. As access gradually improves, more sections of the Wall are opening up to tourism, such as at Huanghuacheng and Jinshaling.

Travellers may also find a number of 'Wild Wall' segments in Beijing and Hebei province. These un-managed, un-maintained sections are less crowded than the better-known tourist spots. Some offer sharp views of the mountains, which from November to February may be white with dustings of snow. Ask first about any local farmers who may try to charge vigilante admission fees.

Great Wall at Badaling

The Ming Tombs

On the way to the Great Wall is the peaceful valley the Ming emperors chose as their burial ground. In 1407 the Emperor Yongle ordered a search for a suitable burial place with auspicious 'wind and water' conditions, as well as appropriate

The 'Bird's Nest' National Stadium can seat 100,000 people

grandeur. This site proved so perfect that all but three of the succeeding Ming rulers were entombed in the same valley.

The route to the 13 **Ming Tombs** (Shisan Ling; daily 8am– 5.30pm summer, from 8.30am winter; charge) begins at a great marble gateway more than four centuries old. Beyond this is the main gate with three archways; the middle arch was used only once in each reign – for the delivery of the emperor's remains to his tomb. Then comes the **Sacred Way** (Shendao), which is flanked by 36 enormous stone guardians. There are a dozen military and civil dignitaries and a dozen pairs of animals, real and mythical, including lions, camels, elephants, unicorns and chimeras.

The largest tomb (Changling) belonged to Yongle himself. Its Hall of Eminent Favours (Lingendian) is Beijing's largest wooden structure remaining from ancient times. The 32 gilded pillars supporting the coffered ceiling were fashioned from a huge tree that took more than five years to ship here from southwest China. The tomb itself has not been excavated, and the emperor and empress still lie undisturbed within the vaults.

Ming Emperor Wanli's crown

The Eastern Qing Tombs

While many visitors to the Ming Tombs find the site rather crowded and uninspiring, there is a fascinating alternative. The **Eastern Qing Tombs** (Dongqingling; daily 8am–5pm; charge; www.qingdongling.com) mimic the older Ming architecture, but are grander and more effectively restored. They are also more than twice as far from Beijing: 125km (78 miles) to the east on slow but interesting roads. Of the nine tombs open to view, those of the two most powerful Manchu emperors, Qianlong and Kangxi, are impressive, and that of Empress Dowager Cixi (1835–1911) is as elaborate as it is strange.

Shanhaiguan

This walled town's strategic location made it the site of many important battles over thousands of years. This is the site where general Wu Sangui let in the Qing armies, effectively sealing the demise of the Ming dynasty. But it is best known as the eastern terminus of the Great Wall. Five huge Chinese characters meaning 'The First Pass under Heaven' mark the two-tiered gate-tower as the starting point of the Wall. Today, huge housing developments and highways surround the small town that is confined by ancient city walls and has streets too narrow for public buses. Just south of Shanhaiguan is Laolongtou, where the Great Wall meets the sea.

Tianjin

The largest port in northern China, just 120km (74 miles) southeast of Beijing, Tianjin is one of China's most important transport and industrial centres. A large number of historical sights can be found in this autonomous governmental municipality of about 12 million people. There is an impressive concentration of concession-era Western architecture along Jiefang Beilu, including a newly restored Italian concession. The city has also restored a Culture Street (Guwenhuajie) of traditional shops selling books, porcelain, carpets, crafts and food, and a Food Street (Shipinjie) with 100 outlets, offering specialities that include fresh *goubuli baozi*, steamed buns filled with meat and vegetables.

Tianjin's once lifeless riverfront has been attracting visitors since it was spruced up before the city hosted football matches for the 2008 Beijing Olympics. The high-speed rail trip to Tianjin from Beijing takes just half an hour.

Old Dragon's Head section of The Great Wall

Chengde

In summer the trip to Chengde, about 250km (150 miles) northeast of Beijing, passes views of fertile fields, stony hills, trees and wild flowers. In the hamlets along

Liuli Wanshou Pagoda

the way, trim houses are roofed with thatch or traditional tile with winged projections. In the fields, the labour is done mostly by hand, and some heavy ploughing is even done by men in harness.

Chengde itself looks, at first glance, like any other northern Chinese industrial town, but the dreariness of this rugged area is interspersed with beautifully sited old temples and an imperial pleasure ground big enough to be protected by a wall 10km (6 miles) long – sections of an immense Unesco World Heritage Site.

The **palaces and gardens** of Chengde provided summertime escape for the imperial courts of the Qing dynasty, beginning with Emperor Kangxi, who created the halls, lakes and hunting grounds here as a second summer palace in 1703. Kangxi was accurate when he called these royal parklands, about 350m (over 1,100ft) above sea level, **Bishushanzhuang** (April 7.30am–5.30pm, May 1–Oct 9 7am–6pm, Oct 10–March 8am–5.30pm winter; charge; www.bishushanzhuang.com.cn), or 'Mountain Villa for Escaping the Summer Heat'.

His interest in Chengde was strategic as well as recreational, for it strengthened his empire's rule over Mongolians and various frontiers.

In line with this strategy, the buildings found in Chengde exhibit an interesting mix of Han and minority architectural styles. Instead of the ornate carvings and large overhanging eaves that characterise Chinese architecture, the summer palace is relatively simple but elegant.

Visitors who don't mind weathering hordes of surly touts will enter this royal resort at the ceremonial Lizheng Gate, flanked by two marble lions. The old palace and royal halls now serve as museums. Among the exhibits are bows and arrows and Chinese flintlocks, rare jade and porcelain, and the sedan chairs in which the emperors were transported all the way from Beijing. The emperor's bedroom is located in the Refreshing Mist-Veiled Waters Pavilion. The halls and courtyards are eminently regal, yet they also inspire a feeling of relaxation appropriate to the setting. The plain wooden corridors connecting the buildings contrast with the illustrated passageways of Beijing's Summer Palace, which occupies just half the space of the Chengde retreat.

The landscape beyond the palace compound features many of the romantic elements of Chinese tradition: interconnected lakes and lotus ponds, forests, causeways and arched bridges, ornate pavilions and towering pagodas. The Tower of Mist and Rain (Yanyulou), a two-storey lakeside pavilion in the southern style, was favoured by emperors for its foggy views resembling those of an old Chinese painting. Tourists can cross the lakes in hand-poled ferryboats or drift at their own pace in a rowing boat. North of the lakes there are hiking trails in the **Garden of Ten Thousand Trees** (Wanshuyuan), where Emperor Qianlong gave an audience in 1793 to Lord Macartney, the first British ambassador to set foot in China.

Beyond the wall surrounding the palace and its gardens rise the exotic roofs of the **Eight Outer Temples**, built by the emperors between 1713 and 1779 to honour and influence Tibetans, Kazakhs and other northern peoples. Most, but not all, are open to tourists. The **Mt Sumeru Longevity and Happiness Temple** (Xumifushoumiao; daily summer 8am–5pm, winter 8.30am–5pm; free) replicates the residence in Shigatse, Tibet, of the sixth

Panchen Lama, who visited Chengde on the occasion of Emperor Qianlong's 70th birthday. It exhibits a blend of Han Chinese and Tibetan architecture. The high red walls surround a pavilion, which has a roof gilded with a tonne of gold.

A short distance to the east, the fantastic **Small Potala Temple** (Putuozongchengmiao; daily 9am–4.30pm; charge) is the largest at Chengde, a reduced copy of the Potala Palace in Lhasa. The highlight, however, is **Puning Temple** (Puning Si; 8am–5 pm summer, 8.30am–4.30pm winter; charge) to the northeast, a Chinese- and Tibetan-styled temple that houses a colossal gilded 22m (72ft) high statue of Guanyin, the Buddhist Goddess of Mercy, carved from five different types of wood.

THE NORTHEAST AND INNER MONGOLIA

Much of China's northeast was once known as Manchuria. Now called Dongbei, this vast land features a variety of attractions, from old treaty ports to Siberian tiger reserves. Although not part of Dongbei, Inner Mongolia is included here for convenience.

DALIAN

Dalian is a thriving port, summer resort and industrial city of about 6.2 million people. Because of a history of foreign occupation, the city is an eclectic medley of architectural styles: China seasoned with a dash of Japan, a pinch of Old Russia and a forcible hint of Soviet Socialist Realism, interspersed with European-style buildings from the 19th and early 20th centuries. Today one themed street hearkens back to Russia, and another marks the recent influx of expatriates from Japan. Dalian's Safari Park is home to Siberian tigers, and performing dolphins can be found in the city aquarium. The coastal locale blesses Dalian with several clean beaches swimmable in the summer, and fresh seafood even at average restaurants.

SHENYANG

In 1625 **Shenyang** ❷ (better known abroad by its Manchurian name of Mukden) became the Manchu capital. Its Imperial Palace (Gugong) was intended to rival the Forbidden City of Beijing; some 70 buildings contain 300 rooms. It now serves as a museum of history and archaeology. In the 1930s the 'Mukden Incident' (a bomb explosion on the railway here) precipitated the Japanese occupation of Manchuria. Today more than half of the Manchu ethnic minority, who resemble the majority Han Chinese in appearance, live in Shenyang. This city of nearly 3.5 million people has high-rises and swanky shops that attest to its role as a commercial hub for the three northeast provinces. Among its attractions are the tomb (Beiling) of the Founder of the Qing dynasty and the monumental architecture of Zhongshan Square.

Harbin's spectacular ice festival

HARBIN

Only a polar bear, you would think, could survive winter in **Harbin** ❸ the capital of China's northeasternmost province, Heilongjiang. The average temperature stays below freezing five months of the year, and the mercury has been known to drop to –38°C (–36°F). It's no surprise that ice-sailing is popular here, or that Yabuli International Ski Resort, with China's best slopes, is nearby. If travelling in the winter, wear thermal underclothes, boots, gloves, a thick cap and a greatcoat even for short walks around town. Almost all buildings are heated.

Siberian tiger

In a country of ancient cities, Harbin is an anomaly. Until the 20th century it never amounted to more than a fishing village. Then the Manchu dynasty agreed to let Tsarist Russia build a branch of the Trans-Siberian Railway through Harbin. Russians and other foreigners peopled the fast-growing transportation hub, which soon boasted hotels and banks, bars and gambling houses. With the Bolshevik revolution of 1917, perhaps half a million Russian émigrés fled through Siberia to Harbin, consolidating the Russian appearance of the city with more pastel-coloured stucco houses and churches with onion domes. From 1932 to 1945, Harbin was under Japanese occupation, followed by one year under the Soviet army. In 1946 the Chinese Communists took control of the city.

Under the People's Republic, Harbin has become an important industrial centre as well as the heart of a rich grain-producing area. With its eclectic mix of Russian domes, traditional Chinese architecture and industrial concrete eyesores, Harbin is aesthetically confusing and often startling, juxtaposing the drab and mundane with the elegant and exotic. Harbin dwellers, most of whom trace their ancestry to other regions, are among the most open and hospitable in China. A short conversation between strangers can lead quickly to a long night of drinking and northern-style hotpots, ending in a friendly scuffle to make sure the other party doesn't pay for it all. Northeast China also claims some of the nation's purest Mandarin accents, a windfall for the beginner language student.

The mighty **Songhua River**, running through the city from west to east, inevitably attracts tourists. In summer months there are sightseeing launches and, for the brave, swimming. On the south bank, **Stalin Park** (Sidalin Gongyuan) is a wide, inviting promenade, with its Flood Control Monument the chief focal point for visitors, a curious architectural mix of classical and Socialist Realist styles. Visible from the shore is **Sun Island** (Taiyang Dao; ferries leave every 15 minutes daily 8am–5pm), in the middle of the river, with health resorts, beach installations and gardens. Also on the island is **Siberian Tiger Park** (Dongbei Hu Linyuan; daily bus tours, 9am–4pm; charge), where endangered Manchurian tigers, dodging the tourist buses, learn to hunt live prey before their release into the wild.

Daoli Old Town

The main walking district, the cobblestoned **Daoli Old Town** (Daoliqu), bordered by Stalin Park, retains much of Harbin's Russian heritage in its onion-domed architecture. Other attractions include the inactive but spectacular **Santa Sophia Church** (daily 8.30am–5pm; charge) and two active temples. Sixth-century stone tablets grace **Wenmiao** (Thur–Tue 8.30am–4.30pm; free), Harbin's temple to Confucius, a charming sanctuary that contains Harbin's only jade bridges, while Jilesi, the **Temple of Bliss** (daily 8am–5pm; charge), the largest in the province, hosts an active community of monks and nuns and opens onto a large, lively street market.

Yabuli Ski Resort

In the snow-covered Changbai mountain range, about 190km (120 miles) southeast of Harbin, skiers can test slopes of up to 32 degrees at China's top resort for the sport, which emerged in about 2000. The Yabuli Resort has drops of 200 to 1,200m (650 to 4,000ft) and up to a metre (3ft) of snow. China's winter sports teams have trained at Yabuli, which was also a venue for the 1996 Asian Winter Games.

One of Harbin's most delightful spots is the **Children's Park** (Ertong Gongyuan), where there is a miniature railway operated by children – the only one of its kind in China. Little trains run daily, roughly between 8.30am– 6.30pm, carrying passengers of all ages in 20 minutes from 'Harbin Station' to 'Beijing Station', a distance of 2km (1½ miles).

A darker attraction altogether is the **Exhibition Hall for the Ruins of the Japanese Troops Invading China** (Tue–Sun 8.30am–4.30pm; free), the site of a secret biological warfare research station set up by the occupying Japanese forces in 1939 to test on the local population. Its existence was hidden until the 1980s. The Japanese blew up the research station before fleeing in 1945, so the exhibits are limited to illustrations of the horrors this site witnessed.

Ice and Snow Festival

Harbin's signature attraction is a celebration of its weather. Every year in January, the place takes advantage of its long-lasting winter freeze to hold the **Harbin International Ice and Snow Festival** (www.icefestivalharbin.com). Its top draw is a city park loaded with colourfully back-lit ice castles and other sculptures. Some are up to 50m (165ft) high and built so people can walk through them (see box).

LANTERNS OF ICE

At the Chinese lunar New Year, or Spring Festival (in late January or early February), Harbin puts on its keynote event: a spectacular show that rivals the famous Snow Festival of its sister city in Japan, Sapporo. While the rest of China is celebrating the New Year with paper lanterns, Harbin is showing off with lanterns carved out of ice in its Ice Lantern Festival, held downtown in Zhaolin Park. Delicate sculptures, human figures and whole buildings meticulously carved out of ice are brilliantly illuminated. The ambience is so festive, you might even forget the sub-zero temperatures.

HOHHOT

The capital of the Inner Mongolia Autonomous Region, Hohhot is a sprawling, booming city with a metropolitan population of approximately 2.8 million. The centre of town looks to the future with new official buildings, housing blocks and wide avenues, but the traffic evokes nostalgia with its parade of donkey carts, ox carts, pony carts and farm tractors.

Horses grazing by yurts

It might come as a surprise to learn that Mongolians are only a small minority here. Most residents of Hohhot are Han (ethnic Chinese). Inner Mongolia's close but tense connection with China dates back several centuries. Some signage in the city is translated into Mongolian script, with a particularly memorable line or two on a KFC marquee. As Mongolia, an independent nation sometimes referred to as 'outer Mongolia', uses the Russian Cyrillic alphabet, China may be the best place to view the original written language.

An unexpected feature of Hohhot is its modern **racecourse** *(saimachang)*, a throwback to the great equestrian tradition of the nomadic Mongols. Under the sky-blue domes of the reviewing stand, visitors are often treated to a Mongolian 'rodeo' of racing and trick riding, and perhaps a procession of Bactrian camels. Elsewhere in town, along the streets near bustling **Xinhua Square**, pedlars shout out their wares with gusto, whether they're selling shirts, vegetables or sunglasses. A bard, banging a cymbal, chants a story, while his partner – a trained monkey – dons the masks and hats of various Chinese opera characters, mesmerising the crowd.

The **Inner Mongolia Museum** (Nei Menggu Bowuguan; Tue–Sun 9am–5.30pm summer, 9.30am–5pm winter; free) covers the region's history from prehistoric times to the Communist revolution, with an ample display of native yurts and riding gear, as well as China's largest dinosaur skeleton. Among Hohhot's sacred sites, the **Xiletuzhao Temple** (Xiletuzhao Si; daily 8am–6pm; free) stands out. It is an active Lamaist Buddhist shrine, with many Tibetan trappings, its main hall filled with brightly coloured dragon carpets and an overwhelming smell of incense. Attractive to photographers is the aptly named **Five Pagodas Temple** (Wutasi; daily 9am–6pm; charge), a striking 18th-century structure capped with five towers. Buddhist scriptures are inscribed on the outer wall in Sanskrit, Tibetan and Mongolian, along with carvings of 1,600 figures.

The **Great Mosque** (Qingzhen Dasi; daily 8.30am–6pm; charge), dating back to the Ming dynasty, serves the large ethnic Hui Muslim population that lives in the neighbourhood. The mosque has a minaret that culminates in a Chinese-style temple roof (topped by a crescent).

Hohhot's oldest historical site, situated 17km (11 miles) southwest of town, is the **Tomb of Princess Zhaojun** (Zhaojunmu; daily 8am–6pm winter, 8am–7pm summer; charge). In 33BC, at the age of 18, this famous Chinese beauty married a tribal chief to bring peace among the nationalities. You can take a stroll to the top of the 33m (98ft) earthen pyramid built above her grave and, from here, look out over the seemingly endless, flat farmland.

Southeast of Hohhot is the 12th-century **White Pagoda** (Baita; daily 8.30am–6pm; charge), known in Chinese as Wanbuhua Yanjingta: the Pagoda of the Ten Thousand Scriptures. The restored seven-tier octagonal structure, isolated amid farmland, was constructed of brick about 900 years ago, when it served as a centre of religious pilgrimages during the Liao dynasty. Although the outside is brilliant white, the interior can be pitch black, making for a treacherous climb.

Street market in Hohhot

THE GRASSLANDS

The most memorable aspect of a visit to Hohhot is likely to be an excursion outside town to the grasslands *(caoyuan)*, where visitors can witness and even join in with distinctively Mongolian activities. The grasslands are found across the desolate Daqing Mountains, where horseback riding is a way of life among Mongolians. A good paved road eases the strain of the zigzag climb that continues up approximately 2,000m (more than 6,500ft) above sea level.

Most visitors end up at either **Xilamuren** or **Gegentala**, a three-hour drive from Hohhot. At these tourist camps, guests sleep in wool-felt yurts with quilts, hot-water flasks and electric lights. Bathing facilities and dining halls are often in separate buildings. Daily activities can include archery, Mongolian wrestling, visits to local villages and horse-riding on the celebrated grasslands. Folk dancing and singing provide evening entertainment. How about butter tea with millet as a nightcap?

Traditional Mongolian Naadam fairs are held in late summer, and at other times. Visitors might be treated to an informal rodeo in which Mongolian horsemen race their energetic ponies. Disarmingly, the cowboys are dressed like ordinary Chinese farmers.

Travellers with more time can venture deeper into the wilderness grasslands, where there is a better chance of sleeping in a real yurt, rather than one which has been specially furnished for foreign visitors. A popular destination west of Hohhot, near the city of Dongsheng, is the **Genghis Khan Mausoleum** (Chengji Sihan Lingyuan; daily 8am–5.30pm winter, 7am–7pm summer; charge) in the Ordoes Highlands. Built in 1954, it supposedly houses the remains of Genghis Khan. A later addition here is a reconstructed Yuan-dynasty village.

From the drab Inner Mongolian industrial centre of Baotou, travellers can reach **Resonant Sand Gorge** (Xiangshawan; daily 8am–7pm; charge), which gives good views of some of the region's vast sand dunes. Another nearby site is the Buddhist **Wudang Lama Temple** (Wudang Zhao; daily 8am–5pm; charge).

NORTHERN HEARTLANDS

This section includes some of the most popular attractions for travellers to China, ranging from Xi'an and its 2,000-year-old terracotta warriors to Luoyang, where the Longmen Caves and Shaolin Monastery are the focus of attention. Here, too, are the historic cities of Taishan and Qingdao.

Beginning a day's journey east from Beijing, at Datong, in the northern part of Shanxi province, we then move south to Taiyuan and Pingyao, with a brief look at Shijiazhuang in neighbouring Hebei province. Then it's east to Shandong province at Jinan, and on to the coast at the port of Qingdao, which still preserves mementoes of its past as the German concession of Tsingtao. Moving inland, Kaifeng, in landlocked Henan province, is a major drawcard, as is Luoyang. Finally, the city of Xi'an is the gateway to Shaanxi province, at the very heart of the country. The famed terracotta warriors are just the best known of this fascinating city's many attractions.

Bactrian camels in the Gobi Desert

DATONG

It takes about seven hours by train from Beijing to reach the city of **Datong ❹**, to the west of the capital in northern Shanxi Province. Datong itself is a poor coal-mining and industrial city on a plateau 1,000m (3,250ft) above sea level. The summers are short here on the edge of Inner Mongolia, and winters are glacial. It's not the sort of place poets would eulogise, yet for nearly a century (398–494) it served as the capital of the Northern Wei dynasty.

Three monasteries and a famous dragon screen recall Datong's once stately history. The **Nine Dragon Wall** (Jiulongbi; daily 8.30am–6pm winter, summer 8am–6pm; charge), a Ming landmark (1392), stands in the old part of town among the narrow streets lined by single-storey houses. This is said to be the largest and oldest screen of its type anywhere in China, at 45.5m (150ft). The ceramic mural shows nine dragons, each in a different dynamic pose. When the sun reflects on the pool that runs along the base of the wall, the glazed tile figures flash to life.

The **Huayan Monastery** (Hwayansi; daily 9am–5pm; charge), was built under the Liao and Jin dynasties by 1140. The main building, the Great Treasure Hall (Daxiongbaodian), is one of the two biggest Buddhist halls still standing in China. The fine ceiling comprises 749 illustrated squares, no two the same. In the centre are enthroned the Five Buddhas of the Five Directions, relics of the Ming dynasty.

The other big temple in town, **Shanhua Monastery** (Shanhuasi; daily 8am–5.30pm winter, 8am–6pm summer; charge), faces the old city wall. The monastery dates from 713, during the Tang dynasty, but it was largely rebuilt after a fire in the 12th century. Standing in the grand, red-walled pavilion are 24 celestial guardians, each of distinct mien. A circular 'moon gate' in the side wall of the monastery leads to the Five-Dragon Wall (Wulongbi).

The city centre is rather bleak, but the authorities have added a pedestrian street featuring old-style northern Chinese homes and restaurants serving the hearty, meaty food that goes down well in Datong's cold climate.

A major attraction near Datong is the **Temple Suspended over the Void** (Xuankongsi; 9am–5pm; charge), situated a two-hour car journey south through a barren sandstone plateau. The 6th-century temple is spectacular, with over 40 halls and pavilions suspended as if by magic on the face of a sheer limestone cliff – some of the rooms supported by only a single pillar – and connected to each other by ornate catwalks. Signs indicate the safe route for visitors to wind up, down and around to reach over 80 statues of Buddha and other treasures.

Three religions

Though Xuankongsi is a Daoist temple, in its Three Religions Hall Buddha, Confucius and Laozi sit side by side.

The Yungang Caves

Datong is best known for the **Yungang Caves** (Yungang Shiku; daily 8.30am–5.30pm summer, 8.30am–5pm winter; charge; www.yungang.org), which are 16km (10 miles) west of Datong and contain one of China's most treasured displays of ancient Buddhist sculpture. When the project was ordered by the Northern Wei rulers to atone for their earlier persecution of Buddhism, some 30,000 artisan families from Dunhuang were forcibly relocated to work on the caves. Thousands of sculptors took 50 years to create about 100,000 statues, carved into the walls of the 20 rock temples. About 50,000 statues remain – from the size of a postage stamp to the height of a five-storey house – despite the rigours of time, weather and marauders. The sculptural style was mainly borrowed from Indian Buddhist art, which itself grew from a synthesis of foreign styles, including Persian, Byzantine and Greek.

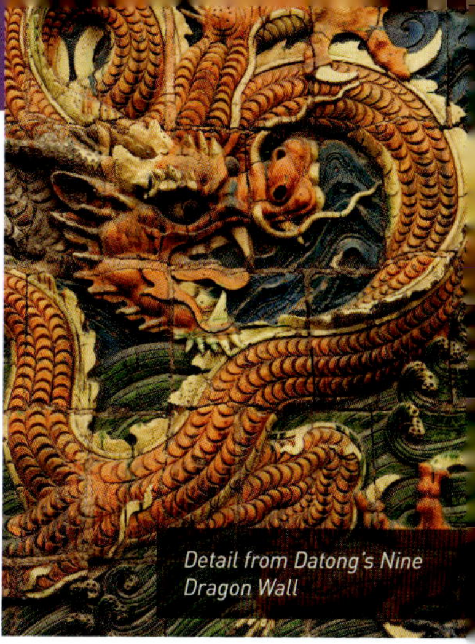
Detail from Datong's Nine Dragon Wall

After running the gauntlet of souvenir shops and stalls, visitors enter the caves through a monastery where 2,000 monks once lived. A wooden structure four storeys high, built in the Ming dynasty, blocks the winds that blast the caves.

The oldest caves of the whole complex – dating from the 5th century – are numbered 16 to 20. In Cave No. 16 are three holes pierced through the outer wall, showing the original positions of three Buddhas appropriated by foreign collectors.

SHIJIAZHUANG

This railway junction has grown into a provincial capital of approximately 2.4 million people. Shijiazhuang's top sight is the remodelled **Hebei Provincial Museum** (Hebei Sheng Bowuguan; Tue–Sun

Jinci temple

9am–5pm; free). Well worth a day trip, Cangyanshan Mountain, with its spectacular Hanging Palace, lies 90km (56 miles) to the southwest. Another day trip possibility is Zhaozhou Bridge, 40km (25 miles) to the southeast, China's oldest surviving bridge (c. AD 600).

TAIYUAN

With a history of more than 2,000 years, this provincial capital in the heart of China's coal country now makes iron, steel, heavy machinery and fertiliser. As such, it's one of China's smoggiest cities. Many of the city's historical sights were demolished during a bloody People's Liberation Army struggle against the Nationalists. The Shanxi Provincial Museum, in the centre of this compact and friendly city, contains revolutionary displays and historic bronzes, ceramics, sculptures and paintings. The **Jinci** temple complex (daily 8am–6pm summer, 8.30am–5pm winter; charge), 25km (16 miles) southwest of the city, is thought to be more than 1,000 years old, consisting of nearly 100 pavilions, halls, terraces and bridges. Most impressive is the ancient wooden Temple of the Holy Mother (Shengmudian), with life-sized statues reflecting a real humanity. North of Taiyuan is one of Buddhism's Four Famous Peaks, Wutai Shan, with scores of ancient shrines.

PINGYAO

The small walled town of **Pingyao** ❺, 100km (60 miles) south of Taiyuan in Shanxi province, invites tourists to walk through a once prosperous commercial hub immaculately preserved in its old splendour. The town that became a banking centre during the Ming and Qing dynasties is enclosed within an intact 6km (4-mile) Ming-dynasty wall. The town is a museum of Ming and Qing architecture, old courtyard houses and family residences. It has been a Unesco World Heritage Site since 1997. Tourists on foot will run into highlights such as the Rishengchang Bank (dating from 1824), the City Wall and the Town Gods Temple (Chenghuang Miao). North of Pingyao, the Qiao Family Courtyard was the setting for director Zhang Yimou's classic film starring Gong Li, *Raise the Red Lantern*. A fee is payable to enter the village, unless you are staying overnight.

JINAN AND TAISHAN

The majority of visitors only pass through Jinan on their way to such traditional sights of Shandong as the holy mountain of Taishan and Qufu, the birthplace of Confucius (see page 26).

Pingyao

Although not well known in the West, **Taishan** (charge; www.mount-tai.com.cn), just south of Jinan, is China's most celebrated peak. Everyone who was anyone in Chinese history, from Confucius to Chairman Mao, has stood on its summit. Because it was long regarded as the Sacred Mountain of the East by followers of Daoism, Taishan served as the supreme altar of worship for millions of pilgrims for over 2,000 years. It undoubtedly ranks as one of the most climbed mountains in the world. Even today it attracts large numbers of visitors, most of them from China.

Situated in Shandong province on the railway line between Beijing and Shanghai, Taishan is only 1,545m (5,070ft) high, but it is a steep climb as it rises for views of the East China Sea. Today there are more than 20 active temples on its slopes, over 800 carved tablets and some 1,000 cliff-face inscriptions, a library of Chinese culture that is carved into the body of nature.

Tai'an, the village at Taishan's base that is some 64km (40 miles) south of Jinan, is home to the magnificent **Dai Temple** (Daimiao; daily 8am–5pm; charge). This walled temple complex, which consists of more than 600 buildings, was the venue for elaborate sacrifices and provided accommodation for the emperor before his ascent of Taishan. The temple's historic treasures include a stone tablet recording the mountain's promotion to the position of 'Emperor of China', as Taishan was designated in 1011 by a Song-dynasty emperor. Rarest of all is the **Qin Tablet**, carved in 209 BC to commemorate the ascent of Taishan by China's first emperor, Qinshi Huangdi. The main temple also contains a statue of the God of the Mountain, Taishanwang, the Judge of the Dead. The **Hall of Heavenly Gifts** (Tiankuang Dian), one of the largest classical temple halls in China, contains a fresco more than 60m (200ft) long.

North of the Dai Temple, the Pilgrim's Road (Panlu) leads to the First Gate of Heaven, the entrance to the mountain. Beyond this point it is mostly massive granite steps. From the First Gate to the Middle Gate of Heaven is about 5km (3 miles), and from the Middle Gate to the top less than 3km (2 miles), but the final mile is the steepest, as the elevation

Pailou gateway on the summit of Taishan

rise is 1,370m (4,500ft). Anyone in a hurry can catch a bus or hire a taxi to the Middle Gate and from there take the cable car to the top.

On the summit one must first negotiate the earthly delights of Tian Jie (Heaven Street), a Qing-dynasty parade of shops and restaurants. The Tang-dynasty **Rock Inscriptions** (Moyabei) were struck in large gold-foil characters to record Emperor Xuanzong's imperial pilgrimage in 726. The Stele without Inscription (Wuzibei) is blank, thought to have been placed here by the first emperor over 2,000 years earlier; everyone who reaches it must touch it for good luck.

The **Temple of the Purple Dawn** (Bixiaci) is the most revered of the shrines on the summit of Taishan. Here presides the Jade Goddess, daughter of the mountain god, who cures blindness and answers the prayers of the childless. And there are hundreds of petitioners and pilgrims even today on the summit of Taishan.

At dawn, the thousands who spend the night in inns on the summit await the famous sunrise. It is precisely here that Confucius observed that the world is small and that Chairman Mao proclaimed 'the East is Red'.

Qingdao seafront

QUFU

The birthplace of Confucius, **Qufu** has been turned into an architectural ensemble on the scale of the Forbidden City in Beijing. The memorial temple, Kong Miao, was begun in 478 BC, the year after the philosopher's death, and improvements continued for another 2,000 years. The compound itself contains ceremonial gateways, palaces, pavilions, shrines and 1,000 carved stone tablets, dominated by the 11th-century Pavilion of the Constellation of Scholars (Kuiwenge) and the 18th-century Hall of Great Achievements (Dacheng Dian), once the venue for sacrificial rites in honour of the sage. The adjacent Confucius Mansions (Kong Fu) consist of hundreds of family halls and rooms. The tombs of Confucius and most of his descendants are set amid ancient pines and cypresses in Confucius Forest (Kong Lin), to the north of the town.

QINGDAO

Imagine Copacabana beach set down on the shore of the Yellow Sea, mix in some century-old German villas and castles, and paint in pinewoods, parks and tree-lined hills for background. Six swimming beaches make the delightful Shandong Peninsula seaport of **Qingdao** ❻ one of China's favourite summer retreats. The sea is refreshing and so, usually, is the air, cooled in summer by the northerly ocean currents. You'll see – or join — the Chinese masses at ease – sunbathing, strolling, having their pictures taken and eating ice cream or dumplings.

Qingdao has an unusual history. Until the end of the 19th century, there was little here apart from fishermen's houses and a minor Chinese naval base. When Germany entered the imperialist age under Kaiser Wilhelm II, Qingdao was selected as a likely port for development. The murder of two German missionaries by Boxers in 1897 gave Wilhelm the excuse for a show of retaliation. German military superiority quickly forced the already weak Manchu government into an agreement to lease the surrounding Bay of Jiaozhou to Germany.

In a short period of time, a modern, German-style city was constructed at Qingdao, with villas, a deepwater port, a cathedral and a main street called Kaiser Wilhelmstrasse. Business was not everything: the Germans used Qingdao as a missionary base, too. It remains one of China's more Christian cities. The twin-spired 1934 **St Michael's Catholic cathedral** (Tianzhu Jiaotang; Mon–Sat 6am, Sun 8am) and the 1908 **Protestant church** (Jidu Jiaotang; daily 8am–4.30pm; charge) tend to be crowded with local people on Sundays and have become tourist attractions.

German Qingdao suffered a curious fate during World War

Tsingtao beer

Qingdao is best known in the West for its most famous export, Tsingtao beer, brewed in the city since 1903. (The brewery, in Dengzhoulu, is open daily for groups only.) The brewers maintain that the high quality of the beer is due not only to German brewing expertise but also to the spring water used, from Laoshan Mountain.

I. Japan, which joined the Allied forces, invaded the city, imprisoned the survivors of the German garrison and occupied Qingdao for the duration of the war. China wasn't able to regain sovereignty until 1922. After the Communists came to power in 1949, industrial development went forward. The city of about 7 million is known today for its vibrant port and manufacturing led by electronics and household appliances. Since 2000, its coastal location has also seen rapid growth in homes with sea views.

As permanent as any of the German contributions to Qingdao is its brewing prowess. The local beer has become China's national brew, exported worldwide in big green bottles or modern cans under the old spelling of the town's name, Tsingtao. Brewery tours can be arranged, and the Qingdao International Beer Festival in the middle of August, the largest event of its kind in Asia, passes for China's *Oktoberfest*. Beer buyers may find plastic bags, not bottles, of Tsingtao sold in local shops. Merchants will tie the corners of the bag around a straw.

German Town

Qingdao is a remarkably walkable city. Some of the German architecture is concentrated in the **Badaguan District** on Taiping Bay, near Beach No. 1. This is a lovely neighbourhood of Western-style mansions, landscaped lawns and tree-lined lanes, capped by what can only be described as a German castle by the sea – the governor's lodge during colonial days (Huashi Lou; daily 8.30am–4pm, charge).

Not far from the old villas and castle is **Qianhai Pier**, once the main berth for German ships. The pier, now known as Zhanqiao, has been lengthened to an impressive 440m (nearly a quarter of a mile), and an octagonal 'Ripple Diverging Pavilion' lies at the far end. Visitors and vendors alike crowd the promenade. Roving portrait photographers hustle tourists, pitching the lighthouse as a background.

Above the beaches, with fine views of the city and the sea, are a number of parks atop steep green hills. In Xinhao Park there stands the opulent residence built for the German governor in 1903. Formerly

Qingdao is famous for its Tsingtao beer

a hotel, the **Qingdao Welcome Guest House** (Qingdao Ying Binguan; daily 8.30am–5.30pm summer, 8.30am–5pm winter; charge) now serves as a period museum. The grand piano in its plush lobby, dated 1876, is German, but the former suites off the lobby area are decidedly Chinese. Occupied for a month in 1957 by Mao Zedong and his wife, they still shelter the Chairman's desk and its secret compartment.

In addition to Qingdao's stunning beaches, which attract some 100,000 sunbathers every summer, the area is renowned for the mountain resort of **Laoshan**, 40km (nearly 25 miles) to the east. Bordering the sea, Laoshan is rich in springs, waterfalls and steep trekking trails. Laoshan mineral water, of vaunted medicinal value, originates here and is sold throughout the country. One of Laoshan's 72 temples is by the sea: **Xiaqinggong**, a Daoist retreat that dates back to 14 BC.

YANTAI

Fishing craft enliven the port of Yantai (known as Chefoo when the British made it a treaty port). There are also a few outdoor markets and a neighbourhood of well-preserved Western-style buildings. The Yantai Museum is architecturally most impressive, and a well-spruced-up crop of former colonial consulates – British, Danish, American, Japanese – can be found on the slopes of Yantaishan Park, along with a Ming-dynasty temple. Yantai also has a number of notable beaches, including a popular sandy one down the coast.

KAIFENG

The ancient walled city of Kaifeng, located in eastern Henan province, lies near enough to the unpredictable Yellow River to have known more than its share of catastrophes – and when it wasn't being flooded it was being pillaged. The most terrible of the invasions, in the 12th century, extinguished the dreams of the Northern Song dynasty and left Kaifeng in ruins. All things considered, it's almost miraculous that several historic buildings have survived to this day. So, remarkably, has much of the city's old imperial dignity.

Kaifeng rose to fame more than 2,000 years ago during the Warring States period, when it was capital of the Kingdom of Wei (265–220 BC). The city's most prosperous and glorious era was between the years AD 960 and 1127, when it was the eastern capital of the Northern Song dynasty.

In northeast Kaifeng, just inside the old wall, is the **Iron Pagoda** (Tieta; daily 8am–5.30pm; charge), Kaifeng's best-known symbol. It looks as if it's made of iron, but the exterior walls are faced with glazed bricks and tiles of an iron-like hue. Built in 1049 and restored in modern times, it is a lucky 13 tiers tall. It was originally part of a 6th-century monastery complex, but the other buildings were washed away in one of the great floods of the 19th century. Another relic of the Song dynasty, the square and imposing **Pota** (Pagoda of the Po Family; daily 8am–5.30pm; charge) reveals none of the high-flying grace of the Iron Pagoda. This might be excused by the fact that the top three tiers of the building collapsed several hundred years ago.

In the northwest part of the city, the **Imperial Way** of the Song emperors has been reconstructed. Tile-roofed souvenir shops and restaurants line the street for three blocks, ending at the entrance to **Dragon Pavilion Park** (Longtingyuan; daily 7am–7pm; charge). The park overlooks two scenic lakes and has a 500m/yd stone pathway that leads to the central pavilion, with upswept golden roofs, which was reconstructed in the 17th century.

On the beach at Yantai

West from Dragon Pavilion Park along the lakeshore is the Stele Forest of the Imperial Academy, an outdoor arena with over 3,000 ancient carved tablets. Nearby is **Qingming Park up the River** (Qingming Shanghe Yuan), a theme park modelled on a 12th-century scroll picturing festive and imperial Kaifeng.

At the centre of Kaifeng, the main attraction is the **Grand Xiangguo Monastery** (Daxiangguosi; daily 7am–5pm; charge), founded in the 6th century. Inside is the gilded statue of the 'Thousand-Armed and Thousand-Eyed Buddha', which (incredibly) has more than the advertised number of arms and eyes. Outside the temple is the city's liveliest and largest open-air market.

Giving the local lore an unusual twist, a community of Jews migrated to Kaifeng in about the 10th century. They established a synagogue in 1163 and maintained a community until a major flood in 1852. Although they have been assimilated, as many as 100 Kaifeng residents still claim Jewish heritage. Stone tablets recording the history of Jews in Kaifeng are stored in the Kaifeng Museum. The grounds of the **Purity**

and Truth Synagogue (Youtai Jiaotang Yizhi), north of a Catholic church and east of a mosque, can still be located with the help of local guides. Bang on the doors and someone will usually let you in.

ZHENGZHOU

This area was first settled more than 3,000 years ago, and traces of the Shang-dynasty city wall can still be seen east and northeast of the city centre. Better-preserved ancient relics can be viewed in the **Henan Provincial Museum** (www.chnmus.net). They include some of the earliest forms of Chinese writing: characters inscribed on bones and tortoise shells as well as fossilised dinosaur eggs from the region. Outside town there is a peaceful, panoramic lookout over the Yellow River.

LUOYANG

During the Sui dynasty, 1,400 years ago, **Luoyang** ❼ shared the imperial court with Chang'an (present-day Xi'an). The city is sometimes known as the Capital for Nine Dynasties, reflecting a political and cultural prominence that originated nearly 4,000 years ago.

In the 10th century the imperial court moved from Luoyang to the northeast. Luoyang later became capital of the central province of Henan, but by the 20th century it was merely a shadow of its former self. After the Communists took power, they decided to revive it as a model industrial centre. Hundreds of new factories were built, turning out tractors, mining equipment, ball bearings and thousands of other products. The city is also associated with the peony: the annual Peony Festival every April showcases over 500 flower varieties in the Royal City Park (Wangcheng Gongyuan).

The **Luoyang Museum** (Luoyang Bowuguan; Tue–Sun 9am–4.30pm; free), housed in a Ming-dynasty temple, contains the fossil of an elephant tusk half a million years old, Stone Age pottery, Shang bronzes and glazed Tang ceramic figures. The **Ancient Tombs Museum** (Gumu Bowuguan; Tue–Sun 9am–5pm summer, 9am–4.30pm winter; free) displays more than 20 royal tombs from the Han dynasty to the Song dynasty.

A short distance to the east of Luoyang stands China's first Buddhist monastery, **White Horse Temple** (Baimasi; daily 7.30am–7pm; charge), which dates from the 1st century AD. The temple's name is a reference to two envoys returning from India with China's first Buddhist scriptures on the backs of their white horses.

Carvings at the Longmen Caves

The Longmen Caves

Counted among the most precious of the grotto complexes in China, the **Longmen Caves** (Longmen Shiku; daily Feb–Mar and Oct 8–Oct 31 8am–6pm, Apr–Oct 7 until 6.30pm, Nov–Jan until 5pm; charge) lie about 14km (9 miles) south of Luoyang. The name Longmen, which means 'Dragon's Gate', might derive from the lie of the land here: cliffs stand like gate towers on either side of the Yi River.

The hard rock here is conducive to delicate carving, which was carried out on a monumental scale for about 400 years from AD 494. More than 1,300 grottoes were constructed, as well as 2,100 niches and nearly 100,000 statues. These range from a height of about 17m (56ft) to a fingernail-sized 2cm (less than an inch). In addition, there are 40 pagodas and more than 3,600 inscribed steles or tablets.

Shaolin

The fighting monks in a thousand kung fu films can trace their origin to the Shaolin Monastery, 40km (25 miles) from Luoyang. In fact, the Chinese martial arts and such offshoots as the gentler exercise forms known as *taijiquan* (t'ai chi) have their symbolic, if not literal, birthplace at this monastery. The branch of Buddhism known as Chan (Zen in Japan and the West) also looks to Shaolin as its source.

With so many traditional arts centred at one historic site, it's no wonder the **Shaolin Monastery** (daily 7.30am–6pm summer, 8am–5.30 winter; charge; www.shaolin.org.cn) has become one of China's more popular tourist attractions. Shaolin now provides movie sets for film crews as well as schools for domestic and foreign classes in self defence. Be it kung fu or karate, taekwondo or judo, these Asian martial arts all originated in ancient China as fighting techniques of one individual against another. It started with the Indian monk Bodhidharma, who came to the Songshan Mountains in AD 527 and founded the monastery. He realised that many Buddhist monks were unable to maintain the total concentration necessary for their demanding meditation exercises. To aid them, he devised a physical training routine, based on his observation of animal movements,

Martial arts at Shaolin

that was designed to concentrate the mind and the body together. From this evolved the inimitable Shaolin boxing that is still practised here today, which in turn gave rise to all the other disciplines.

Shadow magic

It is said the Bodhidharma, the founder of the Shaolin Monastery, sat facing the back wall of a cave and meditated for nine years, until his shadow was finally imprinted on the rock.

Although it is crowded and commercialised, the monastery is still one of China's most interesting historical and religious monuments. In 625 it was expanded by a Tang-dynasty emperor in gratitude for wartime services rendered by the Shaolin monks, who used their fighting skills to send off some usurpers. In the 16th century the monks were called upon again to rid China's coast of Japanese pirates.

In 1928, when warlords carved up sections of the faltering Chinese Republic, one general laid siege to the monastery and set it ablaze. It was ransacked by the Red Guards during the Cultural Revolution, and was closed for years. Now restored, it houses 70 monks.

The Shaolin Monastery has a number of interesting relics and remains. Of the many halls, pavilions and temples linked by broad courtyards, the most important is the **Thousand Buddha Hall** (Qianfo Dian), dating back to 1588.

The outer courtyards of the Shaolin Monastery contain other unusual treasures. The **Forest of Stupas** (Shaolin Talin) is of historic note. Stupas (or dagobas) are small sealed pagodas that hold holy relics and the remains of important Buddhist monks. The 227 stupas represent more than 1,000 years of Buddhist funerals, beginning with that of a Tang-dynasty abbot who was buried here in 746. Just around the corner is the most popular display at the monastery, a courtyard of open-air pavilions containing scores of wooden statues – monks in all the classic poses of a feverish kung fu battle.

The Forest of Stupas at Shaolin

Shaolin offers one more treat for the more adventurous, for the monastery is located at the foot of the western range of the **Songshan Mountains**, part of the mountain cluster that was traditionally regarded as the Central Mountain at the centre of the Chinese Empire. A gondola now whisks visitors to the top, where hiking trails are abundant and views of the Shaolin complex and the vast arid plains of Henan are impressive. On the far side of the range, sheer walls of stone 300m (1,000ft) high tower over the plains, where a series of catwalks and carved footpaths wander through old temples and pavilions into the silence and emptiness beyond.

XI'AN

When ancient Beijing was just a remote trading post, **Xi'an** ❽ was the capital of the Middle Kingdom and the largest city in the world. Palaces, pavilions and pagodas crowned the skyline. Artists and poets (and, of course, cooks) catered for the most demanding imperial tastes. And since this was the starting point of the Silk Road into Central Asia, the most adventurous of foreigners congregated here.

Having made history over several thousand years, the city of today is more populous than ever (at 5.7 million residents) and proud of its modern factories and housing projects. Still, Xi'an and its dusty surrounding countryside preserve the glories of 11 dynasties, and it is as a storehouse of China's Qin, Han and Tang dynasties' treasures that Xi'an has reached the top ranks of international tourism.

On the way to any of Xi'an's archaeological sites, you get a good look at the wind-whipped landscape of the Wei River valley. Militarily and economically strategic since prehistoric times, the area comprises fertile cotton and wheat fields, fallow plains and bizarre terraces of grey clay dotted with caves that provide housing even to this day.

As the rapidly modernising capital of Shaanxi province, Xi'an can look back almost with detachment on its regal past. During the first Zhou dynasty (which ended in 770 BC), several places in the Xi'an district served as capitals. In the 3rd century BC, the Qin settled just northwest of Xi'an, in Xianyang. When the Han took over, in 206 BC, a grandiose new capital called Chang'an ('Everlasting Peace') rose just north of Xi'an. Imperial splendour returned to the region under the Sui (AD 581–618) when a capital known as Daxing ('Great Prosperity') was established on the site of Xi'an. The Tang emperors who followed greatly enlarged and beautified the city, again naming it Chang'an.

The Little Wild Goose Pagoda

The golden age of Xi'an (as Chang'an) ended more than 1,000 years ago, when

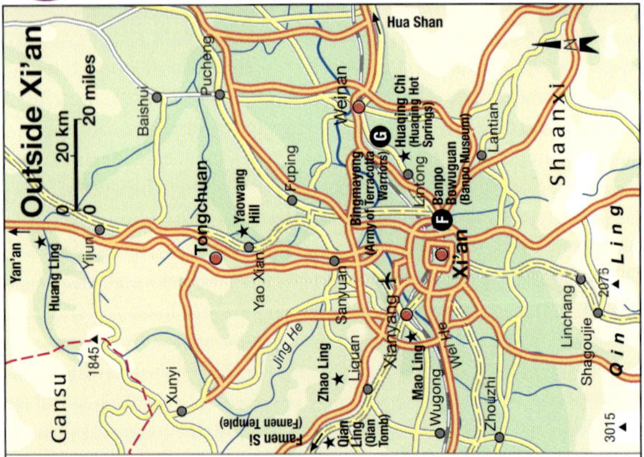
Outside Xi'an
0 20 km
0 20 miles
Hua Shan
Yan'an
Huang Ling
Yijun
Baishui
Pucheng
Tongchuan
Yaowang Hill
Fuping
Weinan
Huaqing Chi (Huaqing Hot Springs)
Bingmayong (Army of Terracotta Warriors)
Lintong
Banpo Bowuguan (Banpo Museum)
Lantian
Xi'an
Yao Xian
Sanyuan
Xianyang
Jing He
Wei He
Zhao Ling
Liquan
Mao Ling
Qian Ling (Qian Tomb)
Famen Si (Famen Temple)
Xunyi
Wugong
Zhouzhi
Linchang
Shagoujie
2075
3015
1845
Gansu
Shaanxi
Qin Ling

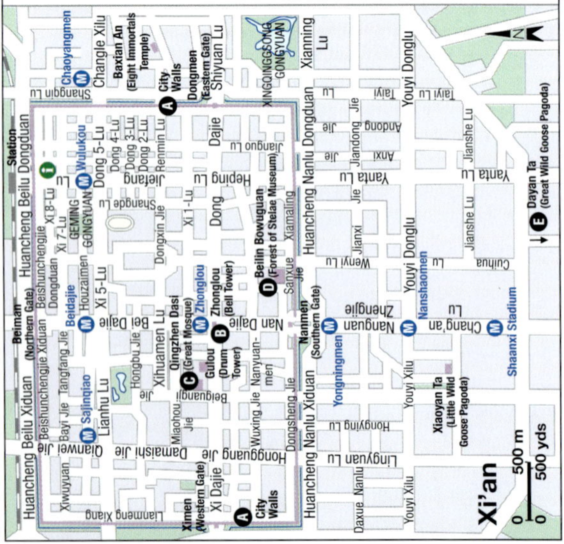
Xi'an
0 500 m
0 500 yds
Huancheng Beilu Xiduan
Huancheng Beilu Dongduan
Station
Beimen (Northern Gate)
Beishunchengjie Xiduan
Beishunchengjie Dongduan
Chaoyangmen
Changle Xilu
Baxian An (Eight Immortals Temple)
City Walls
Dongmen (Eastern Gate)
Shiyuan Lu
XINGQINGGONG GONGYUAN
Xianning Lu
Sajinqiao
Beidajie
Wulukou
GEMING GONGYUAN
Zhonglou
Zhonglou (Bell Tower)
Gulou (Drum Tower)
Qingzhen Dasi (Great Mosque)
Beilin Bowuguan (Forest of Stelae Museum)
Ximen (Western Gate)
Xi Dajie
Dong Dajie
Bei Dajie
Nan Dajie
Lianhu Lu
Xihuamen Lu
Jiefang Lu
Heping Lu
Hongguang Jie
Damaishi Jie
Qianwei Jie
Nanmen (Southern Gate)
Yongningmen
Nanshaomen
Huancheng Nanlu Xiduan
Huancheng Nanlu Dongduan
Youyi Xilu
Youyi Donglu
Xiaoyan Ta (Little Wild Goose Pagoda)
Dayan Ta (Great Wild Goose Pagoda)
Shaanxi Stadium
Chang'an Lu
Yanta Lu
Lingyuan Lu
Hongying Lu
Wenyi Lu
Daxue Nanlu

the Tang succumbed to rebellion and anarchy. The city sank into provinciality, even though impressive new city walls and official buildings were constructed in the 14th century. These features of the Ming era – almost modern by Xi'an standards – are the first to catch the eye.

Tang city grid

The centre of Xi'an still retains its historical layout from the Tang dynasty, with roads laid out in a classical Chinese grid pattern, running due north–south or east–west, and meeting at right angles.

The City Wall

The rectangular Ming-dynasty **city wall** Ⓐ is 14.5km (almost 9 miles) around, and so thick that two-way chariot traffic could travel the roadway on top. Major renovations have restored the ramparts, guard towers and moat, making it an ideal place to stroll.

In the centre of the walled city are several monuments from the Ming dynasty. The **Bell Tower** Ⓑ (Zhonglou; daily 8.30am–9pm summer, 8.30 am–6pm winter; charge) is another of those lofty wooden buildings ingeniously constructed without the use of nails. Three tiers of elegant roofs rise from a solid brick pedestal at the centre of the city, forming one of the emblems of Xi'an.

The **Drum Tower** (Gulou; daily 8.30am–9pm summer, 8.30am–6pm winter; charge), a similar building across a new public square and shopping mall, dates from 1370 and is also open to tourists. The drum is sounded in its tower 21 times at sunrise; the bell is sounded in its tower 21 times at sunset.

Religious Sites

Just around the corner and up a curving alleyway of vendors, the **Great Mosque** Ⓒ (Qingzhen Dasi; daily 8am–7pm; charge) traces its history to AD 742. The serene and spacious complex consists of gardens, temples and pavilions, largely in the Chinese style. The side galleries contain beautifully carved furniture and screens. The triple-eaved Introspection Tower (Shengxin) is a minaret from which many of Xi'an's sizeable Muslim minority, including descendants of Silk Road travellers, are called to prayer. The prayer hall holds over 1,000.

Another attraction in the Muslim district is the food. On one of the main streets, rows of chefs in outdoor stalls cook tempting snacks such as kebabs.

As in so many locations in China, Xi'an's once-glorious temples were devastated during the Cultural Revolution (1966–76), but restorations have led to the reopening of the **Lama Temple** (Guangrensi), founded in 1705; **Wolongsi**, an ancient Zen Buddhist temple; **Dongyuemiao**, a Daoist temple to the mountain god of Taishan; and the **Temple of the Eight Immortals** (Baxianan; daily 9am–5.30pm; charge).

Terracotta Warrior statues

Museums

The **Shaanxi History Museum** (Shaanxi Lishi Bowuguan; Tue–Sun 9am–5.30pm winter, 8.30am–6pm summer; free; www.sxhm.com), south of the city wall, is the most extensive. With a collection rivalled only by the exhibits in the Shanghai Museum (see page 116), the museum presents intelligently arranged pieces that largely focus on the Han, Qin and Tang dynasties. On display are 2,000 relics, including several of the famed terracotta warriors. An underground tunnel houses murals from more than 20 imperial tombs.

Colourful warriors

The terracotta warriors were originally brightly coloured, with rosy cheeks and painted uniforms. Two archers in Vault 2 retain some of their brilliance.

Also of great interest in Xi'an is the **Forest of Steles Museum** D (Beilin Bowuguan; daily Mar–Apr, Oct 8–Nov 8am–6.15pm, May–Oct until 6.45pm, Dec–Feb until 6pm; charge; www.beilin-museum.com), located in the former Confucius Temple. This library of inscribed stone slabs, including a complete edition of the Confucian classics (carved in AD 837), documents the history of Chinese culture and calligraphy. The Nestorian Stele records another history altogether, that of Christianity in China from 635 to 781. The street leading to the old museum along the southern city wall, Shuyuanmen, has been comprehensively restored and offers a fine collection of traditional art and calligraphy shops.

Pagodas

The imposing **Great Wild Goose Pagoda** E (Dayanta; daily 8am–5pm, charge) was built in AD 652 during the Tang dynasty to house precious Buddhist texts brought back from India by Xi'an's most celebrated pilgrim, an intrepid scholar named Xuanzang. Having survived years of sandstorms and blizzards, demons and dragons, Xuanzang was feted on his return in 645. He spent the next two decades translating his stack of holy books from Sanskrit to Chinese. A theme park, **Tang Paradise**, near the pagoda, recreates the old ways of the capital.

Though it's shorter, slimmer and slightly newer than the Big Wild Goose Pagoda, the **Little Wild Goose Pagoda** (Xiaoyanta; daily 9am–5.30pm winter, until 6pm summer; free), built in 707, has more tiers: 13 at the moment. When it was built, it had 15 tiers, but the top came tumbling down in a Ming-era earthquake – the damage is still clearly visible today.

EXCURSIONS FROM XI'AN

The oldest of the region's archaeological wonders is found in a museum erected on the very site where they were discovered. This is at the Stone Age site of **Banpo** **F** (daily 8am–5pm; free), 10km (6 miles) east of Xi'an. Six thousand years ago a village, evidently thriving, occupied this farmland, but traces of habitation came to light only in the 1950s, when workmen were digging the foundations for a new factory.

You have to climb a flight of stairs to reach the covered excavation. From a series of walkways you look down on the outlines of houses, ovens, storage areas and graves. Also on display in the **Banpo Museum** (Banpo Bowuguan; daily 8am–6pm summer, 8am–5.30pm winter; charge; www.bpmuseum.com) are some of the objects found in the course of excavations: axes, fishhooks and pots, as well as artistically decorated ceramics and, most dramatically, the skeletons of these ancient villagers.

Terracotta Warriors

China's greatest archaeological attraction, the **terracotta warriors of the Qin-dynasty army** **G**, stand in battle formation about 30km (18 miles) east of Xi'an in the complex known as the **Museum of the Terracotta Warriors and Horses** (Qinshihuang Bingmayong Bowuguan; daily 8.30am–6pm summer, 8.30am–5.30pm winter; charge). The life-sized (and slightly larger) infantrymen, archers, officers and their horses symbolically guard the tomb of the first Qin emperor.

Well before his eventual death in 210 BC, Qinshi Huangdi conscripted hundreds of thousands of his subjects to construct a suitably impressive tomb. It is said that the workers and supervisors involved in its design and construction were buried alive within the tomb. The novel idea of guarding it with thousands of pottery soldiers was revealed by accident in 1974, when local peasants digging a well created a worldwide sensation. Today the underground army of terracotta warriors is one of the highlights of any visit to China.

Battle formation

What is believed to be the main tomb of the emperor is situated about 1.5km (1 mile) to the west of the terracotta soldiers. According to historical stories, a splendid necropolis apparently depicting the whole of China in miniature is centred beneath the 47m (154ft) high mound. The whole burial site is reputed to cover 56 sq km (22 sq miles). The same accounts also say that the ceiling is studded with pearls depicting the night sky, and that mercury was pumped in mechanically to create images of flowing rivers. Some speculation has it that the emperor was so superstitious and fearful that he had the necropolis built as a decoy and is, in fact, buried somewhere else. However, in order to open up the entire necropolis, 12 villages and about half a dozen factories in the area would have to be relocated.

An arched structure resembling an aircraft hangar has been built to protect the exposed soldiers and horses in Vault 1 from the weather. Walkways permit tourists a bird's-eye survey of the site, revealing the deployment of the troops, 6,000 of them reassembled

Yan'an is a shrine to the Communist revolution

and back in their original ranks. Each warrior is an individual, with his own headdress, moustache or beard and unique expression. It's little wonder that guards patrol the observation deck, discouraging photos. The eager, graceful horses also have distinctive traits. The small museum in the courtyard entrance to Vault 1 contains warriors, their steeds and one of the two half-life-sized solid bronze chariots found near the first emperor's burial mound in 1980.

Vault 2, discovered in 1976 and opened in 1994, is an excavation in progress. It contains imperial cavalry: 900 soldiers, 116 saddled horses and 356 horses hitched to 89 chariots. Vault 3, the smallest so far opened to the public, is a command post with 68 officers in war robes.

Those who want to take home a piece of the action can buy knock-off terracotta warrior statues from vendors outside the vaults.

Huaqing Hot Springs

History and natural beauty mingle easily at **Huaqing Hot Springs** (Huaqingchi; daily 7am–7pm summer, 7.30am–6pm winter; charge), a popular side trip for tourists on the way to or from the terracotta warriors excavations. The spa's hot, mineral-rich waters and its situation on **Black Horse Mountain** (Lishan) attracted a series of royal patrons as far back as the 8th century BC, so the place was provided with delightful pavilions, pools and gardens.

Eager Chinese tourists often descend on the large, mosaic-bottomed Oval Tub used by Lady Yangguifei, favourite concubine of the Tang Emperor Xuanzong (who reigned AD 712–56). Lady Yang was a famous beauty, as a portrait, hanging in her former dressing room, attests. Although she was dear to the emperor, Lady Yang's extravagances and intrigues angered courtiers. When mutinous troops demanded her head, the intimidated emperor acceded to save his throne. After she was taken away and strangled, the grief-stricken emperor wept and then abdicated, giving rise to many classic poems.

Qianling Tombs

Xi'an is surrounded by hundreds of huge earthen mounds – the largely unopened tombs of emperors and their courts. The tombs of notables of the Tang dynasty, dug into a mountainside (Liangshan) 80km (50 miles) northwest of Xi'an, provide an intriguing look at what lies buried around the old capital and at the level of art and culture reached in China during the 7th, 8th and 9th centuries (daily 8am–6pm summer, 8.30am–5.30pm winter; charge).

Several tombs here contain exquisite murals. The famous set of frescoes in the **Tomb of Prince Zhanghuai** (who died in AD 684) depicts an animated polo match, a hunting expedition, a reception for foreign diplomats and (most movingly) a scene in a court cloister with a young concubine looking longingly at a bird in flight. A tomb with a steeply inclined entrance, that of **Princess Yong Tai**, has a mural which is full of intriguing details depicting the court maidens attending the princess (who was to die at the age of 17 in AD 701). These tombs have also yielded brightly coloured ceramic figurines, fine stone carvings and large memorial tablets.

The principal tomb belongs to the third Tang emperor, **Gaozong**, and to his ambitious widow, Wuzetian, who had herself promoted to the rank of empress in 691 – the only woman to hold such power in Chinese history. Gigantic stone sculptures of animals, birds, generals and (now headless) ambassadors line the Royal Way to this tomb, but its entrance remains sealed. The ostentation of the exterior hints at what might lie within.

YAN'AN

This small town in the hills north of Xi'an is one of contemporary China's most celebrated historical sites. In 1937 this was the last stop of the 10,000km (6,000-mile) odyssey of the Long March. Yan'an's stark landscape of windswept sandstone cliffs provided the backdrop for the 'birthplace of the revolution', and was the headquarters of the Chinese Communist Party for nine years. The city now symbolises the heroic and idealistic phase of the revolution, and many tour groups make the same pilgrimage as Mao Zedong and his followers. Revolutionary landmarks, including the caves in which Mao lived, are the attractions here.

SHANGHAI

You couldn't confuse **Shanghai** ❾ with anywhere else in China. It is bigger, more prosperous and more dynamic than any other city; its skyline boasts European-style towers; its shop windows and food stalls seize your attention. Over the past two decades, Shanghai has been Asia's boomtown, and is the most modern, most Westernised city on mainland China. The booming economy is reflected in the ambitious building developments taking place. Shanghai's new airport is serviced by a German-engineered magnetic levitation train, the fastest – and most expensive – transit device in the world. It's also China's wealthiest city.

Before war and revolution changed its face, Shanghai was dominated by foreign fortune-hunters, social climbers and a glittering

Jin Mao Tower

array of sinners. Its very name became a verb in English: 'to shanghai' means to abduct by trickery or force. Nowadays it is regaining much of its old glamour, and the old disreputable edge has been replaced by massage parlours and nightclubs, many aimed at Shanghai's large Japanese, Taiwanese and Western expatriate communities.

With more than 24 million people, Shanghai is one of the most extensive cities in the world. The totally flat metropolitan area covers about 6,300 sq km (more than 2,300 sq miles), which is five times the area of the city of Los Angeles. Administered as a separate region, like Beijing, the Shanghai metropolis includes rich farmland as well as big-city housing complexes and heavy industry. It is not only extensive but expensive: cost-of-living surveys regularly rank Shanghai as one of the world's most expensive cities.

The population, China's most worldly, fashionable and open people, are very individualistic, speaking a dialect that nobody else can understand, eating a different cuisine and generally considering themselves to be light years ahead of their nearest competitor, Beijing (and catching up fast with Hong Kong). People who venture

View of the Bund

from elsewhere in China to seek work in Shanghai stand out right away for their drab clothes and facial expressions that say, 'Am I still in China?'

Shanghai's long-standing position as a great industrial and commercial centre is part of an earlier 19th- and 20th-century colonial tradition. But since around 2000, much of the city's manufacturing industry has moved westwards to cheaper land, allowing Shanghai to remake itself as a financial hub. China's most closely watched financial markets are situated in Shanghai, while financial institutions from throughout the world congregate downtown. Money, not national politics, dominates the public psyche, a striking difference from Beijing. As such, the city has retained a special appeal to visitors as a sophisticated, business-like metropolis.

SHANGHAI IN HISTORY

China's prime port began unpromisingly 1,000 years ago as a fishing village on mudflats near the Yangzi River's outlet to the East China Sea. Shanghai didn't officially become a town until the 13th century, but even then it was largely ignored by the rest of China – but not by Japanese pirates, who were attracted by the overseas trade that passed through the town. After numerous attacks, in the 16th century Shanghai constructed a protective wall, which surrounded the Old City until 1912.

In the 17th and 18th centuries, domestic commerce increased the importance of Shanghai as a port and marketplace. But the authorities firmly resisted foreign connections until British gunboats won an invitation. After the 1842 Opium War, Shanghai became one of five Chinese ports open to foreign residence and trade. Over the next few years the influx of Europeans, Americans and refugees from the battles of the Taiping Rebellion turned Shanghai into a glamorous, if naughty, trading port. Foreign concession areas took up most of what is now central Shanghai, except for the old walled Chinese part of the city.

Soon Shanghai became the place to be – a city with the best culture, the most opulent dance halls, the largest volume of business, the tallest buildings. But little of the prosperity filtered down to the ordinary citizen, who was kept apart. Bitterness at the injustices and corruption of Shanghai society fired the city's revolutionary movement: the Chinese Communist Party was founded here in 1921.

Between 1937 and 1945, Shanghai was occupied by Japanese troops; most of the foreign colony was interned. After the war the Guomindang Nationalists took power, but Communist troops seized Shanghai in 1949. The new regime wiped out organised crime and vice, expropriated factories and built new ones, setting the city on a new industrial course. In 1965 the Cultural Revolution was sparked off

STARES, SMILES, LAUGHTER

A smile in China doesn't always mean pleasure. People who are mildly upset or momentarily confused grin to deflect any unwanted attention. Those who are really happy smile broadly and may laugh. Foreign travellers get the tense grins when trying to speak English with Chinese people who don't understand the language well but feel obligated to try. Travellers may get the bigger smiles if they fall into extended, productive conversation with locals, who seldom have a chance to talk to foreigners. People in much of the country compulsively stare at foreigners. They emphatically don't consider the behaviour rude. To turn a stare into a happiness smile, wave and say, 'Hi.'

in Shanghai, as the political base of Jiangqing, the former Shanghai actress who was Mao's wife. Despite the Red Guards' enthusiasm for demolishing anything that was not defined as Socialist Realism, many buildings from colonial times have survived in the city. After the death of Mao and the arrest of the Gang of Four, Shanghai culture and art experienced a renaissance, and the new economic policies of the reform era benefited Shanghai more than any other city.

THE PORT AND BUND

As an essentially 19th-century phenomenon, Shanghai matured too late to contribute to classical Chinese art or culture. In Shanghai the interest shifts to relics of uninhibited pre-war capitalism and scenes of the city's contemporary energy and flair.

The port of Shanghai sums up the strange and often uncomfortable meeting of East and West, of old and new. The muddy Huangpu River slices through the centre of the city. Foghorns converse into the night, long after the sound of car horns and bike bells has ceased. The river traffic is a motley flotilla of modern container ships and ocean-going junks – their sails the colour of grime blending into a backdrop of polluted skies – of packed ferries and convoys of barges, warships and rusty coasters. Visitors can take a comfortable and endlessly fascinating riverboat tour of the Huangpu from downtown Shanghai to the Yangzi River.

The Bund Sightseeing Tunnel

Returning to the city, you see the astonishingly

un-Chinese skyline of Shanghai. The Waitan, the riverfront promenade on the left bank of the Huangpu, used to be called the **Bund** Ⓐ (and still is by many), from an Anglo-Indian word for an embankment on a muddy shore. It's easy to imagine the elegance of the Bund in its heyday, when the gardens were barred to dogs and Chinese, in that order. This is the place for relaxed people-watching, from early morning when the shadow-boxers work out, until the evening strolls of well-dressed courting couples. The promenade is now also home to smart restaurants and shopping centres.

Facing the river along Zhongshan Road are some grandiose and restored older buildings. These include the Peace Hotel; the Seamen's Club, formerly the British Consulate; the former Chartered Bank of India, Australia and China, now an upmarket shopping and restaurant tower called Bund 18; and the massive 1923 headquarters of the old Hongkong and Shanghai Bank, later transformed into a Chinese bank. And across the river is new East Shanghai, known as Pudong. Here, construction since the turn of the century has given rise to another forest of office towers, including some of Asia's tallest structures. Some buildings allow visitors to the top to take in the views.

AROUND NANJING ROAD

One of the pleasures of Shanghai is to stroll along Nanjing Road, long the most famous shopping avenue in China, to see what's new and what's old. Pop into the **Peace Hotel** (Heping Fandian), on the Bund at the start of Nanjing Road, and peruse the impressive Art Deco lobby of what was originally the Cathay Hotel (opened 1929). The hotel is where Noel Coward holed up to write *Private Lives* and where Steven Spielberg filmed scenes for *Empire of the Sun*. The hotel's jazz band, performing here since the 1930s, still swings every evening in the north wing.

North from the Bund is the **Ohel Moshe Synagogue** (Moxihuitang; daily 9am–5pm; free), built in 1927 to serve Shanghai's Jewish population, which once numbered 20,000. No longer a functioning synagogue, it houses a small museum (daily 9am–4.30pm).

On the south side of Nanjing Road is **People's Park** (Renmin Gongyuan), once home to the Shanghai Race Track (1863) and now adjacent to the elegant **Shanghai Art Museum** (Shanghai Meishu Guan; Tue–Sun 10am–6pm; free; advanced booking required). **People's Square** **B** (Renmin Guangchang) houses the lavish **Grand Theatre**, the illuminating Shanghai Urban Planning Exposition Centre and the incomparable **Shanghai Museum** (Shanghai Bowuguan; daily 9am–5pm; www.shanghaimuseum.net), with state-of-the-art displays and presentation. There are four floors of exhibits with stalls on each floor selling gifts and museum reproductions. Among the chief themes: bronzes and stone sculptures, ceramics, paintings, calligraphy, coins, jade and furniture. Not all of the museum's 120,000 artefacts can be displayed here at one time, but many visitors savour these displays and insist upon a return visit. For a break during museum browsing, there's a tearoom on the first floor.

THE OLD CITY

Just southwest of the Bund is a district known today as the Old City (Nanshi), within the circle formed by Renminlu and Zhonghualu. Shanghai's city walls ran parallel to this ring road until they were knocked down in 1912. Then the moats were filled in and today's streets laid down. Before 1949 the Old City remained under Chinese law and administration, while the rest of Shanghai was carved up by foreign powers, and most of the residents in these old back alleys were Chinese. Eventually it became notorious as a gangster-and-opium slum. Today the vices are gone, but the crowded neighbourhoods, and some of the small houses and tiny lanes still exist, though many have been torn down for redevelopment.

In the centre of the Old City, on Fuyoulu, the **Yuyuan Garden** **C** (daily 8.45am–4.15pm; charge) was commissioned by a Ming-dynasty mandarin. As the main classical Chinese garden in Shanghai, it is an absolute gem of landscaping and architecture

Nanjing Road East, the city's most famous shopping street

– the perfect place for local people to seek tranquillity, so conveniently offered in the heart of Old Shanghai.

Just inside the main gate is a rockery, an artificial hill of inherently interesting stones, held together with glutinous rice powder and lime. From the pavilion on top of this hill, the Ming official could watch all the excitements of river life, though tall buildings now intervene. In front of the **Hall of Ten Thousand Flowers** grows a more than 400-year-old gingko tree. Another carefully created rockery is reflected in a pond teeming with giant goldfish. All the garden's corridors and pavilions, bridges and walls, sculptures and trees are so artfully arranged that it seems many times larger than its actual, compact size.

Outside the garden walls, a large rectangular pond is bisected by the Nine Turnings Bridge, so shaped to deflect evil spirits. The bridge is the only link to the 400-year-old **Huxinting Teahouse** (257 Yuyuanlu; daily 8.30am–9.30pm), which lies in the centre of an illuminated pond. On Mondays a band plays traditional Chinese music in the teahouse.

That pond marks one corner of the Old Chinese City (Nanshi), once deemed a danger zone for European visitors. You might still get lost in this maze of backstreets, reminiscent of a North African souk, but much of it has been renovated, tastefully, into the **Yuyuan Shopping Centre**. However, there are still shops from the old bazaar days selling chopsticks, medicines, bamboo fans, silk and incense.

Also successfully redeveloped is the **Temple to the Town Gods** (Chenghuangmiao; daily 8am–4.30pm; charge), which dates back to the 15th century and now hosts street fairs within sight of the teahouse and Yuyuan Garden, as it did in previous centuries. On the southern edge of the Old City is the restored **Shanghai Old Street** (Fangbang Zhonglu), an attractive (or rather tacky, depending on your point of view) lane packed with teahouses and antiques shops. To the west is a remnant of the 16th-century city wall and the street stalls of the lively **Dongtai Lu Antiques Market**. Shanghai's teahouses, like those elsewhere in China, usually give customers a small sack of loose leaves and access to hot water. A snack tray makes the rounds, and waiters wear traditional Chinese clothing.

THE FRENCH QUARTER

West of the riverside and old Chinese section is a landmark of modern history – the low brick building at **76 Xingyelu** (daily 9am–5pm;

CONSTRUCTION CRAZE

The Chinese love new buildings. Throughout history, empires have demolished and reconstructed things to fulfil a fancy or be remembered. Today that means on just about every urban block something is going up or down. It could be a mere wall or a whole building. Hammering can be heard in the older sections of town as well as in the modern high-rises. Mud-covered workers in hardhats mix with office workers on streets of Beijing and Shanghai. If you stay in your hotel past 8am, the din of drills and hammers may suddenly erupt in a room near yours as the management pursues a remodelling project.

Huxinting Teahouse

free) where the Chinese Communist Party was founded in July 1921. This building was in the **French Concession**, and when the French police learnt of the clandestine meeting, they raided the two-storey corner house. But they arrived too late to find the 12 conspirators, including Mao Zedong. Today, the house is a museum with documents and displays.

Located adjacent is **Xintiandi** **D** (New Heaven and Earth), Shanghai's most upscale pedestrian mall and a household name around China for anyone aspiring to wealth. Xintiandi is both a gourmet's delight and a functioning indoor-outdoor museum of the city's 1930s villa architecture.

Much of the finest European architecture in Shanghai can be seen in the French Quarter, where Art Deco and Tudor villas, neo-Gothic offices and large elegant mansions line many of the small streets. The modern **Okura Garden Hotel** (58 Maominglu) preserves the original lobby area of the Cercle Sportif Français from the 1920s. The **Shanghai Museum of Arts and Crafts** (daily 9am–4pm; free; www.shgmb.com) is housed in a wonderful French

Exhibit at the Shanghai Museum of Arts and Crafts

mansion (79 Fenyanglu) and allows visitors to view artisans at work on embroidery and other crafts.

Other old buildings open to view include **Song Ching Ling's Former Residence** (Songqingling Guju), a 1920s villa where the wife of Sun Yat-sen lived until 1963, and **Sun Yat-sen's Former Residence** (Sunzhongshan Guju), where the founder of the Chinese Republic lived from 1918 until 1924, a year before his death. The **Xujiahui Cathedral**, a Gothic church erected in 1848, now holds Masses in Chinese.

Shanghai's new **Jewish Centre**, with synagogue and kosher restaurant, is also in this district (Villa No. 1, 1720 Hong Qiao Lu; www.chinajewish.org/SJC).

'NEW' SHANGHAI: PUDONG

Immediately across the river from the Bund and Old Shanghai is the Pudong New Development Zone (Pudong Xinqu). The area was home to 1 million farmers before the government designated it the future technology and financial capital of all China. Skyscrapers designed by noted architects have replaced the farms. Shanghai's stock exchange – the first in post-Revolution China – relocated to Pudong, and the city's main international airport is there, too.

Many of Shanghai's skyscrapers are located in Pudong, and some of them are very tall indeed. Towering over them all is the 632m (2,073ft) high **Shanghai Tower** **E**, the tallest building in China and the second highest structure in the world. Nearby is the 492m (1,614ft) high **Shanghai World Financial Center**. Slightly shorter, with 88 storeys, is the 427m (1,400ft) **Jin Mao Tower**. The 468m (1,535ft) high, reddish **Oriental Pearl Tower** **F** (Shanghai Mingzhu; daily 8am–9.30pm) stands out against the formal-looking office towers nearby and allows visitors access to a high-altitude observation deck. You can also find the **Municipal History Museum**, which focuses on colonial-era Shanghai, in the building's basement.

On Zhangyang Lu stands Asia's largest shop, the **Yaohan Department Store** (Nextage), which is 10 storeys high and sells everything from clothing to cars. Pudong even has its own version of the Bund's shore-walk in the **Riverside Promenade**.

One of the city's newest hotspots is a flying saucer-like monolith that staged the Expo 2010 opening and closing ceremonies. This new-age superstructure, **Mercedes-Benz Arena** (www.mercedes-benzarena.com), contains an 18,000-seat show area and 20,000 dining spaces. It has opened to shopping, high-end eating, ice-skating and an interactive National Basketball Association store – displays of urban China's new wealth.

OUTLYING SIGHTS

The **Jade Buddha Temple** (Yufosi; daily 8am–4.30pm; charge; www.yufotemple.com/en), in northwest Shanghai, is not old, but it is Shanghai's leading Buddhist site and quite active, with about 70 resident monks. Its Song-dynasty-style grounds house two priceless white jade Buddha statues, one reclining, the other in the seated position of enlightenment. They were brought from Burma (today's Myanmar) in 1882 and installed in the temple when it was

Inside the Jin Mao Tower

completed in 1918. Most statues in Buddhist temples are moulded from clay with a thin overlay of gold, so these giant jade works attract curiosity-seekers as well as worshippers. Around the back of the altar is a colourful three-dimensional mural. As an extra attraction for tourists, the monks run a restaurant open to the public.

Shanghai's most striking pagoda, part of the lively **Longhua Temple** (Longhuagusi; daily 7.10am–4.30pm, charge) complex in the southwest suburbs, was rebuilt more than 1,000 years ago. The temple grounds contain many centuries-old halls, golden Buddhist statues and copious incense burners for the throngs of daily worshippers. The bell in the Bell Tower can be struck three times for a fee.

ENTERTAINMENT AND CUISINE

Two popular venues for the performing arts in the city are the **Shanghai Centre Theatre** (which also includes the Shanghai Acrobatic Theatre; www.shanghaicentre.com/theatre) and the massive new **Grand Theatre** (Dajuyuan), Shanghai's answer to the Sydney Opera House, which showcases everything from Irish dancing to Russian ballet. The

Yifu Theatre near People's Square presents both traditional Beijing Opera and Shanghai's own Hu-style Opera on Sunday afternoons.

Shanghai is as proud of its food as its wealth and skyscrapers. The best-known Shanghai recipes capitalise on the city's proximity to the sea. Steamed freshwater crabs, in season from October to December, and eel are the highlights for many gourmets. Chefs usually prepare seafood and other meats, including snail, in a sweet vinegary sauce. Bean curd, together with mushrooms and bamboo shoots, lead the vegetarian menu.

THE LOWER YANGZI

The Yangzi River – the world's third longest waterway – has been the lifeblood of China since the distant past. Marking the traditional divide between north and south China, some of the country's most noteworthy historic sights are clustered along the lower reaches of its 6,300km (3,915-mile) course; a number of these are also linked by the ancient Grand Canal, which flows through the centre of Wuxi, known for its classic Chinese gardens. Other places of interest include Suzhou – with its placid waterways and restful gardens – Hangzhou – famed for the lovely West Lake – the magnificent peak of Huangshan, and the great cities of Wuhan and Nanjing. The latter functioned as China's imperial capital for a time and has more visitor appeal than most of the country's large cities.

SUZHOU

For centuries **Suzhou** – rather overenthusiastically dubbed the Venice of the East – has been famous for its canals and classical Chinese gardens, its beautiful women and the musical cadences of the local dialect. An old Chinese proverb, referring to the area's linguistic charms, claims that even an argument in the dialect, which is close to that of Shanghai, sounds sweeter than flattery in Guangzhou. Marco Polo found the inhabitants better traders than warriors, and

Restoration work at Longhua Temple

he described the city as large and magnificent. So much silk was produced, he reported, that every citizen was clothed in it and the surplus was exported. Suzhou remains justly renowned today for its silk products.

Suzhou's canals are part of a larger system started more than 2,400 years ago, the **Grand Canal** (see page 127) , second only to the Great Wall in magnitude as a Chinese engineering achievement. By the 6th century AD it linked Suzhou and other rich farming areas of the south with the consumers of the north – most notably the emperor and his court, who appreciated receiving fresh food regardless of the season.

Suzhou's Gardens

But Suzhou is best known for its perfectly landscaped, classical Chinese gardens, with ponds, caves, bridges and pavilions. Because the city is flat and compact, visitors can walk from garden to garden, although you may be shadowed by touts. More than 150 gardens were laid out, the first over 1,000 years ago, and 69 remain. Largest of all, covering 4 hectares (10 acres), is the **Humble Administrator's Garden** (Zhuozhengyuan; daily 7.30am–5.30pm summer, 7.30am–5pm winter; charge; www.szzzy.cn), built by a Ming-dynasty bureaucrat not otherwise remembered for humility. As befits the City of Plentiful Water, ponds occupy the better part of the terrain. Artificial islands, winding bridges, gazebos, weeping willows and lotus plants work in harmony with the ponds. The lotuses are so abundant that one pavilion is called Hehua Simian Ting (Lotus on Four Sides).

The **Forest of Lions Garden** (Shizilin; daily 7.30am–5.30pm summer, 7.30am–5pm winter; charge; www.szszl.com) dates back to 1336, its rocks from nearby Lake Tai evoking the form and power of the big cats. The Qing-dynasty emperors modelled the rockeries in the Old Summer Palace in Beijing on those they saw in Suzhou's Forest of Lions.

To the west, the **Lingering Garden** (Liuyuan; daily 7.30am–5pm; charge; www.gardenly.com) is a refuge of flowers, trees, courtyards and halls. Aptly named, it is a garden with many nooks and crannies, in which getting lost is a pleasure. This one, too, was built by

SILKEN SECRETS

When the *Bombyx mori* caterpillar is ready to turn into a moth, it exudes a single fibrous strand hundreds of metres long and wraps itself into a watertight cocoon. The caterpillar is the silkworm, the strand is pure silk, and the secret of its cultivation has been known to the Chinese for 4,500 years. From the Neolithic period, Chinese farmers fed silkworms on mulberry leaves and soaked the cocoons in warm water to free the silken yarn. By the 1st century ad, silk production was so prolific that an emperor was able to distribute a million rolls of silk cloth along the northern frontier to pacify marauders. Roman women craved the gossamer fabric carried to Europe along the old Silk Road. Even after a rival silk industry, based on smuggled silkworms, was set up in Syria, damasks and brocades were still exported to Europe from China, where the secret of silk manufacture was so jealously guarded that the penalty for revealing it was death by torture. Today, 10 million Chinese farmers produce over half the world's supply of silk. The thread is wound off the cocoons almost by the kilometre, but it can take up to 1,000 cocoons to produce a single shirt.

A Suzhou garden

a Ming civil servant as a place for meditation. **West Garden** (Xiyuan; daily 7.30am–5.30pm; charge) formed a single area with Liuyuan, until the space was given to a Buddhist monastery. The temple was destroyed in the Taiping Rebellion, then rebuilt.

Probably the smallest of all the Suzhou gardens, situated in the centre of town, is the **Garden of the Master of the Nets** (Wangshiyuan; daily 7.30am–5.30pm summer, 7.30am–5pm winter, 7.30pm–10pm night tour; charge; www.szwsy.com), covering half a hectare (barely an acre) and famous for its peony blossoms in spring. The garden's founder, a retired politician, claimed he had given up public life to become a fisherman. Whatever his interests, he could hardly fail to be inspired by the view from his study. This masterpiece of Chinese classical garden design inspired the Astor Chinese Garden Court in New York City's Metropolitan Museum of Art.

Outside the gardens, a stroll through town leads over bridges that cross the maze of canals. Notice that houses back right up to the canals, allowing residents bound for other parts of town to launch boats straight from the back door.

Among Suzhou's tourist highlights, the highest is **Tiger Hill** (Huqiu; daily 7.30am–5.30pm; charge; www.tigerhill.com), a man-made hill built 2,500 years ago. It is rich in contrived rock formations, vegetation and waterfalls. From the summit rises a seven-level brick pagoda, **Yunyanta**. Like the one in Shanghai, it leans a bit from the vertical, although modern reinforcements should relieve your anxiety. Other sights worth lingering over in the old inner city include the 14th-century **Panmen Gate** (daily 7.30am–5pm; charge), where a magnificent arched bridge crosses a canal linking Suzhou to the Grand Canal and the Rui Guang Pagoda (dating from 1119).

Suzhou is also famous for its silk-making. The **Suzhou Silk Museum** (Tue–Sun 9am–5pm; free) exhibits the 4,500 years of silk history in the region, and the **Museum of Suzhou Embroidery** (Tue–Sun 8am–5pm; free) is a working factory and sales outlet featured on many city tours. The **Suzhou Museum** (Tue–Sun 9am–5pm; free), designed by I.M. Pei, houses thousands of regional relics, and the Ming-dynasty halls of the **Museum of Opera and Theatre** (Xiqu Bowuguan) are stacked with musical instruments, masks and librettos.

The principal religious site, the **Temple of Mystery** (Xuanmiaoguan; daily 7.30am–4.30pm winter, 7.30 am–5pm summer; charge), includes the largest early Daoist hall in China (built in 1179) and today is surrounded by Suzhou's biggest, liveliest outdoor market.

WUXI

Wuxi, a city 30 minutes by train from Suzhou, means 'no more tin', a reference to the depletion, a couple of thousand years ago, of local mines. Wuxi today is a prosperous industrial and marketing centre with a population of 6.5 million, just one light in the Yangzi delta's constellation of cities. Business parks and large-scale demolition of the older part of town have reduced the urban area's one-time historic charm. However, canals and rivers still crisscross Wuxi, and the **Grand Canal**, Wuxi's prime historic attraction, flows right through the centre of town from Lake Tai, Wuxi's prime scenic attraction.

Even a short boat ride through the city on the Grand Canal produces unforgettable sights and photos. People may line the bridges (each of a different design) to wave. Human-propelled ferryboats scurry out of the way as long trains of barges, their decks heaped up with onions, reeds or bricks, labour past. The riverside dwellers, who live in quaint whitewashed houses, wash their clothes in the canal.

The Grand Canal project, begun some 2,400 years ago, created an inland waterway stretching 1,794km (1,113 miles) from Beijing to Hangzhou. For more than 2,000 years successive dynasties linked lakes and rivers to create the single canal, 40 paces wide, that went from Hangzhou, across the Yangzi and Yellow rivers, to the old capital Chang'an (now Xi'an) and on to Beijing. In its heyday, some 15,000 junks, sampans and barges plied this watery highway, carrying grain, timber, salt, fish, cloth, pottery and luxury goods.

THE GRANDEST OF CANALS

The boats and barges that throng the Grand Canal at Wuxi recall the days when this great waterway was China's main north–south artery. For more than 2,000 years successive dynasties linked lakes and rivers to create a single canal, 40 paces wide, that went from Hangzhou, across the Yangzi and Yellow rivers, to the old capital Chang'an (now Xi'an) and on to Beijing. Paved roads built along each bank were shaded by elms and willows. To celebrate the extension of the canal in 610, the emperor sailed along it in his four-decked imperial barge, escorted by a flotilla of dragon boats and followed by a retinue of eunuchs, concubines and officials. In its heyday, some 15,000 junks, sampans and barges plied the water highway, carrying grain, timber, salt, fish, cloth, pottery and luxury goods. With the advent of the railways and coastal steamers, the canal lost its importance. Crops were often grown and houses built in the old canal bed. But today the Grand Canal is being restored and used once again as a means of transport as well as to water the rice fields.

An exhibit in Suzhou's Silk Museum

Today the Grand Canal is used considerably less for commerce and transport. Much of it is not navigable, and some of the water is polluted. But for travellers it can provide an interesting excursion, as local officials from districts along the waterway resuscitate it as a tourist attraction. Canal trips by tourist boat often originate in Suzhou, and chug their way along to Wuxi.

Wuxi's Gardens

Wuxi is also home to two classic gardens. **Li Garden** (Liyuan; daily 7am–6pm; charge) has arched bridges, gaudy pavilions, open walkways, fish ponds, a miniature pagoda and a covered walkway with 89 view-framing windows. The more resplendent **Jichang Garden** (Jichangyuan; daily 8am–5.30pm; free), established in 1520, is a Suzhou-style private garden much admired by Emperor Qianlong, who constructed a similar garden in Beijing's Summer Palace in 1750.

Jichang Garden is contained within **Xihui Park** (daily 5.30am–10pm; charge) on the Grand Canal, site of the seven-tiered Ming-dynasty Dragon Light Pagoda (Longguang) and a spring tulip festival

Lingshan Dafo, the giant Buddha at Lake Tai

with flowers imported from Holland. The park also contains **Erquan Spring**, source of some of the world's best water for tea-brewing, according to the *Classic of Tea* (Chajing), written by the scholar Luyu.

Also notable is the **Dragon Light Cave**, which echoes with the digital whistles and roars of a hundred scattered robotic creatures, all lurking in dark rooms off an intimidatingly long corridor. Walk from end to end, and marvel at surreal, 2m (6ft) singing carrots; fend off twitching Teenage Mutant Ninja Turtles, gasping dinosaurs and motionless penguins; and most importantly, stay away from the huge, whistling and highly dangerous fish-eating insects.

LAKE TAI

Lake Tai (Taihu), China's third-largest freshwater expanse with 72 islets, is the most celebrated lake in Chinese legend. **Turtle Head Island** (Yuantouzhu; daily 8am–5pm; charge) is actually a peninsula at the edge of Lake Tai, a sanctuary of trees, flowers, bridges and lake-viewing pavilions that began as a garden in 1918. The lake, despite its infamy for some of China's most stubborn water pollution, still supports fishing junks and roving sampans. Visitors can easily take to the waters aboard the public ferries (daily Mon–Fri 2.30pm, Sat–Sun 10am and 3pm; hours may vary) to **Three Hills Island** (Sanshandao). Largely an amusement park situated in the middle of the lake, Three Hills (known locally as Xiandao or 'Fairy Island') contains a newly built four-tiered temple with the modern statue of an ancient emperor, providing an enchanting view of Lake Tai from the top. (Ferries run every day, roughly between 8.15am to 5.50pm.)

To underline the monumental character of 2,250-sq km (870 sq mile) Lake Tai in legend and in nature, the world's largest bronze standing statue of Buddha was unveiled in 1997 at Lingshan on the lakeshore 18km (11 miles) west of Wuxi. **Lingshan Dafo** (daily 7am–5pm; charge), to give the giant its Chinese name, is fashioned from bronze plates, weighs 700 tonnes and stands 88m (289ft) tall.

The province's biggest producer of both bamboo and tea, Yixing on Lake Tai is better known for its ceramics. The manufacture of pottery here has a history of more than 3,000 years – longer than local recorded history. The industry's heyday was during the Ming dynasty, but in recent years there has been a revival, with the opening of a Ceramics Research Institute and a Ceramics Museum (daily 8am–5pm; charge). 'Purple Sand' teapots in original designs are highly prized by tea-drinkers and collectors and can be purchased at factories in Dingshan village or at roadside markets.

HANGZHOU

Several dozen lakes in China are named 'West Lake', but only one is so celebrated that it needs no further identification. It is **West Lake** (Xihu) in **Hangzhou** ⑩ near China's east coast. The Song-dynasty poet Su Dongpo likened West Lake to one of ancient China's greatest beauties, Xizi – who was also calm, soft, delicate and enchanting. (The girls of Hangzhou are still famous for their light, clear complexion.)

The capital of Zhejiang province, one of the most prosperous regions in China, Hangzhou is 189km (117 miles) from Shanghai – about 90 minutes by train and two hours by bus or car on the toll road. Historic and cultural monuments are included in most tours. Here you can see how two of China's major inventions, silk and tea, are produced. Today the city of about 2 million people is noted for textiles, among other manufacturing, and its position as an eastern China logistics hub in the Yangzi River delta.

Hangzhou enjoyed 237 years of imperial glory from the 9th century onwards. In 1138 the newly formed Southern Song dynasty took Hangzhou as its temporary residence. The town flourished, with officials, writers and scholars moving here as the dynasty blossomed. In all, 14 kings and emperors held court here.

When Marco Polo visited in the 13th century, he pronounced the city superior to 'all others in the world, in grandeur and beauty as well as its abundant delights, which might lead an inhabitant to imagine himself in paradise'. Hangzhou is the southern terminus of the world's first great canal. That economically strategic, 1,776km (1,103-mile) long **Grand Canal** was expanded in 2012 to increase its shipping capacity by 40 percent. In 2014 it was listed as a Unesco World Heritage Site. It is said that the emperor extended it to Hangzhou so that he could choose the prettiest concubines.

West Lake

The lake and hills around here afford some of the most scenic walking and cycling of any city in China. For a full panorama of **West Lake** and the city, ascend the five storeys of Evening Sunlight at Thunder Peak Pagoda (Leifeng Xizhao; daily Mar 16–Apr 8am–7pm, May–Oct 8am–8pm, Nov–Mar 8am–5.30pm; charge), rebuilt on 1,000-year-old ruins on the lake's southern shore. Another vista spot is located on the summit of the hill on the north side of the lake, where the hauntingly beautiful **Baochu Pagoda** stands. It was originally built in AD 968, and destroyed and rebuilt several times. The present pagoda dates from 1933 and is 45m (148ft) tall.

But the beauty of the lake can best be appreciated at close range: from the deck of a sightseeing boat or from the paths and causeways along its shore. The lake edge is abundantly supplied with flowers and trees.

The highlight of a boat trip across West Lake is the largest of three man-made islands, a 'small fairy island' known as **Three Pools Mirroring the Moon** (Santan Yinyue). The island, created in the Ming dynasty, was ingeniously provided with an island of its own, in the centre of its own lake. A zigzag bridge will get you there. Three small stone pagodas, rebuilt in the 17th century, rise from the main lake just south of the isle. On the night of the Moon Festival, candles are placed inside the pagodas. The flickering light emanating from the small round windows gives the lake 15 reflections imitating the real moon.

Sunset over West Lake

Solitary Hill Island (Gushan Dao), in the northern part of the lake, is reached from the city by a causeway named after a Tang-dynasty poet, Baijuyi. During the 9th century he was demoted from a high imperial position to the job of governor of Hangzhou because he wrote poems satirising the court (which, of course, made him extremely popular with the ordinary people). Leafy **Gushan Park**, in the centre of the island, was established in 1752 as a private imperial resort. The **Zhejiang Provincial Museum** on Solitary Hill (Tue–Sun 9am–5pm; charge; www.zhejiangmuseum.com) is reputed to contain 100,000 cultural relics – including what are thought to be the oldest grains of cultivated rice in the world, harvested around 7,000 years ago.

From Monastery to Plantation

One of the country's best-known Buddhist monasteries, Hangzhou's **Lingyin Temple** ('Spirits' Retreat'; daily 7am–6.15pm summer; charge), west of West Lake, attracts crowds of Chinese tourists and believers. The monks – for this is a working monastery – are kept busy supplying joss (incense) sticks to devout or merely fun-loving visitors. The main hall contains a statue of the Buddha seated on a lotus leaf: carved out of camphorwood, it is 19.5m (64ft) high and thought to be the largest such sculpture in China.

Nearby, the **Peak That Flew from Afar** (Feilaifeng) shelters 380 Buddhist stone carvings created during the Yuan dynasty and four sacred caves. The most famous sculpture is of the **Laughing Buddha** with a bulging belly, a figure fashioned about 1,000 years ago.

Further southwest into the lush West Lake hills is the village of **Dragon Well** (Longjing), where the celebrated Longjing tea is cultivated. Villagers welcome visitors who arrive by local bus or bicycle, sharing cups of tea and selling the precious leaves. On the way, it's worth a stop at the **China Tea Museum** (Zhongguo Chaye Bowuguan; Tue– Sun 9am–5pm summer, 8.30am–4.30pm winter; free), with its displays of ceremonial tea implements and its own model teahouses.

Hangzhou is also renowned for its silks. The **Hangzhou Silk Printing and Dyeing Complex** (Hang Si Lian) is the largest in the country. Daily tours follow the production process from the sorting of cocoons, which arrive by barge in 20kg (44lb) sacks, to silkscreen printing. The **China National Silk Museum** (Mon 12pm–5pm, Tue–Sun 9am–5pm; free; www.chinasilkmuseum.com) lays out the history of silk and sells bolts of the fabric.

Dragon Well tea sculpture

The lakeside promenade provides plenty of shopping and small restaurants, as do

Hubin Lu Pedestrian Street, the upscale pedestrian mall Yihu Tiandi (West Lake Heaven on Earth), and Qing Hefang Historical Street, site of the **Huqingyutang Chinese Medicine Museum** (daily 8.30am–4pm; charge).

Longjing Tea

Ask at the gardens and teahouses along the shores of West Lake for a cup of *longjing* ('dragon well') tea. One serving means a pinch of leaves covering the bottom of a ceramic cup, which will be filled with water that is just below boiling point. Brace for a unique fragrance unequalled by other green teas. A pinch of leaves usually lasts through a second cup of water. Sacks of tea leaves are sold along the lakeshore as well, and prices range from around 40 *yuan* to well over 100 *yuan* per sack, depending on the quality. This farm product is allowed through customs just about everywhere because the leaves are dried and packaged.

NINGBO

Situated down the coast from Shanghai, this port town has a long history of overseas connections. First it was involved in trade with Japan. Then the Portuguese arrived and settled here. Finally, a British consulate was established in the town after the end of the Opium Wars. The sights include a Ming-dynasty library (Tianyi Pavilion) in a pretty garden and a lively pedestrian avenue of old shops and cafés near the Drum Tower. Ningbo is the gateway to one of China's holiest mountains, Putuoshan, the island home of Guanyin, the Buddhist goddess of mercy.

NANJING

Nanjing ⓫, a prosperous and cultured city of 8.3 million, is about 300km (185 miles) west of Shanghai in Jiangsu province. That's two to three hours by train. Here the great Yangzi River narrows to slightly more than 1km (1,100yds), so even before there was a bridge the city had great strategic transportation significance.

This ancient capital of China has suffered so many catastrophes that few historic monuments have survived – and these are widely dispersed. Perhaps this is why so much emphasis is placed on modern triumphs, such as the heroic bridge across the Yangzi River that has become Nanjing's emblem. But past and present are often juxtaposed in Nanjing, like the blue pedicabs competing with the metro line, or the fresh pink and white plum blossoms on the hillsides around the Mingxiaoling tomb.

Nanjing means 'Southern Capital', a name conferred rather late in the city's history. During its early grandeur under the State of Chu, the town was called Jinling, a name still used in literary and other allusions. It served as the capital of six southern dynasties. The last of these, the Ming, made it the national capital, but this was moved north to Beijing in the 15th century.

In the 20th century a series of dramas overtook Nanjing and gave it new prominence. It was here that Dr Sun Yat-sen was elected president of the Republic. Chiang Kai-shek made it his capital until the advance of Japanese invasion forces induced him to head west. When the Japanese troops finally arrived here in 1937, the 'Rape of Nanking' was added to the catalogue of the period's atrocities. The **Datusha Jinianguan** monument and museum (Tue–Sun 8.30am–4.30pm; free; www.nj1937.org), just outside the old city wall, commemorates the victims; around 100,000 died in the first four days alone. The Nationalists regained the battered city after the Japanese surrender in 1945. The Communist army crossed the Yangzi in April 1949, bringing a new order to the old capital.

Nanjing Sights

The **Yangzi River Bridge** (Nanjing Changjiang Daqiao) is an extraordinary engineering achievement. Only a few bridges span the entire river, and at 1,577m (5,174ft) this is the longest. Proudly claimed to be the world's longest two-tier bridge for rail and road traffic, it has greatly improved contacts between north and south China. And

Yangzi River Bridge, Nanjing

it inspired national self-confidence at the time of the Sino-Soviet schism of 1960. When the Soviet Union withdrew its technical experts, the Chinese finished it themselves, in eight years. Today it remains an important symbol for Nanjing, although there is also now a new bridge 11km (7 miles) downstream from the original.

Nanjing claims a little-known distinction – the longest **city wall** (Shence Gate, Taiping Gate, Fugui Mountain, Langi Street 8.30am–5pm; East Water Pass, Jinging Gate until 8pm; free sections all day) in the world, much of it easily visible to the casual downtown pedestrian. In the 14th century, the Ming rulers mobilised 200,000 workers to build fortifications extending 33.5km (nearly 21 miles). It was a formidable redoubt, with tunnels for 3,000 besieged defenders, and was never taken by enemies. The largest of 24 city gates is the **Zhonghua Gate** (Zhonghuamen; daily 8.30am–8.30pm; charge), on the southern edge of Nanjing. It is a good reference point for getting around town.

Also in southern Nanjing, you can see the ruins of the **Palace of the Heavenly King** (Tianwangfu), built when the forces of the Taiping Rebellion captured the city (see page 37). It was the most ambitious

Long River

Chang Jiang, the Chinese name for the Yangzi (alternatively spelt Yangtze), means Long River – and appropriately enough for, at 6,300km (3,915 miles), it is the longest river in China and the third-longest in the world.

architectural project of the mid-19th century. The Western Garden is full of fine touches: an imaginative rock garden, a dragon wall, a children's maze, a bottle-shaped lake for an imperial stone houseboat and a museum chronicling the Taiping Rebellion.

The **Nanjing Museum** (Nanjing Bowuguan; daily 9am–5pm; free; www.njmuseum.com), founded in 1933, is located south of the Zhongshan Gate, the main eastern portal of the city wall. Among art and artefacts from prehistoric times to the end of the empire, the museum displays colourful ancient pottery, jade, ceramics, lacquerware, textiles, bronzes, porcelain, stone figures and a famous burial suit that is 2,000 years old. It is made from 2,600 green jade rectangles sewn together with silver wire.

Back in town, the Ming-dynasty **Drum Tower** (Gulou; daily 8am–6pm; charge) has been restored to its eminence on a hill in the very centre of Nanjing. The drum (since replaced) told the time and warned the citizens of danger. Now there is a tearoom upstairs and a viewing deck. Nearby Gulou Park is open until 10pm and fills with families on balmy evenings.

Visitors keen on a night hike can walk through Xuanwu Lake Park, along lit wooded paths and over causeways, for views of the giant expanse of water anchoring central Nanjing. The paths cover about 100 hectares (250 acres) of wooded land and lead to views over the lake onto the Nanjing skyline.

One of the liveliest temples here is **Fuzimiao** (daily 9am–9.30pm; charge), an ancient Confucian temple located in the heart of Nanjing's main shopping district and pedestrian mall; it is especially interesting to stroll through the area after working hours, when market stalls sell everything from parakeets to clothing.

Nanjing's distinguished history as a political and cultural centre accounts for its considerable local pride. Nanjing claims its salted duck is superior to the more famous Peking duck. Nanjing ducks, it is pointed out, are raised naturally on ponds, not force-fed like their less fortunate Beijing comrades.

Around Nanjing

Chinese pilgrims of all political persuasions come from many countries to honour the founder of the Chinese Republic at the **Mausoleum of Dr Sun Yat-sen** (Zhongshanling; Tue–Sun 8.30am–5pm; charge; www.zschina.org.cn), in the Purple Hills (Zijin Shan) east of Nanjing. The hillside complex roofed with blue tiles, completed in 1929, could scarcely be more grandiose. Following a long, winding avenue planted with plane trees, you continue up the 392 granite steps of the

Fuzimiao Temple

ceremonial staircase to the actual memorial hall. There are statues of Dr Sun standing, sitting (by a French sculptor, Paul Landowski) and recumbent above the vault itself. On the ceiling is a mosaic version of the Nationalist (Guomindang) flag, a white star on a blue background.

Nearby in the Purple Hills is **Mingxiaoling** (daily 6.30am–6.30pm summer, 7am–5.30pm winter; charge), the tomb of Emperor Hong Wu, founder of the Ming dynasty. What with wars and revolutions, there is not much left of the 14th-century complex. But don't miss the **Sacred Way**, lined with large stone statues of elephants, camels, horses, lions and mythical animals, which turns north into an approach road guarded by statues of generals and mandarins.

Meiling Palace (Meilinggong; daily 7.30am–6pm; charge) was the holiday home of Chiang Kai-shek and his wife Song Meiling. It is now a period museum for those nostalgic for the pre-Revolutionary days between the last emperor of the Manchus and the first chairman of the Communist Party.

HUANGSHAN

Although 'Yellow Mountain' is the literal translation of **Huangshan** (not one mountain but a range of dozens of peaks), yellow is not the colour that first comes to mind when describing this site that has been the subject of Chinese poetry and painting for centuries. Green is the colour of the stunted pines clinging to purple cliff faces. Pink are the wild flowers, blue the sky, and white the sea of clouds that rolls in beneath the rocky pinnacles.

Huangshan, a World Heritage Site, is the only region of eastern China's Anhui province that appears on major tourist

A painterly vista

The Huangshan vista that has most inspired painters and photographers is the sight of cottony clouds nuzzling the mountainsides. As the peaks and pinnacles jut above the clouds in the early morning sky, they come to look like islets in a celestial sea.

itineraries. Trains and planes link Shanghai with a terminus at the foot of the mountains, where coaches continue the journey. The scenic mountain resort now has hotel facilities, from extremely basic to comfortable. Chinese tourists – and poets – might spend a week or more exploring the area, but foreign visitors can squeeze it all into a day or two. Huangshan at its peak season can get so overrun with tourists that even the Chinese, who are good at weathering crowds, complain about the 'sea of heads' in front of them on trails.

Huangshan (Yellow Mountain)

The weather can be a critical factor. On average, mid-July to the end of September is considered the most dependable time of year because of the mild temperatures and relatively restrained rainfall. Drizzle rather than heavy rain generally falls from late May to late June, when the spring flowers burst forth, but temperatures are brisk. Mist and fog often enhance rather than obscure the views.

Huangshan has many peaks that are well known by name in China, often through thousands of poems describing these as the country's most beautiful mountains. The three principal summits are **Lotus Flower Peak** (Lianhuafeng), **Bright Summit** (Guangmingding) and the **Heavenly Capital Peak** (Tiandufeng). All are over 1,800m (6,000ft) high and all can be climbed via endless stone stairs, some as steep as ladders. Of the three, Bright Summit is the most accessible; Lotus Flower Peak is slightly more difficult; Heavenly Capital Peak is frequently closed for safety reasons, and is not for the faint-hearted or safety-conscious.

Climbs begin on the east side of the range at Yungu Temple, where a cable car whisks some visitors to the summit while most begin an 8km (5-mile) hike. At the twin summits, the Northern and Western Sea of Clouds, there are small inns and a large hotel, somewhere to get some rest before viewing the sunrise.

The descent on the west side is longer, with up to 14km (9 miles) of paths and stairs, although a cable car also serves this route. A third cable car operates on the north slope.

When hiking becomes too strenuous, Huangshan visitors can recuperate in a hot-spring resort that lies between Purple Cloud Peak (Ziyunfeng) and Peach Blossom Peak (Taohuafeng). Here, piping hot water with a curative mineral content bubbles from the spring year-round. You can drink it, bathe in it, or both.

WUHAN

A lively industrial and intellectual centre, **Wuhan** ⓬ is nearly equidistant from Beijing and Guangzhou, and from Shanghai and Chongqing. Its setting at the confluence of the Yangzi and Han rivers has made it an important junction for railways and shipping.

The story of Wuhan has always been anchored in the vital, muddy Yangzi. So wide and treacherous is the river that, before the construction of the great concrete and steel bridge of Wuhan (the first to cross the Yangzi) in 1957, all communications depended on the ferries, which were often hampered by fog or flood. Now the **Yangzi River Bridge** (Changjiang Daqiao) is shown to tourists as a triumph of the new China. So are the dykes, so tall they cut off the view of the river from the embankment.

Wuhan is a composite name for three historic, contiguous cities: Wuchang, Hankou and Hanyang. Wuchang, the oldest, is bountifully supplied with parklands and wooded hillside college campuses that make up one of China's biggest university districts. Hankou, the financial centre on the opposite bank of the Yangzi, was opened in the 19th century as a Treaty Port; at high tide 10,000-tonne ships

Wuhan martial arts

can reach Hankou's harbour from the sea, some 1,500km (1,000 miles) away. Hanyang, separated from Hankou by the Han River (requiring another, less heroic bridge), is a residential and industrial district.

After the Opium Wars, Hankou was carved up into separate British, French, German, Japanese and Russian zones of influence. Along Zhongshan Avenue, near the Yangzi ferry terminals, some of the old European-style buildings remain. The municipal office buildings on the embankment, administering a city whose population has now grown beyond 4 million, are cast in the German mould.

But Wuhan, the capital of Hubei province, also has a significant revolutionary history. The rebellion of October 1911, which was inspired by Dr Sun Yat-sen, began in Wuchang, and Hankou suffered heavy damage in the fighting. The Central Peasant Movement Institute, where Communist activists were trained in the 1920s and Mao Zedong taught classes, was established in Wuchang. Tourists can see the villa where Mao would spend holidays (Mao Zedong Bieshu; daily 9am–5pm; charge).

Wuhan Sights

The **Hubei Provincial Museum** (Hubeisheng Bowuguan; Tue–Sun 9am–5pm; free; www.hbww.org) owes its excellence to the chance discovery in 1978 of the tomb of the Marquis Yi of the State of Zeng. Located 108km (67 miles) northwest of Wuhan, the grave yielded enough treasure to furnish several museums. About 1,000 items – a mere 15 percent of the total hoard – are now on display here. When Yi died in 433 BC, he was buried with his dog and 21 sacrificed women, as well as tributes ranging from bronze wine vessels to enough musical instruments for an orchestra. The finest musical exhibit in the collection is a set of 65 intricately decorated bronze bells *(bianzhong)*, still possessing perfect pitch and tone.

The museum looks out onto **East Lake** (daily 9am–4.30pm), vaunted as the largest lake in any municipal park in China, with 33 sq km (nearly 13 sq miles) of invitingly clear water. Boating, swimming and fishing are popular here. Of course, no Chinese lake would be complete without its artificial islands, causeways and pavilions, several of which serve as teahouses.

Yellow Crane Tower, Wuhan

Hanyang's main religious landmark, **Gui Yuan Temple** (Guiyuan Chansi; daily 8.30am–5pm; charge), sprawls among pines and cypresses. Built in the 17th century, it was the only one of Wuhan's 20 or more Buddhist temples spared by rampaging Red Guards during the Cultural Revolution (1966–76). The Hall of Five Hundred Disciples is a fascinating gallery of statues. Grinning, yawning, frowning, meditating and leering, each one is different.

The Northern Song-dynasty **Ancient Lute Terrace** (Guqintai; daily 8.30am–5pm; charge) commemorates a 2,500-year-old legend of the deep friendship between a lute-playing mandarin in Chu kingdom, named Yu Boya, and a music-loving woodcutter.

Across the 1.5km (1-mile) Yangzi River Bridge in Wuchang is the **Yellow Crane Tower** (Huanghelou; daily 8am–6pm summer, 8am–5pm winter; charge; www.cnhhl.com), based on another legend. First built in AD 223, the wooden structure burnt down and was reconstructed several times. In 1981, the latest rebuilding project got under way about 1km (2/3 mile) from the original site. The design and decor of the new tower are based on paintings from the Yuan and Ming dynasties and a model of the bridge as it existed in the Qing dynasty.

SOUTHERN CHINA

This section explores the attractions of the southern part of China, and begins and ends in coastal provinces. **Guangzhou** ⓭ (Canton) is the capital and largest city of the province of Guangdong; the city of Shenzhen is also here, just to the north of Hong Kong. We then move down to the tropical island of Hainan, the southernmost province of China, and then to the northwest, into Hunan province. To the east we move to Jiangxi province and, further east, to Fujian province, on the coast opposite Taiwan.

GUANGZHOU

Foreigners have been turning up in Guangzhou for a couple of thousand years, for it was China's first major seaport. It was the first Chinese town to receive Europeans, when a Portuguese fleet arrived in 1514. All this has made for such dramatic historical incidents as the Opium Wars, which broke out when the authorities cracked down on the opium trade here. Fast-forwarding, since

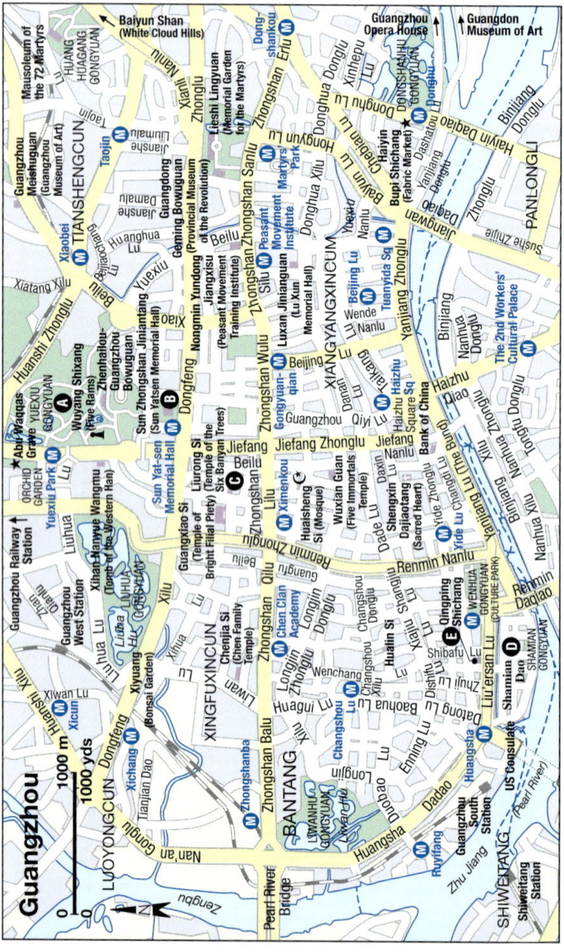
Guangzhou
0 1000 m
0 1000 yds
N
Baiyun Shan (White Cloud Hills)
Guangzhou Opera House
Guangdon Museum of Art
Mausoleum of the 72 Martyrs
HUANGHUAGANG GONGYUAN
Guangzhou Meishuguan (Guangzhou Museum of Art)
TIANSHENGCUN
Taojin
Xiaobei
Xianlie Zhonglu
Lieshi Lingyuan (Memorial Garden for the Martyrs)
Dongshankou
Zhongshan Erlu
Zhongshan Sanlu
Martyrs' Park
Guangdong Geming Bowuguan (Provincial Museum of the Revolution)
Nongmin Yundong Jiangxisu (Peasant Movement Training Institute)
Peasant Movement Institute
Luxan Jinianguan (Lu Xun Memorial Hall)
Donghua Donglu
Donghua Xilu
Xinhepu Lu
Dongshu Lu
Chebian Lu
Baiyun Lu
Haiyin Bupi Shichang (Fabric Market)
DONGSHANHU GONGYUAN
Donghu
Haiyin Daqiao
Binjiang Donglu
Jiangwan Daqiao
PANLONGLI
Sushe Zhijie
Yanjiang Zhonglu
Binjiang Nanhua Donglu
The 2nd Workers' Cultural Palace
Haizhu Qiao
Huanshi Zhonglu
YUEXIU GONGYUAN
Wuyang Shixiang (Five Rams)
Zhenhailou-Guangzhou Bowuguan
Sun Zhongshan Jiniantang (Sun Yatsen Memorial Hall)
Dongfeng
Zhongshan Wulu
Gongyuanqian
Beijing Lu
XIANGYANGXINCUN
Tuanyida Sq
Haizhu Square
Bank of China
Abu Waqqas Grave
ORCHID GARDEN
Yuexiu Park
Jiefang Zhonglu
Jiefang Nanlu
Liurong Si (Temple of the Six Banyan Trees)
Ximenkou
Huaisheng Si (Mosque)
Wuxian Guan (Five Immortals Temple)
Shengxin Dajiaotang (Sacred Heart)
Yide Lu
Yanjiang Lu (The Bund)
Guangzhou Railway Station
Liuhua Lu
Xihan Nanyue Wangmu (Tomb of the Western Han)
LIUHUA GONGYUAN
Guangxiao Si (Temple of Bright Filial Piety)
Renmin Zhonglu
Renmin Nanlu
Chen Clan Academy
Chenjia Si (Chen Family Temple)
XINGFUXINCUN
Zhongshan Qilu
Zhongshan Balu
Qingping Shichang
WENHUA GONGYUAN (CULTURE PARK)
Renmin Daqiao
Guangzhou West Station
Xicun
Xiyuang (Bonsai Garden)
Xichang
LUOYONGCUN
Tianjian Dao
Zhongshanba
BANTANG
LIWANHU GONGYUAN
Changshou Lu
Huangsha
Shamian Dao
SHAMIAN GONGYUAN
US Consulate
Liu'ersan Lu
Huangsha Dadao
Ruyifang
Guangzhou South Station
Zhu Jiang (Pearl River)
SHIWEITANG
Shiweitang Station
Pearl River Bridge
Nan'an Gonglu
Zengbu

1957 the Canton Trade Fair (now the Guangzhou Trade Fair) has attracted throngs of international businesspeople. Expatriates from Africa and the Middle East populate Guangzhou today, using it as a base for trade between China and their homelands. Even in the years of political upheaval, Guangzhou kept open the nation's ties with foreign countries and with overseas Chinese, millions of whom have their roots here in surrounding Guangdong province.

Internet cafés

It may seem ironic that in a country that censors Internet content, cities of any scale allow a proliferation of cybercafés. At these sometimes huge, dark and cavernous establishments with dozens if not hundreds of desktop computers, Chinese youngsters blow off steam for hours by playing Internet games or chatting with friends, online and out of view of their parents. Tourists can use the Net by showing a passport and paying a few *yuan* per hour.

Guangzhou straddles the **Pearl River** (Zhu Jiang), the country's fifth-longest. It links the metropolis to the South China Sea and provides a good deal of charm and excitement. The daily drama of ferryboats, freighters, junks with dirty grey sails, low-lying sampans – even small tankers and big gunboats – unfolds right in the centre of town. The river also serves as the thoroughfare for tourist cruises booked at major hotels.

With a population of over 10 million, industrial Guangzhou turns out buses, ships, agricultural machinery, chemicals and sewing machines. It is one of China's richest cities, with skyscrapers, motorways, metro lines and fashionable shopping centres to prove it. Although the economy has changed radically in recent years, many local traditions live on, including the love of flowers, Cantonese Opera and the local dialect (incomprehensible to fellow Chinese). And then there is Cantonese food, known around the world for healthful flavours. Chefs cook ingredients such as

Prize exhibit, Nanyue Museum

chicken, fish or leafy vegetables, so that individual flavours are preserved and not lost among oils or heavy sauces.

Guangzhou in History

In the 3rd century BC the founder of the Qin dynasty annexed the remote Guangzhou area, thus furnishing China with its first major seaport. By the end of the Han dynasty, foreign trade linked the port with other areas of Asia as well as with the Roman Empire. Foreigners then called it 'Canton'.

By the 9th century, large colonies of Arabs, Jews, Persians and others had settled here. They traded in tea, silk and porcelain, all commodities that were in constant demand abroad. It was to be another seven centuries before Europeans established themselves in Canton. The Portuguese were first, followed by Spaniards, Dutch and British. The Chinese authorities tried to keep the foreigners at arm's length, limiting their activities to certain districts and seasons.

The expansion of trade did eventually bring conflict, because China would accept nothing less than silver bullion in payment for its exports. However, the wily British soon thought of an alternative commodity: opium (see page 36). The Opium Wars ended in 1842 with the Treaty of Nanking (later denounced as 'unequal'). Under the terms of the treaty, China was compelled to open 'Canton' and four other ports to foreign penetration.

When the Qing dynasty fell in 1911, Guangzhou became the centre of the republican movement founded by Guangdong's most famous son, Dr Sun Yat-sen, and the headquarters of the Guomindang (Nationalists), the first modern political party in China. In the civil war of the 1940s, Guangzhou briefly served as the Nationalist capital before the Communists captured the city and gained power nationwide in 1949.

Parks and Monuments

The city's parks and monuments are worth visiting, not least for the chance to mingle with the Cantonese themselves. **Yuexiu Park** Ⓐ (daily 6am–10pm; free), near the Trade Fair in the northern part of the city, covers a 93-hectare (230-acre) site. In addition to its pretty gardens, lakes, pavilions and sports facilities, Guangzhou's largest park also contains the city's oldest building, the red 'Tower Overlooking the Sea' (Zhenhailou). 'Tower' is a misleading description for this building of five storeys. Built in 1380, it now houses the **Guangzhou Museum** (Guangzhou Bowuguan; Tue–Sun 9am–5.30pm; charge;

Guangzhou

Colonial district, Shamian Island, Guangzhou

www.guangzhoumuseum.cn). With signs in English and Chinese, the museum includes artefacts and displays recording the city's contacts with the West (from Bibles to radios). The top floor of this watchtower museum is now a teahouse.

Another famous landmark in the park is the **Statue of the Five Rams** (Wu Yang Shixiang), a granite sculptural representation of five handsome beasts, based on the legend of Guangzhou's founding. Five gods had distributed the rice, blessing the local people with eternal freedom from famine. The gods then disappeared, according to the story, but the five rice-bearing rams turned to stone.

In the northwest corner of Yuexiu Park, the **Orchid Garden** (Lan Pu; daily 8am–6pm; charge) is filled with more than 10,000 pots and 200 varieties of orchids.

Also within Yuexiu Park is the **Nanyue Museum** (daily 9am–4.45pm; charge), displays the contents of the adjacent Tomb of the Southern Yue Kings, who ruled southern China in the 2nd century BC.

Dr Sun Yat-sen (1866– 1925), who began his political career in the city, is honoured in Yuexiu Park by an obelisk 30m (100ft) tall. South of the park is an even more impressive monument, the **Sun Yat-sen Memorial Hall** **B** (daily 8am–6pm; 8am–10pm non-exhibition areas; charge), built in 1931 with sweeping blue-tile roofs. Today's Chinese leadership still looks up to Sun Yat-sen as the founder of a country free of dynastic rule.

For those keen on nature, **Baiyun Mountain** in the rainforests just outside town calls for a fairly rigorous hike. Panoramic city views reward those who gain enough elevation.

South from the centre of the city in Zhujiang New Town is the Guangzhou Opera House, built in 2010. Its deconstructive form resembles rocks from the shores of the Pearl River.

Guangzhou's principal Buddhist monument, the **Temple of the Six Banyan Trees** **C** (Liurongsi; daily 9am–5.20pm; charge), was founded over 1,400 years ago. The trees that inspired the 11th-century poet and calligrapher Su Dongpo to name the temple have since died, but the often-restored complex remains a focus of local Buddhist activities. Overlooking it all is the **Flower Pagoda** (Huata), a slender relic of the Song dynasty.

Given its ties with the Middle East, the city is home to the oldest mosque in China, the **Huaisheng Mosque** (daily 8.30am–5pm; open only to Muslims or tour groups), built in 627 and rebuilt several times since. Its white minaret can be climbed via a spiral staircase for a view of the courtyards, gardens and Guangzhou's modern skyscrapers, but sometimes access to the mosque is not allowed.

The city's leading tribute to the days of imperial splendour is the **Chen Family Temple** (Chenjiasi; daily 8.30am–5.30pm; charge), a memorial to members of a large merchant clan from all over China. This sprawling compound of courtyards, shops, a museum and showy 19th-century pavilions is decorated in a pantheon of finely carved friezes, gates and gold-leaf tableaux depicting scenes of Chinese myth and romance.

Shamian Island

The atmosphere of 19th-century colonial 'Canton' is best evoked by **Shamian Island** **D**, situated in the Pearl River and linked to central

Guangzhou by several bridges. This small residential enclave, shaded by banyan trees, was the closed community of the foreign colony in the era of the Western concessions. The stately European-style buildings, including old banks, factories and churches, have been spruced up, and Shamian's wide streets are free from the incessant traffic that plagues the rest of the city. Pavement cafés, boutiques, traditional craft shops and the high-rise White Swan Hotel make this Guangzhou's leading place for a stroll.

Across from Shamian Island is China's most notorious and colourful marketplace, **Qingping** E (daily 8am–6pm). A maze of alleys crammed with 2,000 stalls, Qingping offers up acres of herbs, spices, jade, antiques, memorabilia, goldfish, songbirds and a sometimes nightmarish display of live animals destined for the kitchen.

Two of the best dining spots are its traditional garden restaurants, Beiyuan and Banxi. Beiyuan, famous for the local noon meal dim sum, consists of over 40 dining pavilions and tearooms, each decorated in intricate latticework. Banxi, on the shores of Liwan Lake, also has a classic decor, with etched glass from the Qing dynasty and delicacies to match.

SHENZHEN

Veteran travellers remember Shenzhen merely as an undistinguished border town on the Hong Kong–Canton railway line. However, it has long been the centre of a Special Economic Zone for joint industrial ventures with capitalists from Hong Kong and Macau. Since 1980, it is one of China's richest cities. The streets are straight and clean, the buildings tall and shiny, and the general atmosphere bustling and rich, although rather characterless and with the mad bustle of any Chinese metropolis. With hot springs, theme parks and a popular golf course so close to Hong Kong, the tourist potential has also been rapidly developed. Day tours from Hong Kong offer Shenzhen as a glimpse of life in modern China and a chance to shop at true factory outlets.

HAINAN

This tropical island off the southern tip of China is the country's smallest, southernmost and newest province (it was part of Guangdong until it became a Special Economic Zone in 1988). **Hainan** ⓮ provides China with coffee, coconuts, sugar and rubber. Since Beijing declared that Hainan would become China's Hawaii, it has been aggressively promoted as an island of tropical resorts located conveniently close to affluent Hong Kong. Some beaches near the tourist city of Sanya look like something out of Thailand,

The Zhangjiajie Glass Floor Bridge

Hunan is Mao's homeland

with coconut palms lining the white sand and gaudy hotels just behind them. The original inhabitants, members of the Li and Miao minorities, live in what's left of the rainforests of the interior, preserving a rich folklore; Han Chinese make up most of the coastal population. The island's biggest city, **Haikou** (on the north shore), has a bustling street life and in 2010 opened the Baishamen white-sand beach. The best beaches are in Yalong Bay National Resorts near Sanya in the south – considered the finest stretches of sand in China – and at the newly developed Boao Scenic Zone to the east. Annual world economic conferences at Boao have helped to raise Hainan's profile, which was already a popular destination for sun-starved Beijingers.

HUNAN PROVINCE

A tour of Hunan province, home of spicy food and crowd-free attractions, starts in the provincial capital, **Changsha**. The city lies along the Xiang River, a wide and often turbulent stream that flows into the Yangzi. The long, thin strip of **Orange Island** (Juzizhou), rich in oranges among other crops, bisects the river and in the early 20th century was home to a small band of Western traders and missionaries.

On the far side of the river, fragrant forests climb the heavily forested slopes of **Yuelu Hill**, a favourite escape from the subtropical heat of the city in summer. A yew tree standing in front of the

However, it has long been the centre of a Special Economic Zone for joint industrial ventures with capitalists from Hong Kong and Macau. Since 1980, it is one of China's richest cities. The streets are straight and clean, the buildings tall and shiny, and the general atmosphere bustling and rich, although rather characterless and with the mad bustle of any Chinese metropolis. With hot springs, theme parks and a popular golf course so close to Hong Kong, the tourist potential has also been rapidly developed. Day tours from Hong Kong offer Shenzhen as a glimpse of life in modern China and a chance to shop at true factory outlets.

HAINAN

This tropical island off the southern tip of China is the country's smallest, southernmost and newest province (it was part of Guangdong until it became a Special Economic Zone in 1988). **Hainan** ⓮ provides China with coffee, coconuts, sugar and rubber.

Fenghuang

Since Beijing declared that Hainan would become China's Hawaii, it has been aggressively promoted as an island of tropical resorts located conveniently close to affluent Hong Kong. Some beaches near the tourist city of Sanya look like something out of Thailand, with coconut palms lining the white sand and gaudy hotels just behind them. The original inhabitants, members of the Li and Miao minorities, live in what's left of the rainforests of the interior, preserving a rich folklore; Han Chinese make up most of the coastal population. The island's biggest city, **Haikou** (on the north shore), has a bustling street life and in 2010 opened the Baishamen white-sand beach. The best beaches are in Yalong Bay National Resorts near Sanya in the south – considered the finest stretches of sand in China – and at the newly developed Boao Scenic Zone to the east. Annual world economic conferences at Boao have helped to raise Hainan's profile, which was already a popular destination for sun-starved Beijingers.

HUNAN PROVINCE

A tour of Hunan province, home of spicy food and crowd-free attractions, starts in the provincial capital, **Changsha**. The city lies along the Xiang River, a wide and often turbulent stream that flows into the Yangzi. The long, thin strip of **Orange Island** (Juzizhou), rich in oranges among other crops, bisects the river and in the interesting sights are on the walk down; if you don't mind company, it is a good idea to ride the cable car up (daily 8am–5pm) and walk down with the tour groups.

Another western Hunan hotspot, **Fenghuang**, unites the province's mountain scenery with a village where ethnic-minority Miao people still carry baskets on their heads and wear clothes unlike anything seen in Chinese cities. Cafés and craft shops line a river through the village centre. Visitors can go on river tours, or walk further into town for views of traditional houses perched precariously on steep hillsides. For those who stroll far enough, the remains of a Ming-dynasty wall may eventually loom into view.

Flamboyant upswept roofs surmount Yueyang Tower, a Tang-dynasty landmark that has been rebuilt in Song-dynasty style. This three-tiered tower overlooks Lake Dongting, the second-largest freshwater lake in China and prone to summer flooding. In summer months huge lotus flowers rise above the surface of the water. Junshan, an island in the lake endowed with many hills (and numerous legends), produces the rare and fragrant 'silver needle' tea.

T'AI CHI

T'ai chi combines meditation with physical exercise, but leaves out the 'combat' element common to most other martial arts. It is practised by an individual using 'postures' that mimic techniques of attack and defence, such as 'ward off' and 'elbow strike'. The movements are thought to have been formulated by a monk named Zhang San Feng in the 14th century, but the basic principles of t'ai chi are reflected in the instructions of the Daoist sage Laozi: 'Yield and overcome; bend and be straight.' A probable precursor to the art was a system of exercises introduced during the Three Kingdoms period and imitating certain animal movements to help exercise every joint in the body.

JINGDEZHEN, JIANGXI PROVINCE

Jingdezhen has been producing famous pottery on the banks of the Yangzi River since the Han dynasty. White clay from a nearby mountain made possible the very thin, durable, translucent porcelain. (The mountain, **Gaoling**, gave its name to kaolin, the clay used to make porcelain.) Most of the tourist attractions are pottery-oriented: a traditional porcelain producer, a museum, an ancient kiln and modern factories that turn out copies of classic designs.

MT LUSHAN

This conifer-insulated scenic retreat draws a constant flow of tourists on minibuses that zigzag up two-lane roads from the highway between the Nanchang airport and the industrial Yangzi River port city of Jiujiang. An entrance fee allows each traveller to stay in the 302-sq km (116-sq mile) **Mt Lushan National Park** ⓯ (daily 6am–6pm; charge) for hours or days to hike through some of China's best-preserved public forests, from over 1,400m (4,500ft) above sea level. One of the more striking vistas is Dragonhead Cliff, where clear days yield panoramas of steep-sided mountains in the distance enhanced by the sound of waterfalls. The mountain has offered shelter and retreat for monks and priests of various religions for more than 1,000 years, which is why over 300 temples and churches speckle the park. Mao Zedong used Lushan's sanctuary to hold three secretive, strategic meetings between 1959 and 1970. In 1996 the park was declared a World Heritage Site by Unesco. Visitors can stay the night at several hotels in the park.

XIAMEN

China's cleanest major city (according to an official poll) and one of its most charming, **Xiamen** is a booming port in Fujian province, just 160km (100 miles) from Taiwan across the East China Sea. Long a relatively prosperous place owing to its close connections with overseas Chinese investors (many of whom emigrated from the area),

Xiamen has wisely spared much of its Old Town and harbour from the bulldozers of progress.

From the busy harbour square, overlooked by the balconies of the venerable Lujiang Hotel, you can stroll into Old Town areas along Zhongshan Road, past dozens of antiques shop-houses and cafés. Or you can head south along Minzu Road and take in the life of the fishing boats and warehouses on the quays.

Fuboshan ('Whirlpool Hill') in Guilin

If you walk long enough (or hail a taxi), you end up at **Nanputuo Temple** (daily, Outer Mounatin Gate 3am-8pm, Inner Mountain Gate until 6pm, free), nestled in the hillside on the east shore of the harbour. This Buddhist complex is in immaculate condition, its marble a gleaming white. Locals are always on hand, burning incense and praying for good fortune. The rocky cliffs behind the temple make for fine hiking and picnicking.

South of the temple and past **Xiamen University** (founded in 1921 by a local who made good in Singapore) is the **Huli Mountain Cannon Platform**. In 1921 the Germans placed their artillery here to defend the colonial port of Amoy, as Xiamen was known to Westerners. From here, if you look across the Taiwan Strait on a sunny day, you can make out the disputed island of Jinmen (Kinmen). Once known to Western politicians as 'Quemoy', this heavily militarised island featured in the Nixon–Kennedy presidential debates of 1960. Today, the 'cold war' between China and Taiwan, once waged on the outlying islands with loudspeakers and leaflet bombardments, as well as live fire in the 1950s and 1960s, is on hold and Jinmen is courting tourists as its soldiers are moved elsewhere.

Gulangyu Island

Xiamen's chief pleasure for any visitor is **Gulangyu** (https://kulangsuisland.org/), a small island in the harbour that was once home to foreign colonials. Passenger ferries connect downtown Xiamen to the island. Gulangyu is a pedestrian-only island. The terrain is hilly, with twisting cobblestone streets forming a compact maze, but you're always within sight of the shoreline. A sandy beach next to warm-ish waters allows swimming in the calm ocean. The lanes are full of villas and grand European buildings. Beginning in 1842, Western traders allowed in after the Opium Wars built Gulangyu into a virtual European town, with their own schools, churches and hospitals. The British Embassy still stands on a hill above the ferry landing, and beyond it the Roman Catholic church, completed in 1882 and still in use. The Sanyi Protestant church, built by the British in 1904, is also active. These days, the colonial villas are occupied by local Chinese.

A statue of the patron saint of Xiamen, Koxinga (Zheng Chenggong), stands on the tip of the island. A warrior, he expelled the Dutch from Taiwan in the 17th century. Not far from Koxinga's heroic image are the guesthouse villas and sandy beaches where locals relax and sometimes even take a dip in the warm waters of the East China Sea. Above the beaches is the island's most famous garden, **Shuzhuang** (daily summer 5.30am–9pm, winter until 8.30pm; charge), built in 1913 by a wealthy Taiwanese merchant and admired for its pond and rock design: 'a garden in the sea, a sea in the garden'. It houses Asia's largest piano museum (charge), honouring an instrument once commonplace in the isle's homes.

The best views are from the towering **Sunlight Rock** (Riguangyan; charge) in Yanping Park, at 93 metres (305ft) the highest point on Gulangyu and well worth the climb. From here, you can see across the long harbour to downtown Xiamen. And of course you can see Gulangyu itself, a dense sea garden of flowers, red-tiled villas and tiny seafood cafés – a bright home to just 12,000 residents. (By comparison, the city of Xiamen has over 636,000 citizens and is a rampaging metropolis.)

The **Xiamen Museum** (Tue–Sun 9am–5pm; free; www.xmmuseum.com), housed in Gulangyu's most striking red-domed building, contains a sprinkling of different exhibits on its four floors, including printing presses, Tang-dynasty porcelains, wooden rifles, assorted gifts from sister cities around the world, and photographs of the island's dazzling colonial architecture.

FUZHOU

On the coast halfway between Shanghai and Guangzhou is Fuzhou. It is the capital of Fujian province and was one of the Treaty Ports open to foreign settlement in the 19th century. The population is a fascinating mix of Minbeihua-speaking locals of Portuguese descent, economic migrants from the poverty-stricken countryside and Shanghainese looking for profit in a rapidly expanding city. Fuzhou is famous for its lacquerware products, which have as many as 80 coats of lacquer. The city's West Temple and its Black Pagoda and White Pagoda date from the 10th century.

Elephant Trunk Hill

SOUTHWEST CHINA

This section tours four provinces of China's southwest, starting from the beautiful limestone rock formations of Guilin and Yangshuo – both in

Guangxi province, which borders northern Vietnam. We then journey north to Guizhou province, for more natural wonders at Huangguoshu Falls, before turning northwest to Sichuan, with its cultural and natural attractions, and spicy cuisine. The section ends in Yunnan province, where the numerous sights range from the Stone Forest (Shilin) rock formations to the stupendous mountain scenery, picturesque old towns and ethnic minorities on the borders of Tibet.

GUILIN

China's most famous landscapes, the subjects of thousands of paintings, are in **Guilin** ⓰. Poets, artists and tourists have made this China's number one natural attraction for its mountains and rivers. The climate is subtropical, with an annual rainfall of 190cm (75in), most of it between April and July. Autumn visitors will see and smell osmanthus (cassia) blossoms all over town; in fact, the name Guilin means 'Cassia Woods'.

Tourists are so numerous in the otherwise relaxed shopping district of Guilin that the pedestrian crossings have signs in English as well as Chinese. Another cosmopolitan influence comes from the area's many minority peoples: Guilin is part of the Guangxi-Zhuang Autonomous Region, which borders Vietnam. The proliferation of so-called Muslim restaurants is explained by the presence here of thousands of people of the traditionally Muslim ethnic Zhuang people.

The geological history of Guilin, the key to the wonder of its moody mountains and caves, goes back several hundred million years. The area was under the sea when an upheaval raised it to the status of terra firma. Later it was flooded, then lifted again in further cataclysmic events. The alternation of sea water and air through the millennia created limestone formations called karst, which eroded into pinnacles, mounds and peaks.

Guilin was settled more than 2,000 years ago when a canal was built, linking the great Yangzi and Pearl rivers. The Ling Canal, one of the world's longest, still exists and can be easily seen at Xi'ang,

65km (40 miles) northwest of here. Guilin's connection with one of humankind's most ambitious engineering projects was important, but otherwise little was heard from the town. It served as a provincial capital for several hundred years, and in modern times, thanks to the profusion of caves to hide in, was a centre for resistance during the war with Japan – and as a result Guilin was razed by the Japanese army in 1944. Today, rebuilt from the rubble of war, the city is thriving, thanks in large measure to its spectacular scenery and the tourists it attracts. Guilin's best shops and restaurants are located downtown in the modern **Central Square**, especially along Yiren Lu and the pedestrianised street, Zhengyang Buxing Jie.

Limestone Pinnacles

The best way to appreciate Guilin's unique setting is to climb to the summit of one of its limestone pinnacles: for example, 150m (640ft) **Solitary Beauty Peak** (Duxiu Feng; daily Mar–Apr

Reed Flute Cave

Scenery at Yangshuo

& Oct–Dec 7 7.30am–6pm, May–Oct 7 7.30am–6.30pm, Dec 8–Feb 8am–6pm; charge) near the centre of town, or the hill called **Diecaishan** (daily 8am–6pm winter; charge), to the north. The latter name means 'Piled Silk Hill', or 'Folded Brocade Hill', a metaphor suggested by the layers of rock. Hiking to the lookout point at the top is strenuous, but catching your breath is only one good reason for stopping along the way: Breezy Cave, which cuts through the hill from south to north, is permanently cooled by a refreshing breeze, to the relief of crowds on hot summer days. The many inscriptions carved into the cave walls over the centuries are much admired by connoisseurs of calligraphy.

At the summit, at an altitude of 223m (732ft), stands the charmingly named **Catch-Cloud Pavilion** (Nayunting), which gives a 360-degree panorama. The view is worth savouring: the winding river, the tile-roofed cityscape, the green, flat farmland and the mist-shrouded hills fading into the distance.

Elephant Trunk Park (Xiangshan Gongyuan; daily 6.30am–9.30pm in summer, 7am–9.30pm in winter; charge) features Guilin's most famous peak, **Elephant Trunk Hill** (Xiangbi Shan). The leafy limestone pachyderm stands at the meeting point of the Li River and the Peach Blossom River. On top of the peak stands the **Puxian Pagoda**, built during the Song dynasty as an offering to calm the flood-prone river. The hill is illuminated at night.

So too is **Fuboshan** ('Whirlpool Hill'; daily 8.30am–4.40pm), another natural stone tower closer to the city centre, with a view as well as other distractions. According to legend, a General Fubo, who passed this way 2,000 years ago, tested his sword in the Sword-Testing Stone, a stalactite formation that comes down to within inches of the ground. Further on, the Thousand Buddha Cliff is carved with several hundred figures dating from the Tang and Song dynasties.

The **District of the Two Lakes**, in the southern part of town, has been made into a delightful public park with gardens, walkways and pagodas. Originally, Banyan Tree Lake (Ronghu) and Fir Tree Lake (Shahu) were a single expanse, forming part of the moat which protected the city wall. The Song-dynasty-era Green Belt Bridge across the middle created the two lakes.

Reed Flute Cave (Ludiyan; daily 7.30am–6pm summer, 8am–5.30pm winter; charge) takes its name from the reeds – which were used to make flutes – that once grew at its entrance. Today the entry is marked by a ticket booth, where guides meet visitors to take them on an illuminated tour 500m/yds into the mountain's interior. The cave's largest chamber, called the Crystal Palace of the Dragon King, can accommodate 1,000 people, and was where many local citizens sheltered during the Japanese bombing campaign.

Huangguoshu Falls

On the eastern bank of the Li lies **Seven Star Park** (Qixing Gongyuan; daily 6am–7.30pm summer, 6.30am–7.30pm winter; charge). It acquired its name from the position of its seven hills, which suggest the pattern of the Plough (Big Dipper) constellation. In the centre of the park rises Camel Hill (Luotou Shan), which indeed does uncannily resemble a camel. Another attraction is the **Forest of Steles**, a cliff where poems and pictures have been carved into the rock over the past 1,500 years.

But the true star of Seven Star Park is **Seven Star Cave** (Qixing Dong; daily 8am–5.30pm; charge) – a mere million years old and a tourist attraction for more than 1,000 years. Some of the scenic formations of stalactites and stalagmites have names like Old Banyan Tree Welcoming Guests and Dragon Splashing Water, providing an idea of the poetic licence enjoyed by Chinese cave explorers.

Li River Boat Trip

The transcendent tourist experience of Guilin is a boat trip on the **Li River**. The limestone scenery could hardly be more romantic. The 83km (52-mile) cruise on the Li takes only four to five hours, but there is no river trip like it.

But life along the river is also quite fascinating: washerwomen squatting on the shore, water buffalo ambling down for a dip, and the improvised ferryboats. Captive cormorant birds, their necks ringed to prevent them from swallowing all their catch, await orders to go fishing from bamboo rafts.

Large, flat-bottomed tour boats that can fit 100 people usually leave early in the morning from the quay near the Liberation Bridge in central Guilin. (In the dry season, when the river is at its lowest, the first part of the journey is by coach.) River traffic keeps amateur photographers snapping in all directions at flat-bottomed tubs, hand-poled bamboo rafts, sampans and towboats.

Images unroll before the eye like a painted scroll as your boat continues downstream: Tunnelled Hill, Pagoda Hill (also known as Battleship Hill), Washing Vase Hill and Fighting Cocks Hills (facing each other across the river). A large village on the left bank, **Dragon Gate Village**, is noted for water chestnuts and its 1,000-year-old banyan tree.

To the south is a much larger village, **Daxu**, with a high bridge from the Ming period called 'Longevity Bridge'. Here and elsewhere, the rich, flat land produces the ingredients for a formidable fruit salad: oranges and grapefruit, chestnuts and persimmons, plus exotic tropical delicacies all but unknown outside Asia. Adding to the entrancing beauty of the scene, great stands of a feathery variety of bamboo grow along the riverbanks, forming huge cascades of green.

Beyond the village of Yangdi unfolds the uncanny scenery that prompted a Chinese poet more than 1,000 years ago to write, 'The river is a green silk belt, the mountains emerald hairpins.' Peaks and pinnacles crowd the river, white goats cling to steep mountainsides, and an eagle soars high above the cliffs. The river itself flows green and transparent due to a high content of carbonic acid.

Mural Hill is so called because the sheer cliff face comprises so many patches of colour that it might be a fresco.

Qingyanggong ('Green Goat Temple'), Chengdu

YANGSHUO

The boat trip ends at **Yangshuo**, set among extraordinary limestone pinnacles. Dominated by the same river-cut conical mountains but with less group tourism and attendant hassles, the town has become almost as popular as Guilin. The scenery around it attracts droves of independent travellers. Eerie yet photogenic landscapes are closer at hand, and there are superb views from the hilltop pavilion in the

WHEN THE BAMBOO FLOWERS...

The giant panda has been known to science for little more than 100 years, yet it might vanish before another century passes. The future of these furry black and white beasts is linked with the forests of bamboo that cover the mountains of southwest China, their only native home.

The varieties of bamboo on which the panda feeds flower and then die off over vast areas, at intervals of decades, sometimes even a century. After this happens, it takes many months for the plants to grow again. Several hundred pandas once died of starvation when large tracts of bamboo flowered. There could be another bamboo famine soon.

Sixteen areas have been set aside as panda reserves; a research station is studying the movements and feeding habits of the animal; and Chengdu Zoo, which already breeds pandas, is geared to provide refuge and food for stricken creatures during a bamboo crisis. Today, there are thought to be just under 2,000 giant pandas left in the wild. In 2016, WWF downgraded them from 'endangered' to 'vulnerable', after their population increased by 17% in a decade.

Zoos overseas, from Taipei to Washington, DC, are doing their part to keep the species alive. Although their pandas are goodwill gifts from China, the zoos often try to breed cubs with the option of returning them to China.

city park, from the port and from the bridge to the south.

Many travellers jump on bicycles (available to hire everywhere) and head out of town. Perhaps the best trip is to **Moon Hill** (Yueliang Shan; charge), 50 minutes outside town by bike. Make your way to the top while fending off hawkers for unparalleled views of the Yangshuo countryside. Other popular activities in Yangshuo include rock-climbing, trips up the River Li and cave exploration.

Giant panda in Chengdu zoo

The trip back to Guilin from Yangshuo by minibus provides yet another chance to see more beautiful scenery.

HUANGGUOSHU FALLS, GUIZHOU PROVINCE

China's premier run of cascades and waterfalls, Huangguoshu Falls is as wide as 81m (263ft) and drops a resounding 74m (230ft) in the course of 2km (1¼ miles). There are also caves to explore, tunnels to walk and a minority people, the Bouyei, to meet. Between the great falls and the nearest cities, Anshun and Guiyang, the lush karst landscape of Guizhou province contains a number of underground marvels, including Zhingin Cave, China's largest.

Guizhou is home to large numbers of minority ethnic groups, each preserving a strong sense of identity and tradition. The main groups are the Miao, numbering more than 8 million, the Dong, who live mainly in the south of the province, and the Bouyei, of eastern Guizhou. The Miao in particular are known for their colourful festivals, where traditional clothing is worn, with each Miao subgroup having

Dafo (Great Buddha) at Leshan

its own distinctive costume. Miao girls also wear remarkable silver headdresses at the *lusheng* (bamboo-pipe) festivals. The minorities have also preserved their languages.

CHENGDU

North of Guizhou province is Sichuan, the natural habitat for 80 percent of the world's dwindling population of giant pandas. Temperate, often misty weather keeps the provincial capital, **Chengdu** ⓱, green and full of flowers year-round. It's the climate in which bamboo – the staple diet of the panda – thrives (see page 168). Unless you have time to journey to the Wolong reserve in the wild mountains of western Sichuan, the best place to spot these endangered beasts is a short distance northeast of central Chengdu, at the **Giant Panda Breeding Research Base** (daily 7.30am–6pm; charge; www.panda.org.cn), where 83 pandas have free run of some 30 hectares (80 acres) of bamboo groves. There's also a panda museum here. In closer confines, the **Chengdu Zoo** (daily 8am–5pm summer, 8.30am–5pm winter) has more resident pandas – about a dozen – than any other zoo in the world. The thin bamboo stalks they find so delicious are grown in the zoo's grounds. As befits their celebrity status, the giant pandas are assigned high-ceilinged, spacious cages and outdoor play areas.

At the time of the era of the Three Kingdoms, in the 3rd century, Chengdu was capital of the feudal Kingdom of Shu, and politics, not pandas, was the prime attraction. The principal monument from that era is the **Temple of Marquis Wu** (Wuhousi; daily 8am–6.30pm winter, 8am–8pm summer; charge), a complex of halls and gardens in the southern suburbs built to commemorate the kingdom's prime minister. Known in his lifetime (AD 181–234) as Zhugeliang, he was posthumously ennobled for his role in unifying the region and developing its economy and culture.

Chinese literary pilgrims are drawn to another of Chengdu's historic sites, the thatched **cottage of Dufu** (Dufucaotang; daily 8am–8pm summer, 8am–6.30pm winter; charge), a shrine, museum and park at the spot where the poet of the Tang dynasty lived in exile from the capital for several years. Dufu lived from 712 to 770 and wrote more than 1,400 poems, many of them regarded as the greatest in the Chinese canon.

In May 2008 the city experienced a magnitude 7.9 earthquake which killed some 68,000 people. The quake eliminated villages in the mountains north and east of Chengdu and drove the government to declare a nationwide day of mourning. Ask about conditions before venturing to or even through towns such as Beichuan, Dujiangyan and Mianyang. In Beichuan, you can visit the Chengdu Beichuan Earthquake Memorial, located at the site of the old Beichuan High School, commemorating the human tragedy of 2008.

Chengdu's most popular Daoist temple, **Qingyanggong** ('Green Goat Temple'; daily 8am–6pm; charge) is a lively, garish complex where two bronze 'good luck' goats at the main altar have been rubbed smooth by those seeking their fortunes. Not far away is the centre of Zen (Chan) Buddhism in Sichuan, the 1,300-year-old **Wenshu Temple** (daily 8.30am–5.30pm; charge), which maintains its own woodcarvers as well as a vegetarian restaurant and outdoor teahouse.

Chengdu's largest and most renowned religious monument, located 28km (17 miles) to the north of the city, is the **Divine Light Monastery** (Baoguangsi; daily 8am–5pm; charge). The most photographed element of this vast establishment is the stupa, a slightly crooked 13-level pagoda. It was built of stone at the end of the Tang dynasty, replacing an ancient wooden pagoda on the same spot.

By long tradition, Chengdu is China's pre-eminent city of teahouses. Many still operate along the north bank of the Jin ('Brocade') River, serving covered cups of flower tea. Customers linger at courtyard tables, watching trinket vendors and pipe and tobacco salesmen ply their trade along the river promenade, or sometimes enjoying free performances of Sichuan Opera or instrumental music.

Another restful locale is **Wangjianglou** (the River Viewing Pavilion Park; public areas daily 6am–9pm; free; daily 8am–6pm cultural relics area; charge), along the south bank of the Jin River. More than 100 kinds of bamboo grow here. As in other traditional Chengdu parks, there are pavilions and towers, rock gardens, ponds and shady paths. This irrigation and flood-control project was constructed around AD 256 by Li Bing, the governor of the Shu prefecture. Amazingly, it is still in use, irrigating some 2,400 sq km (930 sq miles) of agricultural land. There is a 3m (10ft) tall statue of Li Bing in the Pavilion of the Dragon's Defeat (Fulongguan), which was erected in the 3rd century to commemorate the governor's achievement.

In the centre of town some neighbourhoods retain a medieval look. Two-storey shophouses, some sagging with age, line the narrow streets. They have shops on the ground floor and living quarters above, with wooden balconies and distinctive carved designs. But 'progress' is inevitable: on the site of the ancient viceroy's palace, in the very centre of Chengdu, a giant statue of Mao Zedong graces the entrance to **Tianfu Square**, a vast pedestrian mall. Visitors find that the Chengdu locals tend to smile and greet strangers more often than Chinese elsewhere.

By way of local colour, you shouldn't turn down a chance to see a performance of Sichuan Opera. It's all sung in the local dialect, but you can just relax and watch the spectacle of mime, dance and acrobatics. Backstage tours are arranged these days by private tour operators.

Sichuan cuisine is one of the four great schools of Chinese cooking. One of the most famous dishes, *mapo dofu*, consists of bean curd infused with chilli peppers in a manner that numbs the tongue on impact. Most food in Chengdu is moderately spicy yet fragrant.

Barges ply the Yangzi River at Chongqing

Chengdu is the gateway to the **Great Buddha at Leshan, Mt Emei** and the Daoist mountain of **Qingchengshan**. About 100km (60 miles) northwest of Chengdu, the stunning **Wolong Nature Reserve** is an unspoilt region dedicated to the preservation and propagation of pandas. You may not actually spot any pandas in the wild, but they can be seen at the research centre.

Travellers often start land trips to Tibet from Chengdu. Roads run through Kangding into the high mountains of Sichuan, which are populated largely by ethnic Tibetans. The Tibet Autonomous Region is just beyond. Make sure to arrange permits to pass Kanging, as the police don't let in just anyone.

LESHAN

From the provincial capital of Chengdu, a three-hour motorway drive through populous Sichuan (Szechuan) province ends at the town of **Leshan**, the base for visits to a monumental riverside Buddha and to Emeishan, one of four sacred mountains of Chinese Buddhism. A 13th-century poet wrote that the most beautiful scenery of China is found in Sichuan, and some of the best of that scenery is concentrated in Leshan. Three rivers converge and flow along the city wall, and far away in the mist rises Mt Emei.

Boats ferry visitors from Leshan to the site of the **Great Buddha** (Dafo; daily 9am–4.50pm; charge). Whether seen from the river or, later, from the hillsides, the world's largest seated Buddha is an impressive spectacle. Carved from the cliffside by a monk starting in AD 713, its height is 71m (233ft). The statue's feet are so big that 100 people can sit on each one.

The boats tie up some distance from the Buddha and passengers climb from the shore to **Dark Green Temple** (Wuyousi), with magnificent views of the surrounding rivers and Mt Emei. Below the temple are some Han-dynasty tombs and a modern reclining Buddha, at 170m (559ft) the world's longest. The Stairs of Nine Turnings wind steeply down one side of the statue to the feet. Another honeycombed stairway carved from the cliff leads back up the other side, coming out level with the statue's massive crown.

MT EMEI

Mt Emei (Emeishan) reaches an altitude of well over 3,000m (over 10,000ft). You don't have to climb all the way to the summit of Emeishan to appreciate its charm and mystique, but the higher you go, the more chance you'll have of sighting the rich fauna of the hill forests, from gregarious golden monkeys to red pandas. This was the traditional Buddhist 'Peak of the West', the mountain shrine to countless pilgrims, emperors included.

At the foot of Mt Emei, foreshadowing the many temples ahead, are the **Crouching Tiger Temple** (Fuhusi) and the 16th-century **Loyalty to Country Temple** (Baoguosi). The latter is filled with plant life, home to many small gardens and bonsai. It also contains the Shengji Bell, reputedly the second largest in China (after Beijing's Great Bell), inscribed with Buddhist scripture. There are monasteries and famous scenic spots every few kilometres along the paths to the summit, but this is a climb (for the energetic only) that requires several days. Many tourists have time to spend only a night on the mountain in one of the basic inns, such as those at the **Shrine of Limpid Waters** (Jinshui), before being driven to the summit before dawn to see the renowned sunrise.

Chongqing's cityscape

At sunrise on **Golden Peak** (Jinding), pilgrims and tourists alike gather in the hope of seeing an optical phenomenon called 'Buddha's Halo'. They are looking for their shadows perfectly framed inside a bright halo formed when the rising sun penetrates a morning sea of clouds.

CHONGQING

Although the city's history goes back thousands of years, **Chongqing** ⓲ is more of an industrial than a cultural centre. Travellers will see the daily life of a major Chinese working-class city with a number of endearing quirks, such as hills and hotpots based on the spiciest pepper oil in China. Chongqing is also the launch point for excursions on the legendary Yangzi River.

The city was a capital under the Qin dynasty in the 3rd century BC, and during the Tang period (618–907) it was known as Yuzhou – it is still called Yu for short. The emperor Zhao Dun, of the Song dynasty, renamed it Chongqing ('Twin Fortune') after two lucky events: he first became prince of the prefecture, then later emperor of China. Until the past few years it was spelt Chungking, by which name the city was best known in the West as the political and military capital

The Three Gorges Dam

of the Nationalist government from 1939 to 1945, the wartime redoubt of Chiang Kai-shek. For several summers during the war, the town was bombed by the Japanese; but in the winters, enemy planes were prevented from doing any damage by the heavy fog that typically rises from the rivers, shrouding the town.

Chongqing was once part of Sichuan province, but since 1997 it has been an autonomous governmental municipality (as are Beijing, Shanghai and Tianjin), with a population of over 32 million people. Set on a promontory where the Yangzi and Jialing rivers converge, this stark city of smokestacks is crucial to transportation and commerce in southwest China. Foreign carmakers and other manufacturers have sited new factories in the city alongside traditional iron, steel and machine tool-makers. With the increase in investment has come growth in office space and trade shows. The cost, naturally, is a nagging smog problem. Air pollution, compounded by high summer heat, makes the city as famous among Chinese as its economic expansion.

Chongqing presides over the portion of the Yangzi upstream from the massive Three Gorges Dam project (see page 178).

Chongqing Sights

The sightseeing you remember best might be the lively free market lining the hundreds of steps that descend higgledy-piggledy from the hills of central Chongqing to the river. Bustling peasants hawk the rich harvest of the surrounding farming country: cabbages and oranges, eggs and live chickens (they are weighed while flapping), river fish and squirming eels, and table after table of the most fragrant spices. Men in the markets will offer to carry your heavier wares away on a shoulder pole, for a few *yuan*.

Stalls and hole-in-the-wall cafés throughout town serve the city's number-one dish, the famous Sichuan hotpot. Even in the heat of summer, hotpots seethe in oils into which the diner dips and boils to perfection a personal selection of meats, vegetables and bean curd.

At the tip of the peninsula where the two rivers meet is a small pavilion known as the **Gate to the Sky** (Chaotianmen), with a steep stone stairway leading down to the water's edge. At the bottom of this long descent there is a terminal for the funicular that returns you to the top of this town, which is so hilly that bicycles are almost unknown. For another view of the rivers, visitors can join local commuters in riding cable cars over either the Yangzi or Jialing.

Sights worth seeing in town include the **Chongqing People's Hall** (daily 8.30am–5pm; charge), built in 1953. It blends the styles of the Ming and Qing dynasties with the needs of a modern conference hall. Just opposite of the Hall is the **Three Gorges Museum** (Tue–Sun 9am–5pm; free; www.3gmuseum.cn). It showcases Chinese art and artefacts saved during the construction of the Three Gorges Dam, instructs on the construction of the dam, the history of Chongqing, and presents the Anti-Japanese War from the perspective of the city. Perhaps the liveliest sight in the Chongqing is the 1,000-year-old **Luohan Temple** (Luohansi; daily 8am–6pm; charge), where blind fortune-tellers and followers of Buddha converge from dawn to dusk. The restored template is known for 500 painted terracotta sculptures called *arhat*.

In the domain of darker political history, two former Nationalist prisons outside town are open as monuments to the revolutionary cause. The **Refuse Pit Prison** (Zhongmei Hezuosuo, also known as the US/Chiang Kai-shek Criminal Acts Exhibition Hall; daily 9am–4.30pm; free), includes cells and torture chambers once used to hold and interrogate suspected Communists. A smaller detention centre, the **Bai Mansion** (Baigongguan; daily 9am–4.30pm; free) has an equally dark past. It is found 3km (2 miles) down the hill.

Because of Chongqing's torrid summer weather, hills and parks are a very welcome refuge. **Loquat Hill** (Pipashan), the city's highest spot, has gardens, a teahouse (Hongxing) and some splendid panoramas. The Northern and Southern Hot Springs parks (Beiwenquan and Nanwenquan) are also popular gathering places, with well-kept public gardens. During the years of Japanese air raids, hundreds of air-raid shelters were dug

A CONTROVERSIAL DAM

The Three Gorges Dam – 181m (594ft) high and 2,309m (7,575ft) long – houses 26 hydro turbine generators and holds back a reservoir more than 660km (410 miles) long, stretching upriver into the municipality of Chongqing. Its purpose is to control the Yangzi's occasionally devastating floods and provide electricity for central China. Construction forced the relocation of 1.3 million local people, reduced farmland, submerged sites of historical interest and threatened rare species. The Yangzi river dolphin is believed to have become extinct in 2004. The Chinese alligator, Chinese sturgeon and Siberian crane are on the endangered list. There are worries, too, about the degenerating water quality in the reservoir, as much of the waste from settlements along the Yangzi is discharged directly into the river. And without constant dredging, the tonnes of sediment transported by the river may pose a threat to the dam's smooth operation.

into the mountains here, and some have been turned into cafés and restaurants.

Chongqing's newest attraction is **Ciqikou Old Town**, a restored Ming-dynasty-era district of shops, cafés and teahouses. These mostly pedestrian streets rise up a steep riverside at the less populated edge of town.

Music practice

EXCURSIONS FROM CHONGQING

Yangzi River Cruise

Despite the inevitable impact of the dam project on the surrounding scenery, China's most exciting boat trip remains the **Yangzi River cruise** through the spectacular **Three Gorges** (Sanxia). The most awesome scenery on the two-day stretch between Chongqing and Yichang is concentrated between the Sichuan city of **Baidi** and **Nanjin Pass** in Hubei province.

Tourists can choose between ordinary Chinese passenger boats or more luxurious cruise ships. The riverboats largely for locals lack frills, amenities and guides. The luxury craft charge much more but offer a good range of tourist services, including meals. Often reserved in part for package tours, these ships are also open to independent travellers, and staterooms can even be booked in advance from overseas with such lines as Victoria Cruises or Viking River Cruises.

For the latest information on the **Three Gorges Hydropower Project**, and its impact on cruises and the landscape, visitors considering taking the trip should contact their specialist travel agency or local operators such as CITS or China Highlights Travel.

In 2003 the Yangzi was blocked by the closure of 22 sluice gates, and the water in the reservoir behind was allowed to rise from 66m (215ft) to 135m (443ft). In May 2006 construction of the main wall of the dam was completed, and by the project's completion in 2009 the water level in the reservoir was able to rise as high as 175m (574ft).

The 185m (607ft) high dam and 1,045-sq km (403-sq mile) reservoir behind it had stirred controversy over the forced relocations of 1.3 million people who lived in the affected area. Threats to the riverside ecology, the disappearance of cultural sites and the spectre of an accidental breach that might flood huge communities downstream also contributed to a debate that was tolerated more often than not by Chinese authorities.

The Dazu Caves

One of China's great artistic wonders is the Buddhist sculptural treasure of **Dazu** (daily 8.30am–6pm; charge). This district was so inaccessible in earlier times that many thousands of statues were never exposed to pillage. Today, it still takes two hours to cover the 112km (70 miles) from central Chongqing.

The stone carvings of Dazu were begun late in the 9th century, during the Tang dynasty; the work lasted well into the Southern Song period, hundreds of years later. Although Buddhism is their central theme, there are also sculptures representing historical and human-interest subjects.

KUNMING

Flights into **Kunming** ⓳, the capital of Yunnan province, land on an unexpectedly long runway that has a dramatic history, commemorated neither by plaques nor monuments. This was once the end of the line for the Flying Tigers, the American pilots who supplied China during World War II. Kunming was also the Chinese terminus for supplies travelling down the tortuous Burma Road; milestone '0' – otherwise unmarked – can be seen on the right side of the road

21km (13 miles) from the centre of Kunming, on the edge of the Western Hills.

May Day Parade in Kunming

One of Kunming's best attractions is its benign climate. The city lies at an altitude of 1,900m (more than 6,200ft), and up here temperatures are pleasantly mild, producing what is described as perpetual springtime. During one season or another the camellia, azalea, magnolia and begonia are in flower, and the region is renowned as China's pharmacopoeia. The thatched roofs of farmhouses near the modern city are draped with drying corn and chilli peppers.

The total population stands at over 6.6 million, of whom half live in the city proper. A high proportion of the citizens belong to minority nationalities, who trade or study in the provincial capital. The city's leading university, the Institute for Nationalities, has more than 20,000 minority students. **Yunnan Provincial Museum** (Tue–Sun 9am–5pm; free) has displays of minority arts and crafts, as well as early bronzes from the region. Travellers usually cannot tell who's from what ethnic group, as most have East Asian features and wear the same clothes, unless a ceremony or performance calls for something more native. Kunming denizens are relatively polite, gentle and unlikely to stare at foreigners, as they are used to mingling with people from different cultural and linguistic backgrounds.

Downtown Kunming has modernised rapidly, but there are still a few touches of the old, the exotic and the scenic: a colourful bird and flower market, the blind masseurs who work outside in the public square at the Workers' Cultural Hall, the still-active **Nancheng Ancient Mosque**. A few older neighbourhoods remain around the city's main park, **Green Lake** (Cuihu), and the lake is pleasant, particularly on a Sunday when families visit and in winter when the 'laughing gulls' stop over on their way from Siberia. Small shops throughout town sell the region's unique green teas, which customers can sample before deciding what, or whether, to buy.

Kunming's most interesting temple, Qiongzhusi, or the **Bamboo Temple** (daily 8.30am–5pm; charge), lies 13km (8 miles) northwest of the city centre. It houses the surreal work of a 19th-century sculptor who created a version of the 500 *arhats* (followers of the Buddha) that is unequalled at any other Buddhist temple in China.

Lake Dian

Kunming's prime scenic and recreational area is at **Lake Dian**, where tour boats cruise the crystal waters. **Grand View Park** (Daguan Gongyuan; daily 7am–7pm; charge, on one shore of China's sixth-largest lake, provides the flowers that make Kunming famous as a floral centre, along with arched bridges and pavilions. On the opposite shore, the rich green slopes of the Western Hills (Xishan) rise abruptly. Also situated by Lake Dian is the **Yunnan Nationalities Village** (Yunnan Minzu Cun; daily 9am–6pm; charge; www.ynmzc.cc), an ethnic theme park exhibiting 24 minority mini-villages, probably the best of its kind in China. Here people dress as if they were readying for traditional ceremonies.

A strenuous climb up the sheer face of the Western Hills via tunnels and stair treads carved from stone ultimately leads to **Dragon Gate** (Longmen; daily 7am–6pm summer, 8am–5pm winter; charge). During the Ming dynasty the emperor was carried all the way up from the lakeside by four bearers. There are several excellent places to stop and catch your breath on the way up, including a teahouse, a former concubines' residence and an emperor's temporary living quarters. The gate itself is wide enough for only one person to pass through at a time. Caves painstakingly cut into the mountainside contain colourful painted carvings, all the work of a single-minded Daoist monk of the 18th century and his followers.

Stone Forest rock formations

THE STONE FOREST

From Kunming it's 80km (50 miles) southeast to Yunnan's most popular attraction, the **Stone Forest** (Shilin; daily 7am–6pm; charge; www.chinastoneforest.com). This geological park is an otherworldly fantasy of twisted limestone formations that comprise the world's largest natural stone maze. Geologists say the structures originated 200 million years ago with the interaction of limestone, sea water, rainwater and seismic upheavals. The bizarre pinnacles that resulted are of the distinctive type of limestone called karst, the same rock that one finds in Guilin. Some stones are massive, with dark, narrow passageways through which visitors can walk. Between some of the stones are patches of planted grass that give the forest the feel of a golf course.

The Stone Forest covers about 260 sq km (100 sq miles) of Yunnan province, but most tourists confine themselves to a manageable area of concentrated rocks. Here there are paved paths, protective railings and a few painted signs, but it is indeed possible to lose one's way inside this massive labyrinth. Near the starting point, women from the neighbouring village (members of the Sani tribe of the Yi nationality) sell embroidered blouses, bags and assorted knick-knacks. The Sani also work as freelance guides.

Bai music and dance festival at Santasi (Temple of the Three Pagodas), Dali

The biggest open space in the Stone Forest, a lawn surrounded by cherry trees, is the site of a Sani festival each June. For 48 continuous hours, the tribesmen devote themselves to singing and dancing, wrestling matches, bullfights (actually, water buffalo fighting each other), feasting and romancing.

Those who spend an evening in the Stone Forest are usually entertained with a Sani folklore show. Among the instruments in the orchestra are flutes, zithers and a giant banjo with a hollow bottom. Women dancers wear red, white and black conical hats, while the men sport floppy black turbans. Through song and mime they recount legends of the forest.

DALI

The attractive Old Town of **Dali** ⓴, about 250km (155 miles) northwest of Kunming along the historic Burma Road route, captivates independent backpackers. The surroundings are spectacular, with Erhai ('Ear Sea') Lake to the east and the steep Cangshan mountain range to the west.

The town, capital of the Bai Autonomous Region (named for the region's predominant ethnic minority), has sections of a medieval wall with formal gates on the north and south ends. Within the walls are a few intersecting main streets whose tile-roofed shops and houses now serve as souvenir shops, private travel agencies, hostels, and – above all – small, intimate cafés serving a truly international mix of inexpensive dishes. Although the Bai are the dominant ethnic group, Han Chinese who look very much like them and Tibetans from higher ground in the west have also set up shop. The push to profit from tourism has filled Old Dali with touts so aggressive they may sit at your café table, uninvited, or knock on your hostel door. Travellers wanting to escape might like to book horse rides or charter boats across the lake.

The chief monument at Dali is the **Temple of the Three Pagodas** (Santasi; daily 8am–7pm summer, 7.30am–6.30pm winter; charge), founded in 825. The tallest, and oldest, of the three rises to 16 tiers and 70m (230ft). The pagodas have survived several earthquakes, though the original temple has not. Excavations during a 1979 renovation unearthed a trove of exquisite artefacts – gold Buddhas, silver phoenixes, bronze mirrors and copper utensils.

Independent travellers should be aware that in local parlance there are actually two Dalis. The old walled town, where most foreign visitors stay, is known as Dali Gucheng (Dali Old City), while the newer, larger Dali, 20 minutes south by road, is usually marked on maps as Xiaguan, but sometimes as just 'Dali' or Dali Shi (Dali City). Whatever it is called, it's a less than charming urban sprawl. Each centre has its own railway station.

AROUND DALI

Erhai Lake, the second-largest in Yunnan, is a 30-minute walk from town, and its main village, Caicun, is a maze of unpaved alleys and mud houses. Ferries cross the lake to even more remote villages, including the temple dedicated to Guanyin (goddess of mercy) on **Putuo Island**. Any of dozens of local travel agents can quickly arrange an excursion to lakeside villages, including the market at **Wase**. One popular diversion is the Monday-morning outdoor market at **Shaping**, 30 minutes up the eucalyptus-lined road by minibus from Dali. It's a vast market of country wares, batik and horse-trading, with hundreds of local people dressed in their traditional bright Bai jackets, tunics and plumed caps.

On the other side of Dali, a day hike leads to temples and pagodas in the steep foothills of the Cangshan (Green Mountain) range. Although seldom open, they provide the perfect ornaments for a hike from vista to vista over this long, narrow valley that reaches west to Tibet.

LIJIANG

Lijiang ㉑, in the highlands of northwest Yunnan province, was once an outpost for adventurers in search of Shangri-la, that magical place whose definition varied from explorer to explorer. That was just a few years ago. Now the well-preserved Naxi minority village is a tourist magnet, and Shangri-la in the mountains beyond has become ominously well defined. Lijiang has built an airport and watched tourist arrivals, most of them domestic, surpass 4 million per year.

The old part of Lijiang – cut with waterways, decorated with attractive local architecture and populated with blue-clothed members of the Naxi minority – has held on to its native character. It was designated a World Heritage Site by Unesco in 1999, three years after a severe earthquake prompted a huge reconstruction effort.

At the north end of town in **Black Dragon Pool Park**, the **Naxia Dongbei Cultural Museum** (daily 8am–5pm; free) is devoted to Chinese ethnic minorities; 25 of the 55 nationwide are found in Yunnan. On clear days, massive snow-capped mountains come into full view from the park.

Naxi musicians and dancers hold a variety of evening musical performances in Lijiang, with the most famous staged by the Naxi Orchestra. Some of the dances are Tibetan, while some of the musicians use archaic instruments seldom heard elsewhere.

Rising up outside town is the dramatic 5,500m (18,000ft) **Jade Dragon Snow Mountain** (Yulongxue Shan), which you can ascend by cable car to a considerable altitude. Photos with local yaks and romps in the snow await those who make the trip. Annual music festivals sometimes headlined by China's original rocker, Cui Jian, electrify Snow Mountain in the summer. Ask around about the dates.

Lijiang Old Town

For those seeking depths as well as heights, Lijiang functions as a jumping-off point for the popular two- to three-day hike along the 30km (18-mile) long **Tiger Leaping Gorge** (Hutiaoxia; daily 9am–6pm; charge). The hike can be dangerous in parts, depending on the weather, so enquire in Lijiang about conditions along the gorge before setting out. Shorter hikes, taking less than a day, are also possible.

SHANGRI-LA

Deeper into the mountains, on the region's enduring 'teahouse road' trade route in Yunnan's Diqing Tibetan prefecture, lies the real Shangri-la. This county, formerly called Zhongdian, was renamed after James Hilton's fictional land – featured in his 1930s novel *Lost Horizon* – by government order in 2001 to promote tourism. Spectacular mountain scenery and varied ethnic groups living in peace and harmony made Hilton's Shangri-la synonymous with an earthly paradise. Visitors to this Shangri-la enjoy similar scenery and rent bikes to visit a nearby Tibetan monastery.

Bus rides to the county from the Yunnan provincial capital, Kunming, take 12 hours; flights from there are considerably shorter and more comfortable, but not always cheap.

XISHUANGBANNA

Tourism is in full throttle in this prefecture on the border of Myanmar and Laos. Its population is mostly of the Dai nationality (closely related to the people of Thailand). Large areas of rainforest survive in the humid tropical climate, with thousands of species of trees and plants, and many rare mammals, birds and insects. Wild elephants, gibbons and the endangered golden monkey are among the protected species. Popular tourist excursions include visits to Dai stilt villages, especially during the mid-April Water-splashing Festival, and safaris to the Banna Wild Elephant Valley in the Sanchahe Nature Reserve. More adventurous souls can hire a personal guide in Jinghong and explore the jungle and remote villages independently.

Han-dynasty bronze horse at the Gansu Provincial Museum

NORTHWEST CHINA

The ancient trade route of the Silk Road connects two of the provinces visited in this section: the sprawling central western province of Gansu, with its wide open spaces and varied minority groups, and its western neighbour, Xinjiang, a vast, sparsely settled region that will have you wondering if you really are still in China. It is populated by the Uighurs, a Turkic-speaking, mainly Muslim people. To the south lies the high-altitude plateau of Tibet, another profound contrast with China proper, whose people have preserved a strong sense of identity separate to that of the Han Chinese.

LANZHOU

Two legendary thoroughfares pass through the northwestern Chinese city of **Lanzhou** ㉒: the broad, powerful Yellow River and the ancient trade route known as the Silk Road. Today this big, busy city has broad new boulevards as well as intriguing old streets of shops and houses. Adding local colour, Tibetans and members of the Muslim Hui people contribute their own customs, costumes and cuisine to the cosmopolitan mix. Of particular interest in Lanzhou is the large concentration of Hui, who resemble the Han Chinese and speak primarily Mandarin, due to their wide distribution and legacy of intermarriage. Most Hui in west China are Muslims.

Lanzhou is the capital of largely dry, barren and geographically massive Gansu province, which extends from the farmland of the Yellow River Basin through the narrow Gansu Corridor, with its steep rocky mountains, to China's far west deserts and oases. Lanzhou received its name under the Sui dynasty more than 1,000 years ago. In recent times its role as a transport centre has strengthened with the spread of the railways and air routes. Industrial development here since 1949 has transformed the city. The population of the metropolitan area is now more than 3.6 million.

The **Gansu Provincial Museum** (Gansu Sheng Bowuguan; Tue–Sun 9am–5pm; free), just across the street from the big Soviet-style Huaiyi Hotel, houses Silk Road treasures and perhaps the most famous sculpture in China, the galloping *Flying Horse of Wuwei*. With its right rear leg touching a symbolic bird, the horse is the subject of countless reproductions.

For a view of the muddy, swiftly moving Yellow River and the city along its banks, go along to **White Pagoda Hill Park** (Baitashan Gongyuan; daily 6am–6pm; charge), once a military stronghold. The temple itself, an octagonal seven-tier structure, was rebuilt in the 15th century. **Five Springs Hill Park** (Wuquanshan Gongyuan; daily 6.30am–8pm; free) climbs a steep mountainside on the opposite bank of the river. To break up the climb there are temples, pavilions and teahouses to visit and a big pond crossed by a crooked bridge. The temples date from the 14th century; one artefact, a 5-tonne bronze bell, was cast in 1202. Lanzhou and other western Chinese cities offer China's best views of the Yellow River, because this legendary waterway often dries up downstream in the dry season due to the heavy demand for its water.

Hui Muslims in Lanzhou

West of Lanzhou are the magnificent **Thousand Buddha Temple and Caves** (Binglingsi Shiku; daily 8.30am–4pm; charge), with hundreds of statues and some of China's best-preserved Buddhist cave art, and, at Xiahe, the **Labrang Monastery** (Labulengsi; daily 8am–6pm Grand Sutra Hall and Gongtang Pagoda, 8am–4pm other halls; charge), one of the largest and most active lamaseries outside of Tibet. Southeast of Lanzhou, requiring an overnight stay, is one of the greatest of China's Buddhist grottoes, the **Maijishan Caves** (Maijishan Shiku; daily 8.30am–5.30pm summer, 9am–5pm winter; charge), dating back to the 4th century.

DUNHUANG

It used to take 24 hours by train, plus a two- to three-hour bus or jeep journey, to reach the desert town of **Dunhuang**, in Gansu province. Now an easy plane ride from Xi'an or Beijing, it has come a long way since the days when the Silk Road camel trains stopped here. Camels still work in and around Dunhuang, pulling ploughs or transporting cargo. Although some donkey carts and bicycles occasionally impinge on the tranquillity of the main street, the 10,000 townsfolk have plenty of time to stand around and gossip.

In China even provincial museums can be treasure troves. The **Dunhuang County Museum** (Dunhuang Bowuguan; daily 9am–6.30pm summer, 9am–6pm winter; free) in the centre of town overflows with Silk Road relics, from works of art to 2,000-year-old chopsticks. The first hall is devoted to calligraphic rarities found in Cave No. 17 of the Mogao Caves. Paper documents have survived for 1,000 years in the dry climate of the cave. In the second room, sacrificial objects unearthed in ancient tombs are shown alongside pots, a plough and armour. Ancient handicrafts displayed in the third hall include a Tang-dynasty chess set, a present from the governor to the emperor. At the edge of town stands the **White Horse Pagoda** (Baima Ta; daily 8am–6pm; charge), reminiscent of Beijing's White Dagoba. This is where the white horse of the famous travelling Indian monk Kumarajiva (344–413) is said to have died.

The Mogao Caves

Tourists head for this 2,000-year-old town to see the Mogao Caves, which contain China's most magnificent ancient murals and painted statues, 25km (15 miles) away.

Xiahe Labrang Monastery

The **Mogao Caves** (daily 8am–6pm summer, 9am–5.30pm winter; charge), hewn from a desert cliffside, tell the story of the great flowering of Buddhist art in China. They were created in fits and starts over 1,000 years: the first caves are said to have been built by the monk Lezun in AD 366, the last ones carved out at the time of the Mongolian conquest in 1277. After that, Mogao sank into oblivion, until the monk Wang Yuanlu settled here at the beginning of the 20th century. The first cave he opened is the one now numbered 16. In the adjacent cave, No. 17, he found more than 4,000 manuscripts.

Statistics aren't everything, but consider that there are 45,000 sq m (484,000 sq ft) of mural paintings. They cover the walls and ceilings with brightly coloured pictures of men and gods and speculations about eternity. The clay of Mogao, unlike the cliff boulders of grottoes further east, is ill-suited to large carvings, so artists created stucco figurines and frescoes. And in the same caves stand over 2,000 painted sculptures, realistic or fantastical. Of the several hundred grottoes still intact, only a few dozen are open to the public. And even these are kept locked so that visits can be supervised. The outer walls of the caves have been reinforced, with walkways added. Tours cover various itineraries. Here are some highlights:

Northern Wei dynasty (386–534). Statues with Persian or Indian faces. Lifelike animal paintings with three-dimensional effects.

Sui dynasty (581–618). Illustrations of religious stories. Notice the emotions revealed in the characters' faces; also, Chinese robes have replaced foreign dress.

Tang dynasty (618–907). Don't miss Cave No. 96, a nine-tiered temple from the 7th century. The seated Buddha statue inside has toes as long as your arm. Cave No. 158 is filled with a statue of the reclining Buddha, the face particularly peaceful and godly when seen from the far left. You'll be struck by the imagination, life and colour of the Tang wall paintings.

Later dynasties. Murals from the 10th century onwards provide valuable details of everyday life in medieval China.

Crescent Moon Lake

Most of central China's desert is a sea of gravel out of which stark, rocky mountains appear. But everybody's dream desert can be seen a few kilometres south of Dunhuang. With oases in sight, awesome dunes rise in waves to 250m (800ft) crests. As the sun and clouds move, the colours and textures of the sand hills change.

Hidden between the hills is a small, clear lake – **Crescent Moon Lake** (Yueyahu, daily 5am–8.30am; charge). It's not a mirage. Reeds grow at the edge of this cool blue spring and tiny fish swim in it. You can reach the lake from the edge of the desert on the back of a camel or (if you like walking in sand) on foot. Twenty minutes each way should do it. Beside the pool is a magnificent pavilion tower with a teahouse. For a rare desert experience, climb to the top of a dune and listen to the musical – or thunderous – sound as the sand slides down. This is the same sound that Marco Polo heard – the Singing Sand Dunes (Mingshashan) – when he passed this way on his own camel caravan 700 years ago.

JIAYUGUAN

Located on the far western edge of Old China in the Hexi Corridor, **Jiayuguan** is the remote western terminus of the Great Wall. Jiayuguan Fort, built in 1372 under the Ming, retains its fortifications and towers. A Great Wall Museum has been added, and there are some 10,000 underground tombs of royal officials nearby, including the 1,700-year-old Wei-Jin tombs now open to visitors.

TURPAN

The pavements of **Turpan** ㉓ would turn to mud if it ever rained, but it almost never does. Here in the middle of the great desert in Xinjiang (Sinkiang) Autonomous Region, only 16mm (½in) of rain ever reaches the ground in an average year.

THE STRICT RULES OF THE CAVES

A notice at the entrance of the Mogao Caves lists all the things you may not do. It is forbidden to sit down or to lean on the barriers, or to carry bags, cameras, hats or sticks, for fear that these might scrape against the murals. And children shorter than 1.4m (4ft 7in) are not allowed in the caves. Although around 40 of the grottoes are open to the public, you can only see them on a guided tour, which will allow a dozen or so to visit (different caves on different days).

The murals have survived for over 1,000 years thanks to the desert climate and the pigments used – and the fact that they have not been exposed to the light. For this reason, they are not permanently illuminated today, and flash photography is strictly prohibited. Guides may shine torches on selected frescoes, adding a hint of archaeological adventure to the proceedings, and you may also use your own torch – briefly – to examine features in detail. Postcards, slides and picture books, as well as copies of the wall paintings produced by local artists, are on sale in a shop on the site.

Inside the Mogao Caves

Because of Turpan's location in the Tarim Basin – at 79m (260ft) below sea level, the second-deepest continental basin in the world – it's startling to discover here a sizeable city where houses are supplied with electricity and running water and shady trees line the streets. It's an oasis of civilisation in a cruel climate.

Turpan's secret is underground water, utilised today as it has been for thousands of years by a system of interconnecting wells *(karez)* that use gravity to relay water from the Heavenly Mountains (Tianshan) underground to the oasis. (If the aqueduct were above ground, the water would almost all be lost through evaporation.) Over the whole region, these water tunnels, all dug by hand, stretch for perhaps 3,000km (more than 1,800 miles), with some individual tunnels running as far as 40km (25 miles).

Thanks to the wells, Turpan grows cotton, melons and grapes of great sweetness and renown. And the surrounding desert is kept at bay by bountifully irrigated stands of elm, poplar and palm trees. The *karez* is an engineering feat on a par with that of the Grand

Canal, and an exhibition centre at one well site allows visitors to enter several of these hand-dug wells for a close-up view.

The climatic conditions of China's 'oven' are nevertheless hostile to humans. In the summer, when the temperature exceeds 40°C (104°F) for days at a time, the locals take refuge in cellars until the night breeze comes up. In winter the mercury plummets and residents dress for the big chill.

Turpan is about 200km (125 miles) southeast of Urumqi, the regional capital (see page 198) and reachable by car or bus. Visitors can also fly from Urumqi to the Turpan airport, which opened in 2010. It's so dry and (except for winter) hot in the oasis that tourists are advised to drink as much tea or juice as possible to prevent dehydration.

Two thousand years ago, the Silk Road traders stopped in Turpan to find water and rest. The **bazaar** of today might give you the impression that little has changed. There are outdoor butcher shops, cobblers, dentists and a shooting gallery, plus merchants selling medicinal herbs, embroidered skullcaps and tobacco by the pocketful. Makeshift restaurants dish up spicy kebabs and the bread called *nang*. The customers, mostly of the Uighur nationality – Uighurs make up 80 percent of Turpan's residents – give this Silk Road oasis a most un-Chinese atmosphere.

Minarets outnumber pagodas here, and just east of the city is **Emin Minaret** (Sugong Ta; daily 8.50am–8pm; charge), a 44m (144ft) tower of clay brick that was erected in 1778. The attached white stone mosque, with its plain interior, is the largest in the region and can hold up to 3,000 worshippers. It is only used during important Muslim festivals, although a square for vendors was also built here.

Excursions from Turpan

The most remarkable sites in the area are the ruins of two ancient desert capitals. The city of **Jiaohe** (daily 9am–6pm; charge), 10km (6 miles) west of Turpan, was founded in the 2nd century BC and laid out in a grid. Destroyed at the end of the 14th century, its sand and brick still preserve the haunting outlines of a great city that stretched for a mile, with a Buddhist temple and headless statues at the centre. There are remains of underground dwellings, which offered protection from the elements.

The underground irrigation system at Turpan

Gaochang (daily 8am–5pm; charge), a second ancient city, 46km (29 miles) east of Turpan, has an imposing city wall with a perimeter of 5km (3 miles). Gaochang reached its prime during the Tang dynasty, when it became the capital of China's western territories. During its heyday, it had 30,000 inhabitants and more than 3,000 monks in over 40 Buddhist monasteries. When Islam overtook Buddhism here in the 13th century, Gaochang was abandoned. Visitors today usually hire a donkey cart for a tour of the earthen remains.

A few miles from Gaochang is the royal **Astana Cemetery** (Astana-Karakhoja Mu; daily dawn–dusk; charge), a burial ground for Gaochang's dead, with well over 500 tombs, the oldest dating from AD 273. The cemetery was discovered by accident in 1972. Because of the almost total lack of moisture, the murals in the tombs have retained their original lively colours. Visitors can enter several of the underground burial chambers, including one where a couple buried together 12 centuries ago lie side by side, their hair and fingernails grown long.

Northeast of Turpan, the road skirts the **Flaming Mountains** (Kizilatak in Uighur, Huoyanshan in Chinese; daily 8am–9pm summer, 10am–6.30pm winter; charge). Facing south, the slopes attract and store the sun's heat – temperatures here have reached

Dinosaur finds

A number of joint Chinese-Japanese expeditions to the Xinjiang region in western China have uncovered important dinosaur fossil fields, especially from the Jurassic period.

as high as 55°C (131°F). On a sheer cliff in a gorge in these mountains perch the **Bezeklik Thousand Buddha Caves** (charge), with carvings and frescoes dating from the 5th century. These grottoes have been largely emptied by rival religious groups and by archaeological looters from the West, and the 40 painted walls and ceilings that remain have almost faded into the grey dust of the desert.

URUMQI

In Mongolian, **Urumqi** ㉔ means 'Fine Pasture'. In Uighur, it's written with umlauts: Ürümqi. The Chinese make four syllables of it. However you read or write it, Urumqi is the most distant major city in the world from any ocean or saltwater sea. The population was once mostly made up of minority and nomadic peoples, but it has been developed by the Han Chinese into a modern industrial city. The Han now make up 75 percent of its 3.5 million residents.

Though the races get along on the surface day by day, tensions simmer, making the central government nervous about separatist tendencies in this region annexed to China in 1951. Tension boiled over in 2009 with a deadly race riot targeting the Han Chinese.

Urumqi is the capital of the Xinjiang Uighur Autonomous Region, which covers one-sixth of China. The region borders Afghanistan, Pakistan, India, Tajikistan, Kyrgyzstan, Kazakhstan and Mongolia on the old Silk Road route through Central Asia, and more than half of the province's population belongs to minority groups, led by the Uighurs (see Kashgar, page 200). The greatest attractions lie well outside the city, in scenic highlands where nomads still reign.

Urumqi lies 900m (2,950ft) above sea level. City-centre avenues are broad and tree-lined, there are dozens of mosques, and the packed street markets provide splashes of colour. At the largest covered market, the **Erdaoqiao Bazaar**, vendors sell handmade goods from boots to carpets, and herds of sheep and donkey carts ply the alleyways. The most irresistible items are edible: kebabs, home-made noodles and round flatbreads, cooked on the spot over coal fires. When walking the streets, be sure to keep your valuables in a front pocket.

Xinjiang Museum (Xinjiang Bowuguan; Tue–Sun 10am–6pm summer, 10.30am–6pm winter; free), with explanatory cards in English, Chinese and Uighur, contains Silk Road coins, earrings, tiles, silks and a collection of mummies, embalmed as long ago as the 13th century BC. There are also life-sized models of the houses and tools of the most important nationalities in the region, and some 3,000-year-old corpses of European and Mongolian ancestry. The museum shops carry the main local products: Persian-style

Emin Minaret, Turpan

Silk Road circuit

Silk Road enthusiasts fly from Beijing or Xi'an in central China to Urumqi in the far west, returning via the exotic desert oases of Turpan and Dunhuang for the Buddhist cave treasures and camel rides to sand-locked lakes.

carpets, ornate skullcaps, deadly looking knives in bronze scabbards (which many of the local people carry), stringed instruments and white jade.

Two sites with Chinese characteristics on the Urumqi River, **Red Hill** (Hongshan, daily 10am–9pm; free) – topped by the 18th-century Zhenglong Pagoda – and **Hongshan Park**, on the west bank, are favourite leisure grounds for the locals.

Around Urumqi

In the **Southern Mountains** (Nanshan), 74km (46 miles) south of Urumqi, the Kazakhs move their families on horseback and set up their yurts on the high pastures to graze their sheep. At the end of the road, near an Alpine waterfall, the Kazakhs, who once rode with Genghis and Kublai Khan across these grasslands, open their village to visitors and in July stage a six-day summer fair *(nadam)* with horse races and wrestling.

A more famous scenic spot is **Heavenly Lake** (Tianchi), 120km (75 miles) east of Urumqi. It is surrounded by yurts, grazing sheep and snowy peaks, capped by Mt Bogda. Kazakh locals may be happy to share their food, shelter and horses with paying guests who want to ride the lake rim or spend the night in a yurt. The road between Urumqi and the lake passes through some lovely scenery.

KASHGAR

It's almost impossible to go any further west and still be in China. Or is it China? The airport and a Mao Zedong statue around the new city centre might make you think you could be anywhere in the country. But Old **Kashgar** ㉕ (Kashi) is pure Central Asia. The city is a two-hour flight from Urumqi, which in turn is a four-hour flight from Beijing.

Situated beside the great Taklamakan Desert, Kashgar was once an important stopover for Central Asian traders. The old part of town consists of earth-coloured low-rises, and ethnic Uighurs, most of whom are Muslim, are in the majority here. Although some Uighur women wear veils, female visitors do not need to follow the custom.

Next to the Old Town, the sprawling **Id Kah Mosque** (daily 8.50am–10pm; charge) allows visitors into its courtyard, gardens and yellow-tiled buildings – enough space for 20,000 worshippers. The mosque, built in 1442, has been restored after being damaged in the Cultural Revolution. Its highlight is a particularly ornate ceiling painting. Beyond the mosque is the new part of Kashgar, including the better hotels and a redeveloped Uighur theme street. Authorities are still chiselling away at the old Kashgar, slowly but surely rendering it more Chinese.

All of China belongs to the same time zone. But because of the distance from China's east coast where the zone makes the most sense in terms of light and dark, Kashgar uses an informal clock that runs three hours behind. Your flight will leave on Beijing time, but other appointments may be quoted in local time.

Uyghur men trade livestock in Kashgar

LHASA

Only tourists in good physical condition should venture to **Lhasa** ㉖, the capital of the Tibet (Xizang) Autonomous Region, for the altitude of 3,600m (nearly 12,000ft) taxes heart and lungs. Apart from the majestic Himalayan scenery, the top attraction in Lhasa is the **Potala**– a 1,300-year-old, 13-storey building combining the functions of palace, fortress, monastery and dungeon. The monolith spans 41 hectares (100 acres) and rises 119m (390ft) on top of Red Hill in central Lhasa. Today's complex stems from reconstruction that began in 1645 and ended only in 1936. In the 17th century it became the home of the Dalai Lama – considered in centuries past the top political and spiritual leader of Tibet – and the hub of Tibet's religious and political activities. In 1959 China turned it into a public museum (daily 9.30am–3pm; charge). It is also now a World Heritage Site. Potala's Red Palace contains stupas, Tibetan monuments to previous Dalai Lamas. Its White Palace was the Dalai Lama's residence. Visitors will find Tibetan books and records of Buddhist history in the region.

A gathering of Tibetan monks

Outside the palace, visitors can tour some of the 22 buildings in Zhol City, which once functioned as a city government centre with a mint, jail and administrative offices. Zhol City today features exhibits, some hands-on, of Tibetan arts, crafts and cooking.

Other temples, reopened since Beijing granted the Tibetans greater religious freedom in 1980, are now on the itinerary led by Jokhang Temple, Tibet's most active shrine. There is also a **Tibet Museum** (closed for renovation; expected to re-open in 2020) with costumes, *thankas* (scroll paintings) and a yak-skin boat. Increasingly Lhasa is taking on the cast of a modern Chinese city, embracing private enterprise and tourism.

To Lhasa by rail

The completion in 2006 of the highest railroad in the world, from Golmud to Lhasa, made rail service between Lhasa and Beijing possible for the first time in history. Some 80 percent of the rail route from Lhasa to Golmud, in neighbouring Qinghai province, is at an elevation of 4,000m (13,000ft). Carriages are equipped with tanks of oxygen for passengers who react badly to the altitude.

A walk through Lhasa gives an insight into the lives of ethnic Tibetans, whose appearance, language and lifestyle differ strikingly from that of the Han Chinese. Many wear colourful garb, some carry knives and most believe strongly in Buddhism, monuments to which occur on every block. A few try to talk with foreign tourists about the Dalai Lama, the spiritual leader exiled to India and ever at odds with Beijing over the future of Chinese-controlled ethnic Tibetan areas. Lhasa is also a jumping-off point for four-wheel-drive trips into the Tibetan outback, where some of China's poorest people live. Dependent on herding for a living, they are cut off from basic utilities.

After early 2008 riots over the Chinese government's role in Tibet, Beijing tightened rules for foreign tourists. Many foreign visitors join officially sanctioned Tibet tours and then break away to do their own thing if the guide doesn't mind. Check with a travel agent before booking a passage to Tibet to make sure you can legally complete the proposed trip.

Nanjing Road

WHAT TO DO

Most visitors to China come to see the nation's many excellent historic and cultural sites. But there is much else of interest in this vast land to make the journey truly enjoyable. You will want to bring home at least a few souvenirs, and you will have opportunities to attend presentations of a range of only-in-China performing arts.

SHOPPING

Most large towns now have huge department stores, and vast hypermarkets, such as the French chain Carrefour, can be found in major cities. Many of the big cities have multi-storey shopping centres with brand names and fancy cafés. Electronics can be bought from big-name domestic stores like GOME, while a range of cheaper electrical goods are sold in big supermarkets. Silks, teas, jade and porcelain are sold in shops and markets in tourist areas. Many of the bigger department stores take credit cards, but it is advisable to bring cash just in case. Shopping malls generally have a cluster of ATMs on the ground floor which usually allow withdrawals on overseas debit and credit cards for a steep bank fee. Shopping around should certainly give you the chance of finding similar items at better prices. (Avoid buying artworks and souvenirs from hotel shops, where prices tend to be inflated.) The big department stores are no longer state-owned, and new stores and malls are opening all the time. Department-store prices have risen quickly along with the country's wealth, leapfrogging some of those in the West. Symbols

Checking prices

Prices are fixed by the government at department stores, so it is useful to check prices there before purchasing a similar item on the free market.

Haggling

Rule No. 1: Anyone can do it, even foreigners.
Rule No. 2: Haggle anywhere, not just at market stalls; even the department stores expect customers to suggest a lower price. Many merchants have already inflated the original asking price so are ready to haggle.
Rule No. 3: Start at 10 percent of the asking price in a market, or at 50 to 60 percent in a store. Vendors will be neither surprised nor offended by a low bid or a polite refusal to accept the final offer.

of the consumer revolution include the enormous Oriental Plaza on Dongchang'an Jie in Beijing and the vast Nextage in Shanghai's Pudong district.

In many cities, arts and crafts department stores showcase the output of local artisans. Antiques shops specialise in old pottery, jewellery, carvings and calligraphy, as well as high-quality reproductions. Since the distribution system is unpredictable, old China hands say you shouldn't take a chance: if you find something you like, buy it, for it might not be on sale anywhere else.

Fruit, vegetables, fish and meat are sold at markets. In the free markets, where prices are more flexible, and sometimes higher (reflecting better-quality goods and greater availability), there are often other items such as wicker baskets, metalwork and clothes such as work shirts that may easily last for years. In the bigger cities, street traders offer their wares well into the evening.

WHAT TO BUY

Antiques. From fossils to ancient coins, Chinese customs regulations prohibit the export of any cultural relics dating from before 1795, the end of the reign of Emperor Qianlong during the Qing dynasty. Even more recent antiques may not be legally exported unless they are marked with a special red wax seal. All other antiques are the property of the People's Republic of China and, without the seal, will be confiscated without compensation if you try to take them out of the country. Even so, browsing for antiques is fascinating. Remember that many knowledgeable buyers will have preceded you. Remember, too, that producing fake 'antiques' (accompanied by fake official seals) is a thriving industry in China and that much of what you see is likely to be counterfeit. That said, knockoffs often look just like the real thing and can be taken out of the country.

Bamboo products. In the southern regions where bamboo grows, cottage industries turn out bamboo tea boxes, fans, flutes, chopsticks, walking sticks and furniture.

Brocades and silk. Since the time of the Han dynasty, China has been exporting delicate silk fabrics in brilliant colours. These days visitors can buy inexpensive raw silk by the metre or exquisite brocades, as well as beautifully made silk items, such as scarves, ties, shirts and blouses.

Bronzeware. Modern versions of traditional hotpots are useful in the home, as are bronze pitchers, plates and tea kettles. Vases may be engraved with intricate dragon or floral designs.

Carpets and rugs. Luxurious and colourful, Chinese rugs of wool or silk are a tempting buy. Big stores catering to tourists can arrange for shipping.

China (porcelain). Reproductions of classical designs or modern teapots, cups, plates, bowls, spoons and vases. Shrewd buyers point out that price tags always indicate the excellence

Shopping for fabric in Shanghai

Silk shop in Beijing

of porcelain (and of cloisonné ware, too). In the line of Chinese text before the actual price, look for the Chinese symbols for the numerals 1, 2 or 3 (one, two or three horizontal lines), meaning first, second or third class. If there's no number at all, it means first class.

Chopsticks. You might want to collect the appropriate utensils. Elaborate chopsticks are sold in their own fitted carrying cases – handy for a picnic or an emergency.

Cloisonné. The Chinese have been doing this type of enamelware decoration very well for several hundred years. Cloisonné is applied to plates, vases, sculptures and other items.

Ethnic novelties. Artisans from China's ethnic-minority groups produce a good share of exotica: ornaments and figurines, ceremonial knives and swords, skullcaps and other headgear, colourful dresses and shirts, and shaggy sheepskin coats.

Fans. One factory in Hangzhou alone manufactures 10 million fans per year, most of them for export. They come in several hundred varieties, but the best-known folding fans are made of fragrant sandalwood or black paper.

Figurines. Ceramic polychrome figurines of historic or legendary personages are very popular, as are little animals, especially the giant panda.

Furniture. Screens, chairs and chests made of boxwood, mahogany or bamboo and decorated with elaborately carved designs recreate the atmosphere of Old China. Shipping abroad can be arranged. Some wooden pieces come from the homes of farmers displaced by demolition and redevelopment. Prices for those may be under 100 *yuan*, especially for a hard bargainer.

Ginseng. The Chinese medicinal herb is becoming well known and popular in Western countries as a tonic. Small doses of ginseng in tea, wine or soup are claimed to be the secret of enduring vitality.

Herbs and spices. Every market has stands selling fragrant spices. Look above all for varieties that are particular to the region; in Chongqing, for instance, you might buy Sichuan dried peppers. A few *yuan* will buy an exotic gift that may be unknown or unavailable at home.

Jade. One of the hardest of stones, jade has intrigued the Chinese for at least 3,000 years, and has been used to make everything from Han-dynasty funeral robes to Qing-dynasty vases. This stone, which occurs in a range of colours, is a symbol of nobility and is worn for several reasons: as good luck, as a protection against sickness and as an amulet for travellers. Do not buy from open-air private markets unless you are confident that you know real jade from imitation.

Avoid ivory

You should not export – or even buy in the first place – objects made from wild animals, especially from ivory, as the trade is largely banned under international agreements. Ivory carvings of remarkable intricacy are a Chinese speciality, but today substitute materials are used to good effect. You are unlikely to find anything made from genuine tusk. If you did – and could afford it – it would be confiscated when you arrived home.

Kites. In windy Beijing and many other Chinese cities, high-flying kites are a favourite of both children and adults. The designs are colourful, original and elaborate.

Lacquerware. Lacquerware has been produced in China for 2,500 years. Numerous layers of lacquer, individually polished, are applied to trays, cups, vases and boxes. Lacquer also makes the ideal finish for tea and coffee services, since the material resists boiling water as well as the tannins and other chemicals in tea and coffee.

Luggage. One answer to the problem of excessive buying of souvenirs might be to buy additional luggage to carry them all home. The Chinese make good, cheap, sturdy suitcases of all sizes. Or you can pick up a local imitation of a Western executive attaché case in most public markets.

Musical instruments. Such European and Chinese musical instruments as the violin, guitar, flute and pipa (a plucked stringed instrument) are well made and usually well priced in China.

Traditional themes are reproduced by modern painters

Paintings. Squadrons of Chinese artists copy traditional drawings and paintings by hand. A long scroll can take 10 days to complete, brushstroke by brushstroke, with the details of a landscape intended to be viewed in sections, not all at once. The scrolls have the advantage of being ready rolled, which makes them easy to pack.

Paper art. The Chinese, credited with inventing paper, are thought to have devised the decorative art of paper-cutting nearly 2,000 years ago. With great skill, scissors-wielding paper-cutters produce intricate scenes suitable for framing.

Pearls. Sweet-water pearls are best bought in Beijing, while Guilin is famous for the South China Sea pearls. As with jade, you should be wary of buying these at open-air private markets.

Open-air markets are a great place to find bargains

Rubbings and reproductions. Stone rubbings of inscriptions from ancient temples, or of classical calligraphy on stone pillars, make popular (and portable) souvenirs. In some museums you will find shops selling reproductions of their most famous archaeological exhibits (for example, the flying horse of Wuwei in Lanzhou). Tiny facsimiles of the Xi'an warriors are now available all over China.

Seals. These ink stamps (also called 'chops') are the traditional Chinese substitute for handwritten signatures. You can have one carved specifically for you, with your name incised – perhaps in ancient Chinese block characters – in soapstone, plastic or jade.

Tea. A collection of Chinese teas (black, green, semi-fermented and flower-petal) makes an inexpensive and useful souvenir. Tea is often packaged in special, artistically decorated containers.

Toys. Inexpensive and unusual toys, from cuddly animals to mechanical games, are sold widely.

Woollens, clothes and shoes. An unexpected bargain in many places across China is cashmere sweaters, which are available in a wide range of styles and colours. Button-down shirts, jackets for all seasons and throwback styles of leather shoes sell for modest prices in markets and department stores, although quality can be patchy.

ENTERTAINMENT

Evening entertainment tends to start early and end early... the next morning.

CHINESE OPERA

The Chinese hospitably assume that foreigners can't bear more than about 10 minutes of traditional Chinese Opera. You might, indeed, find the voices shrill and the mannerisms maddening. But if you persevere, you will begin to understand what the Chinese see in this age-old art form. If you fail, you've still enjoyed the splendid costumes and make-up, the acrobatics that enliven some regional versions, and the experience of sharing a theatrical occasion with local people. Chinese Opera combines amusement with edification in a glittering package few Western impresarios could afford to mount. Beijing Opera is the version that is most familiar

COUNTERFEITS

Chinese manufacturers fake everything from car parts to the labels on tropical fruits. They often counterfeit with such precision that consumers cannot distinguish between fake and real except by price. Naturally the issue outrages foreign brands, such as Microsoft, whose CD-ROMs are widely pirated in Beijing, and Europe's top handbag-makers. Foreign governments routinely plead with China to step up enforcement. If a price on a North Face coat or a Gucci bag sounds too good to be true, it probably isn't true. Bulk buyers of pirated CDs or DVDs beware – customs back home may search your bags and confiscate them.

A performance of The Legend of the Red Lantern

to Westerners, but other regions, such as Guangdong and Sichuan, have their own styles.

If possible, familiarise yourself with the plot in advance. Ideologically uplifting operas were the only ones permitted during the Cultural Revolution; classical stories were banned. Ideological dramas can still be seen on television or live as spoofs. But today both classical and modern works are presented. The words of the songs are projected onto screens alongside the proscenium to clarify the nuances of a tonal language set to music.

Apart from the set pieces, most of the music is percussive and serves to support and reflect the action and mood. Props are minimal and the action is subtle: an actor closes an invisible door with a mime gesture, anyone walking with a riding crop must be understood to be mounted on a horse, and carrying an oar shows that the action takes place on a boat.

The costumes are similarly stylised and symbolic, and based on court costumes of the Han, Tang, Song and especially Ming dynasties. Make-up is equally important: the make-up artists can create more than 300 different types of mask-like faces, including likenesses of women to be worn by men. Audiences need not go to the same sartorial lengths: normal day clothes are quite acceptable at the opera.

PUPPETS, ACROBATS AND FOLKLORE GROUPS

Popular with adults and children, Chinese shadow play (a 2,000-year-old art form) dramatises familiar legends. The two-dimensional puppets, manipulated by puppeteers behind a silk screen, can jump and fly, giving the colourful silhouettes an advantage over the actors in Chinese Opera. The busy puppeteers give voice to their characters, often in song. Professional and amateur shadow-play troupes also put on shows with marionettes.

Trapeze artists are often first-class, and so are the contortionists and human pyramid acts. They also include jugglers, magicians, animal acts and even clowns, and you don't have to understand a word to join in the laughter. Almost every large town has its troupe of acrobats, many of which tour the country. In big cities such as Beijing, Shanghai and Guangzhou, there are permanent performances.

THE GREATEST NAME IN OPERA

Mei Lanfang (1894–1961) remains without question China's most celebrated opera singer. Famous from the age of 20, he sang more than a thousand dan (heroine) roles during his long career (this key female character in Beijing Opera is traditionally played by a man). Not only a performer but also a choreographer, he became the foreign ambassador for this ancient Chinese art: he appeared in Japan, in Russia and in the US, where he toured in 1929 – and forged a friendship with Charlie Chaplin. Bertholt Brecht attended the performance that Mei gave in Moscow in 1935. Today, his son Mei Baojiu continues the family tradition.

Some 'Chinese folklore' performances are organised especially for tourists. Shows feature the costumes, songs and dances of the national minority groups – often as foreign to a Chinese audience as they are to visitors from abroad.

Traditional acrobatic shows are staged throughout China

CONCERTS AND BALLET

During the Cultural Revolution, Beethoven and Tchaikovsky were banned and many Chinese musicians sent to the countryside for 're-education'. Today music from China and abroad can be heard in concert halls in the major cities. Most professional Chinese musicians have not yet reached world standards, but a few, such as Beijing-born Mandarin pop star Faye Wong, are on their way.

Ballet, which was a vehicle for ideological indoctrination during the 1960s and 1970s, has re-emerged over the years. Folk legends are often a source of inspiration, and classical European works are sometimes performed, with elaborate sets, costumes and lighting effects.

NIGHTLIFE

In Beijing, Shanghai and Guangzhou, a selection of English-language free magazines aimed at expatriates feature local nightlife and entertainment listings. Beijing has its own *Time Out* magazine as well as *City Weekend*. These publications, as well as some state-run weeklies, list restaurants, cafés, bars, concerts and art galleries, and can usually be found in Western-style bars and restaurants and some of the bigger hotels. Nightlife in China's tier-two cities is usually anchored

The Lantern Festival marks the end of the New Year holiday

by late-night restaurants-cum-beer halls and loud music bars near universities. Bartenders may be inexperienced, so if ordering a mixed drink be specific about the contents and proportions.

In the larger cities many bars and clubs have opened in recent years, and are meeting places for affluent youths. Beijing, Shanghai and Guangzhou, in particular, have big modern clubs, regularly attracting top overseas DJs. It's not unusual for parties to start late and end at dawn. Unable to find a day's listings, adventurers in Beijing might try Ladies' Street, and those in Shanghai prowl around Hengshan Road, as both have large clusters of bars and clubs. Many hotels have their own discos, which may also stay open until the early hours of the morning. Big cities also have a number of gay bars, often with drag shows at the weekend. Some hang a sign; others you just need to know about. Beijing has also accumulated a number of lounge-like clubs that have spartan cubist decor and play techno or new-age music.

The Chinese also love karaoke. Most karaoke bars are recognised by the letters 'OK' among the characters for their names. Some of these bars are intended for rich local businessmen; some are fronts for prostitution.

With varying degrees of success, the tourist hotels try to meet foreigners' demands for a quiet place to have an evening drink and a chat. Only the newest hotels, those built with international cooperation, contain bars reminiscent of those found in Europe or America. The others are likely to be quaint rather than cosy.

TRADITIONAL FESTIVALS

All official Chinese holidays are of modern invention, commemorating the triumphs of the international working class or the Chinese Communist Party (see page 244). The festivals listed below, however, are traditional rather than 'official', and provide excellent opportunities for visitors to experience Chinese culture at its best.

Chinese New Year or Spring Festival. The year's most important festival, the Lunar New Year, is also called the Spring Festival in China. On the Gregorian calendar it starts in late January or early February. The festival runs for two weeks, one of which is a government-sanctioned holiday. It is a family occasion, a time for buying new clothes, giving and receiving gifts, paying debts and eating well. The holiday ends with the Lantern Festival, a carnival of light and noise. If travelling during this holiday, book early to avoid a homecoming rush for train and air tickets.

Qingming (tomb-sweeping). This April festival is a time for honouring ancestors. The traditional sweeping of graves is not as solemn as it sounds.

Dragon Boat Festival. On the fifth day of the fifth lunar month – usually in June – this celebration recalls the ancient poet and statesman Qu Yuan (340–278 BC), who drowned in Hunan province in spite of all efforts to save him. The population threw rice cakes into the river, to try to stop the fish devouring his body. Today sweet rice cakes made with dates or nuts are served. Some cities organise dragon-boat races.

Mid-Autumn Festival. The date depends on when the harvest moon reaches its fullest – usually around mid-September. Everyone turns out to toast the full moon and hope for a big harvest. The shops do great business in 'moon cakes' (pastries filled with gooey sesame paste, red-bean and walnut filling) and *tang yuan* (glutinous rice-flour balls with sweet fillings in sugar syrup).

Confucius Festival. Late September is normally the time when Chinese communities celebrate the memory of Confucius.

Christmas. November and December are relatively quiet months in China, but Christmas is gaining momentum as a consumer celebration, even though the government does not recognise it and business goes on as usual if 25 December falls on a weekday. In Beijing, it is fashionable to exchange Christmas cards and presents, and there are even sightings of Santa Claus in some shops.

EATING OUT

While Europeans were still dining on porridge and gnawing bones, the art of good cooking was becoming an important part of China's cultural heritage. French *haute cuisine* competes with it for subtlety and sophistication, although the Chinese have been gourmets a couple of thousand years longer. It's no surprise, then, that Chinese food spans a vast variety of dishes using a wide choice of ingredients presented with sensitivity and flair.

Almost every country in the world now has Chinese restaurants. But the authenticity of the food suffers greatly when essential ingredients are hard to come by and the chef compromises with locally sourced substitutes. The most authentic Chinese food remains in China.

Skewered scorpions at a street market

WHAT TO EAT

Hard times and desperate hunger inspired the Chinese to make the most of foods others might have deemed inedible, including snakes, certain fish, and the lining gathered from swifts' nests. Large animals that require pasture lands – cows and sheep, for example – are not as common as poultry and pigs. Without doubt, pork is the most popular meat, and when a menu doesn't specify which meat is used in a particular dish, it's usually pork.

In addition, both fresh- and saltwater fish are highly prized.

The range of vegetables cultivated in China is vast, particularly in the warmer south, and includes exotic delights such as a huge range of leafy greens, bamboo shoots, water chestnuts, taro and lotus root.

Restaurants range from the traditional to the modern

The most common method of cooking is stir-frying in a wok over a very high heat. Not only does this save fuel, but it results in both crisp texture and maximum vitamin retention. Deep-frying, steaming and braising are also popular, but slowly roasted or baked meats are not, and are usually produced only in restaurant kitchens.

Few Chinese dishes feature any one ingredient exclusively. The blending of ingredients and balance of seasoning is important; common seasonings are soy sauce, ginger, garlic, vinegar, sesame oil, soybean paste and spring onions. The Chinese revel in culinary contrasts: bitter and sweet, crunchy and tender, the yellow of the pineapple and the red of the pepper.

All the dishes are shared at a typical meal for two or more; thus, the more people there are in your party the more chance you will have to sample many flavours. Using chopsticks lengthens the reach, so serving dishes don't have to be passed around, although tables sometimes have revolving platters to facilitate distribution of food.

Restaurants

Even if your hotel food is good, you're missing the adventure of a real Chinese restaurant. As you travel through China, look for restaurants specialising in regional dishes: Peking duck in Beijing, seafood in Shanghai and dim sum in Guangzhou. Your guide or hotel clerk can advise you in choosing a restaurant, ideally one rich in traditional atmosphere. If it's the high season, or if you are part of a large group, call ahead to reserve a table.

Watch out for restaurants that provide foreigners with an English menu displaying prices in excess of the Chinese version. Don't expect to be able to pay for meals by credit card. Tips are not expected in cheaper eateries, but a service charge will probably be levied in smarter establishments. Make sure that the restaurant is clean and that the food has been freshly prepared.

Bringing your own chopsticks is not considered an insult. Restaurants in southern China are often not heated, even in winter, so it is advisable to dress warmly.

When to Eat

Hotels serve breakfast 7am–8.30am or 9am, later in the far west to compensate for the delayed dawn. Breakfast is the only meal in hotels that normally offers a choice of Western-style or Chinese food. Lunch is served noon–2pm, and dinner is usually eaten 6pm–8pm or 8.30pm. Even banquets in China start early and finish by 9pm or 10pm. Some of the big hotels have restaurants that stay open after hours, for those who can't adapt to the Chinese timetable. Restaurants often shut down between meal times to give staff a break.

Chopstick basics

With a little practice, anyone can use chopsticks. Wedge one stick in the V between your thumb and index finger, resting it on your ring finger. Hold the other between the tips of your thumb, index and middle fingers. This is the one you pivot to grasp food.

Surviving a Banquet

Tourist groups are often offered banquets or formal

Freshly steamed dim sum

dinners, in which protocol problems compound any uncertainty over the food being served. The Chinese don't expect foreigners to know every bit of dining etiquette but feel better when the basic rules are followed. Here are a few guidelines to help you avoid making a faux pas.

Don't be late. Don't touch any of the food or drink until your host gives the sign that the proceedings have begun. Drink the firewater (usually *mao tai*) in your smallest glass only when toasting or replying to a toast. Taste a bit of every dish offered, but start sparingly, for there might be as many as 13 courses. There's no need to try something you don't like a second time. One by one, the prepared dishes are placed in the centre of the table. You should help yourself with a serving spoon, if provided, or with your own chopsticks. Don't take the last morsel from a serving dish; this might imply that not enough food has been provided. Don't ask for rice, which is not served at banquets; it would be tantamount to demanding a sandwich at a formal dinner. However, rice usually shows up anyway.

Regional Cuisines

Profound regional variations developed in Chinese cooking as some ingredients were readily available in one area and not another: tastes, like the climate, differ from place to place.

Most Chinese restaurants overseas feature Cantonese food because it was people from the southern Guangdong province ('Canton') who emigrated widely, opened restaurants and introduced new tastes. Cantonese chefs are renowned for a willingness to incorporate foreign ingredients. They make abundant use of fruit and many types of vegetables, as well as seafood such as prawn, abalone, squid and crab. Steaming and stir-frying methods capture the natural flavour of Cantonese food. Look for steamed dumplings filled with meat or shrimp, deep-fried spring rolls and, of course, sweet-and-sour pork or prawns. Steamed rice is the usual accompaniment.

Wheat, not rice, is the staple in the north of China, where meals involve noodles or steamed bread or dumplings. Most northern cuisine stems from Shandong province. Beijing is the place to try Mandarin fish and Peking duck. Every day, Beijing restaurants turn out thousands of roasted, crispy-skinned ducks. Diners wrap pieces of skin and meat, sprinkled with green onions and anointed with a sweet bean sauce, in the thinnest of pancakes.

In Shanghai, chefs deftly fuse contrasting flavours:

Fast-food invasion

American-style fast food has become so popular in Chinese cities that parents are concerned about the effects it is having on their children's health. Well-known American brand names are rampant, due largely to aggressive advertising. Younger Chinese also gravitate there for the bright lights, clean seating and promotional freebies. Greasy noodle bowls and other fast food from Japan and Hong Kong are catching up with the slickest of Americana.

Peking duck

sweet or salty, plus hints of garlic or vinegar. Meats are often marinated, then braised at length in soy sauce, wine and sugar. However, Shanghai is best known for its seafood, with such dishes as steamed freshwater crab, honey-fried eel, braised yellowfish and sautéed shrimp (prawns). Nearby Hangzhou has a subtle novelty, shrimp in tea sauce, permeated with the flavour of tea.

Sichuan province is the source of the peppery Szechuan recipes, which are more complicated than the first fiery taste would indicate. They combine many elements in unlikely coexistence: bitter, sweet, fruity, tart and sour. Even beancurd, which many tourists consider bland, takes on real character in the hands of cooks in Chengdu or Chongqing. But not everything on the Sichuan menu is hot; for a bit of relief, try sautéed shredded pork with spring onions and soybeans.

Neighbouring Hunan province also revels in the invigorating possibilities of the chilli pepper. But dishes here turn out less oily than in their Sichuan counterparts. The gourmets rave about Hunan's chilli-smoked pork or chicken. Another typical Hunan dish is a whole steamed fish topped with chilli peppers and crunchy beans.

Wherever you travel in China, look for the local specialities: roast lamb and pilaf rice in far-west Xinjiang, great hunks of mutton in Inner Mongolia, Yunnan's delicately smoked ham served in the thinnest slices, and sweet-and-sour fish along the Yangzi.

In the northeast, Jilin province is famous for stewed chicken with ginseng. Neighbouring Heilongjiang province offers boiling hotpots into which lamb, beef or tofu is dipped. Chefs in Shanxi blend flour noodles with meats, greens and tomatoes for spaghetti-like dishes.

If you see 'fragrant meat' on the menu, be aware that this is a euphemism for dog meat, a favourite of diners in Guangdong and in ethnic Korean regions of the northeast.

Conventions of the Table

In provincial or non-tourist restaurants, you'll notice the Chinese habit of wiping chopsticks and bowls with a paper napkin before a meal. No one takes offence at this precaution. In many parts of the country, it is common, and not considered rude, to eat rice by bringing the bowl to the lips and shovelling it in with chopsticks. It's also fine to slurp soup straight from the bowl. And don't be surprised when diners at the next table chew with their mouths open.

Roast duck

Roast duck is one of the most famous and most widely eaten delicacies of China. It usually comes with plum sauce, green onions, cucumber slices and mini pancakes into which it all gets folded and eaten. The best duck chefs are in Beijing and Guangdong. Duck doesn't have to cost much, though tour guides often steer visitors towards one of the more famous (and expensive) chains. Common restaurants, out-of-the-way hotels and even university diners may serve it.

WHAT TO DRINK

The Chinese have been enjoying wine for millennia. Each province or region has its own wine or liqueur, usually sweet and high in alcohol. It's made from local fruits, flowers or herbs.

In a Beijing teahouse

Connoisseurs recommend red and white wines from Shanghai and the dry white wine of Yantai. Rice wines come in many varieties; the most venerable is distilled at Shaoxing in Zhejiang province. In Xi'an you will be offered Xifeng wine, a colourless drink that was first made during the Tang dynasty.

Like the wines, Chinese spirits display regional variations, incorporating ingredients as ingenious as bamboo leaves, chrysanthemums and cloves. The best-known spirit, and the staple for banquet toasts, is *mao tai*, a brew from Guizhou province that hides its potency behind a rather fragrant taste.

Beer-drinkers can almost always buy Tsingtao, the hearty German-style lager brewed, the company says, from the spring water of Laoshan Mountain in Shandong province. Local brands such as Yanjing and Hapi can also be found in various regions.

Mineral waters are also available, as are fruit juices and soft drinks based on fruit flavours.

China invented tea as a beverage and has thousands of years of brewing experience. Teahouses can be found everywhere and may often feature musicians or storytellers who are on hand to entertain customers. Note that the Chinese drink their tea without sugar or milk. Among the varieties available are flower tea *(hua cha)*, fragrant green tea, tea scented with jasmine or magnolia, and slightly fermented oolong tea.

A–Z TRAVEL TIPS

A SUMMARY OF PRACTICAL INFORMATION

A Accommodation 227
Airports 228
B Bicycle Hire 229
Budgeting for Your Trip 229
C Car Hire 230
Climate 231
Clothing 232
Crime and Safety 232
D Driving 233
E Electricity 234
Embassies in Beijing 234
Emergencies 235
G Getting There 235
Guides and Tours 235
H Health and Medical Care 237
L Language 238
Laundry and Dry Cleaning 240
LGBTQ Travellers 240
Lost Property 240
M Maps 240
Media 241
Money 242
O Opening Hours 243
P Police 243
Post Offices 244
Public Holidays 244
T Telephone, email and internet 245
Time Zones 246
Toilets 247
Tourist Information 247
Transport 248
V Visa and Entry Requirements 250
W Websites 250
Y Youth Hostels 251

A

ACCOMMODATION

Accommodation for visitors on package tours is arranged in advance, sometimes in conjunction with the China International Travel Service (www.cits.net). Overseas travel agents can book rooms with many international-class hotels in China's main cities. Individual travellers can make their own advanced bookings through a number of international hotel chains: Holiday Inn and Shangri-La have the largest range of hotels in China. Increasingly, Chinese-run hotels take online bookings. A comprehensive listing can be found on www.trip.com. Hotels are busiest – and sometimes full – in the peak months of May, September and October. Low season runs from after the Lunar New Year, usually in February, to late March, when conferences and tour groups occupy many rooms. But if you have confirmed reservations, your room will be kept for you, as hotels rarely overbook.

Chinese hotels range from first-class – complimentary breakfast, in-room Wi-Fi, cable TV, business centre open late – to grimly spartan. The newest hotels, often built with foreign cooperation and with foreign management, bear a close resemblance to their counterparts in Europe or North America, although service standards frequently fall short. Usually the prices of these better hotels are in line with hotel prices in the West. Among the top in their class are the funky Hotel G in Beijing and the imposing got-it-all Portman Ritz-Carlton in Shanghai.

The more spartan places, often near railway or bus stations, may refuse foreign guests due to Public Security Ministry restrictions. Paid homestays and B&Bs are rare.

Worth mentioning are a few well-preserved hotels built by the colonial powers in some cities. They include the Peace Hotel (Heping) in Shanghai, the People's Hotel (Renmin Dasha) in Xi'an and the Astor Hotel (Lishunde Dafandian) in Tianjin.

In almost every room you'll find cups and a large thermos of hot water for making tea; a small container of tea is often supplied as well.

Bottled water or water coolers are provided in most quality hotels. As a rule, never drink water from the tap, though some of the top hotels may provide potable tap water. China's toilets and showers are notorious for flooding, even in the most luxurious rooms. Rooms may come with cable TV, but media restrictions reduce the full range of channels.

Postal and tour desks, a foreign-exchange facility, at least one restaurant, a café and gift shops are usually on the ground floor.

Single room **Danren fangjian**
Double room **Shuangren fangjian**

AIRPORTS

All internal flights are handled by China's domestic air carriers, which now fly advanced Western-purchased aircraft to most major destinations and a number of newer ones such as Kashgar and Lijiang. Beijing's Capital Airport (airport code: PEK) has cafés, restaurants and a teahouse in addition to the usual facilities. Banks inside the arrivals hall can change foreign currency, and local currency can be withdrawn on several ATMs. Flights from Beijing to Shanghai take about 90 minutes, to Hong Kong just under three hours and to Urumqi in the far west more than four hours. The 2008 opening of Beijing's third terminal, which is cut off from the other two, complicates transit for some. Be sure to ask in advance from which terminal your flight will leave.

Airport transport. The fastest way to get to the city centre is by train (Airport express line). The journey takes no longer than 20 minutes: the cost of one way ticket is 25 RMB. Airport buses run from Beijing's terminals to the city centre and suburban areas. Taxis are also available for the 40-minute journey into town. Many international hotels provide some form of airport shuttle or transfer. Make arrangements with hotels well ahead of your arrival. Near the main entrance there are desks where transfer to city hotels can be arranged. If you are taking a taxi, join the queue of people waiting for a cab on the pavement just outside the terminal. Drivers and touts mill about outside the customs area and on the kerb, but they should be avoided, as they charge twice or three times the going rate for the ride.

Buses run by CAAC (the Civil Aviation Administration of China) link airports with their offices in many towns and cities. Shanghai's Pudong International Airport is linked to the metro system by a high-speed MagLev train. Several airports in China, such as Chongqing and Nanjing, are situated far from the city centre, so it is important to calculate how long it will take you to reach the airport by taxi or bus.

Arrival. Customs procedures are generally straightforward, and foreign tourists are usually paid little attention. Standard rules found in almost any country apply to what travellers may bring into China.

Departure. Be sure to arrive at the airport two hours before check-in time, as crowds can form and flights are often delayed, rescheduled or even cancelled shortly before takeoff. Departure tax is now usually included in the price of the ticket.

B

BICYCLE HIRE

You can hire bicycles in many Chinese cities at bike shops, via tour agents or online. Cyclists may pick out bikes in advance at www.bikechina.com, among other English-language websites. It is advisable to get a strong U-lock or park your cycle at a guarded parking space for a small fee. China has almost as many bicycle thieves as bicycles!

BUDGETING FOR YOUR TRIP

Prices for tourist accommodation, meals, sightseeing and entertainment bear no relationship to the local cost of living. To give an idea of what to expect, here are some approximate figures; note that they are subject to regional, seasonal and inflationary variations.

Airport transfer. Taxi from Beijing Airport to city about 85 *yuan*.
Car and driver. 400 *yuan* per day (8 hours or 120km/75 miles).
Entertainment. Formal theatre or Chinese Opera performance 100–200 *yuan*.
Entry fees (museums, scenic spots, temples and walled cities). 2–180 *yuan*.
Haircuts. Under 50 *yuan* at local places, 100 *yuan* plus at top joints.
Hotels (double room with bath). Luxury international class 1,200– 2,500 *yuan*; moderate 600–1,200 *yuan*. Smaller cities charge less, often just half the rate for the same amenities with less pomp. Budget hotels, usually not far from rail and bus stations, may charge well under 100 *yuan* per night for a simple bed. Rates vary according to the season.
Meals and drinks. Lunch for one in moderate restaurant 20–60 *yuan*; in expensive restaurant 80–150 *yuan*. Dinner in moderate restaurant 50–150 *yuan*; in expensive restaurant 100–400 *yuan*. Imported spirits 50 *yuan* per drink; Chinese beer in bar 15–30 *yuan*; in shop approx. 3 *yuan*; imported beer 40–60 *yuan*. Cup of coffee 10–35 *yuan*.
Transport. City bus 0.5–3 *yuan*. Taxi from Beijing railway station to Tiananmen Square 11 *yuan*; taxi from Beijing Hotel to Temple of Heaven 25 *yuan*; from central Shanghai to Pudong Airport, about 150 *yuan*.

C

CAR HIRE

For visitors, China is not an easy country in which to drive, and, although rentals are available (www.zuche.com, http://chinaairportcarrental.com) and officially posted road rules generally match those found in the West, driving conditions are appalling and highly dangerous. Taxis are the usual choice, both readily available through hotels and on any major street in larger cities, especially near railway and bus stations. It's often possible to arrange for a taxi by the hour, half-day or full day, for a rate seldom exceeding 400 *yuan*. Taxis are fairly inexpensive for getting around town (usually 15–50 *yuan* per trip, depending on the distance travelled). Receipts can be provided; insist that the taxi drivers use their meters and hand over receipts for any road tolls, oil price surcharges and other incidentals.

CLIMATE

China is a vast country, encompassing a variety of different climates. Summer lasts more than six months of the year in Guangzhou (Canton), but flits past in only 15 days in far western Urumqi. In January the mean temperature in Harbin, in the northeast, is –19°C (–2°F) while Guangzhou, in the south, basks at 14°C (57°F). Summers bring continental monsoon rains, high heat and a degree of humidity to all but the far north and high elevations, with temperatures well over 30°C (86°F). The hottest cities are along the Yangzi – Nanjing, Wuhan and Chongqing. Beijing can also top 40°C (104°F) at the peak of summer. In general, the best seasons all over China are spring and autumn, when most areas have moderate temperatures. Some average monthly temperatures, factoring in daytime highs and overnight lows:

		J	F	M	A	M	J	J	A	S	O	N	D
Beijing	°F	25	28	39	55	68	77	79	77	68	55	39	27
	°C	-4	-2	4	13	20	25	26	25	20	13	4	-3
Guangzhou	°F	57	59	64	72	79	81	84	84	81	75	68	59
	°C	14	15	18	22	26	27	29	29	27	24	20	15
Shanghai	°F	37	39	46	57	66	75	82	82	75	64	55	43
	°C	3	4	8	14	19	24	28	28	24	18	13	6
Xi'an	°F	27	36	46	57	68	79	81	79	68	55	45	34
	°C	-3	2	8	14	20	26	27	26	20	13	7	1
Guilin	°F	46	48	56	65	74	79	83	82	78	69	59	50
	°C	8	9	13	18	24	26	29	28	26	21	15	10

CLOTHING

Be sure to pack sweaters and rainwear. For winter, a warm overcoat is essential and thermal underwear is a definite boon; gloves, scarves and hats make worthy accessories. All can be bought in China, if necessary, at reasonable prices.

Tourists may dress with relative informality, with shorts acceptable in warmer months and especially on beaches, although business visitors should wear suits and ties for important meetings or banquets. In general, try to avoid dressing shabbily. Dark colours are safer than flashier ones. Men should be careful with green clothes, especially caps, as the colour symbolises being abandoned by one's wife. Perhaps the most essential item is a durable pair of walking shoes.

CRIME AND SAFETY

Crime exists in China, as it does in all countries, but official statistics show the incidence of violent crime is low in comparison with Western societies. Attacks do occur, however. It is wise to be wary of pickpockets and petty thieves around tourist sites, on public buses and in markets and in poorly lit underpasses. Use a money belt or front pockets. Avoid accompanying strangers who strike up conversations and offer to act as your guide; not all of them have honourable motives. Stay out of public brawls or arguments following minor accidents, as a foreigner's involvement may offend face-conscious Chinese people.

Chinese men are generally not intimidating towards women, though plenty will stare, and female travellers usually feel safe travelling in China. You can usually walk freely at any time of day or night without fear, especially in a group. The most common hassles are fending off hustlers eager to sell you something, and avoiding beggars, who may give chase and grab at your pockets.

Victims of theft or violent crimes can file reports at police dispatch stations or call 110. Chinese bystanders will often offer to help.

Call the police! **Jiao jing cha!**
Help! **Jiu ren a!**
Danger! **Wei-xian!**
Police officer **Jingcha**
Dispatch station **Paichusuo**

Visas. Every visitor to China must possess a valid passport, and most from Western countries must get a visa issued in advance by Chinese authorities outside mainland China. Travel agencies, particularly in Hong Kong, can arrange visas for groups and individuals. Be sure to determine your need for a visa well in advance of your departure.

Independent travellers should apply in advance to the China International Travel Service (CITS), China Travel Service (CTS) or the nearest Chinese Consulate or Embassy. Additional charges are levied for urgent service, if required. The minimum time for delivery varies from overnight in Hong Kong to 10 days in most other places.

Health requirements. No special inoculation certificates are required, except for visitors arriving in China within six days of leaving or passing through an area infected by yellow fever, though the odds of an officer demanding the certificate are low.

Leaving China. Antiques may not be exported from China unless a special wax seal is attached (and antiques dating from before 1795 may not be exported at all). To change money on departure, you might need to show exchange receipts.

DRIVING

Chinese drive on the right side of the road, though the rules are not strict and cars may be found straddling lane dividers, including the centre. Laws suggest that drivers pass on the left. China regularly posts speed limits, from 40km/h (25mph) on smaller highways to 120km/h (75mph) on expressways. Foreign drivers who have accidents should call the police on 110 and be prepared to show a passport and driver's licence for insurance purposes.

E

ELECTRICITY

In principle the electricity supply everywhere in China is 220 volts/ 50 cycles. In practice the voltage lapses significantly from time to time. Blackouts periodically occur outside major cities. Socket types and sizes vary, but most are two-pronged, and larger hotels can usually lend adaptors.

EMBASSIES IN BEIJING

Australia: 21 Dongzhimenwai Dajie, Beijing, tel: (10) 5140-4111; fax: (10) 5140-4204; www.china.embassy.gov.au

Canada: 19 Dongzhimenwai Dajie, Beijing, tel: (10) 5139-4000; fax: (10) 5139-4449; www.canadainternational.gc.ca/china-chine/offices-bureaux

France: Faguo Zhuhua Dashiguan, 60 Tianze Lu, Beijing, tel: (10) 8531-2000; www.cn.ambafrance.org

Germany: 17 Dongzhimenwai Dajie, Beijing, tel: (10) 8532-9000; fax: (10) 8532-9281; www.china.diplo.de/cn-de

Republic of Ireland: 3 Ritan Donglu, Beijing, tel: (10) 8531-6200; fax: (10) 6532-6857; www.dfa.ie/irish-embassy/china/

Italy: 2 Dong'er Jie, Sanlitun, Beijing, tel: (10) 8532-7600; fax: (10) 6532-4676; www.ambpechino.esteri.it/ambasciata_pechino

New Zealand: 1 Dong'er Jie, Ritan Lu, Beijing, tel: (10) 8532-7000; fax: (10) 6532-4317; www.mfat.govt.nz/en/countries-and-regions/north-asia/china/new-zealand-embassy

South Africa: 5 Dongzhimenwai Dajie, Beijing, tel: (10) 8532-0000; fax: (10) 6532-0181; www.dirco.gov.za/beijing/

UK: 11 Guanghua Lu, Beijing, tel: (10) 5192-4000; fax: (10) 5192-4239; www.gov.uk/government/world/organisations/british-embassy-beijing

US: 55 An Jia Lou, Jianguomenwai Dajie, Beijing, tel: (10) 8531-3000;

fax: (10) 8531-4200; https://china.usembassy-china.org.cn/

Embassy **Dashiguan**
Passport **Huzhao**
Visa **Qianzheng**

EMERGENCIES

When in doubt about an emergency, phone 110. Ambulances can be reached at 120, and traffic police respond to 122. Most duty officers do not speak English, though it doesn't hurt to try it.

G

GETTING THERE

By air. Most international airlines have direct or connecting flights to Beijing, Shanghai and Hong Kong. CAAC, the Civil Aviation Administration of China, consists of more than 20 small airlines; of these, the three largest – Air China (www.airchina.com.cn), China Eastern (http://noa.ceair.com/) and China Southern (www.csair.com) – offer regular international flights to most major cities in Asia, Europe and North America.

Airport **Feijichang**
Railway station **Huoche zhan**

GUIDES AND TOURS

Many tour operators in Europe and the United States offer group tours to China. The cost usually includes flight, full-board accommodation in China, excursions, internal travel in China, services of local guides and interpreters. Groups consist of between 12 and 50 people. Visits to farms, factories, hospitals, schools and other places difficult to visit on one's own may be included on a group tour, as well as trips to the top historic and scenic locations. Evening entertainment might include ethnic dance and music or a Chinese Opera. The nation's main tour operator for foreigners is China International Travel Service (www.cits.net).

Special interest and adventure tours. Alternative itineraries (but still in group format) are available for travellers with specialist interests: from acupuncture to archaeology, martial arts to minority cultures. On these sorts of tours, time might be spent in meetings with professional counterparts or visiting relevant institutions or sites. For those with a yen for adventure, there are tours featuring trekking, mountain-climbing, wilderness exploration and cross-country cycling. Eco-tourism has also caught on in China. You can find a list of possibilities at www.viator.com.

Independent travel. Those travelling independently will have more opportunity to wander off the beaten track. Many independent travellers enter China from Hong Kong. Part of China since 1997 and known officially as the 'Hong Kong Special Administrative Region' (SAR), this is the easiest place to obtain last-minute visas and make travel arrangements. There are air, rail, road and sea links between Hong Kong and many major destinations in China.

Private English-speaking travel agents in Hong Kong offer a variety of all-inclusive China tours, from a one-day excursion across the border to Shenzhen to a full two- or three-week agenda taking in major cities and sights. Independent travellers can also make arrangements in Hong Kong through the local offices of China Travel Service (CTS) or China International Travel Service (CITS). In general, CTS handles travel for Overseas Chinese, while CITS (Guoji Luxingshe) is responsible for foreign tourists of non-Chinese descent, although this distinction is fading. Flights into China can also be booked using Hong Kong-based Cathay Pacific (www.cathaypacific.com), Dragonair (www.cathaypacific.com), or China Southern (www.csair.com).

H

HEALTH AND MEDICAL CARE

Respiratory diseases are always on the prowl due to the dense population and sub-par hygiene habits. The minor ailments that most often seem to strike foreign tourists are coughs, colds and sore throats. Digestive upsets occasionally result from drinking contaminated water or eating unhygienically prepared food. Avoid partially cooked or raw food, except the salad in top hotels. Drink only boiled or bottled water. Avoid ice cubes unless you're sure they come from treated water sources.

Take with you any essential medications, as it is difficult or impossible to find Western medications and treatments outside major cities. If you plan to visit a region in which malaria occurs, you must begin treatment before your trip and continue for a specified time after leaving the affected area.

Should you require medical care in China, your guide, hotel desk clerk or local CITS office will call a doctor or arrange for you to be taken to a hospital. Considering the language problem, it's a relief to have an interpreter when discussing symptoms and treatment. Most Chinese doctors, especially those treating foreign visitors, are extremely well qualified in Western medicine and can give expert care. Among the clinics in China more popular with foreigners is International SOS (www.internationalsos.com), which has 24-hour centres in Beijing (tel: 10-6462-9100), Shanghai (tel: 21-5298-9538), Guangzhou, Nanjing, Tianjin and Shenzhen.

You can find other clinics as well as multi-discipline hospitals staffed by Western-trained doctors in cities with large expat populations, such as Beijing, Guangzhou, Shanghai, Tianjin and Qingdao. Treatment may be expensive, so taking out appropriate insurance ahead of travel is highly recommended. Treatment can involve both modern and traditional medicine if you request it.

Chinese pharmacies usually operate independently of hospitals, but are clustered near the larger ones. They carry a growing range of prescription and non-prescription drugs, Chinese herbal cures and basic toiletries. If there is no pharmacy sign in English, look for white characters on a background. Many pharmacies are open late into the evening.

Pharmacy **Yaodian**
Hospital **Yiyuan**
Doctor **Daifu/yisheng**

L

LANGUAGE

Chinese is the native tongue of more people than any other language. The written language that binds them is universal, but spoken Chinese is fragmented into dialects, some of them mutually incomprehensible. The vocabulary and much of the grammar are the same, the writing is the same, but the pronunciation differs so much that a native of Guangzhou, for instance, cannot understand a citizen of Shanghai and vice versa unless they speak the national language, Putonghua (better known in the West as Mandarin). In the interests of national unity and understanding, the government encourages the use of Putonghua, which is based on the dialect spoken in Beijing.

Every syllable of Putonghua is pronounced with one of four tones (high, rising, falling-rising and falling), and is paired with a distinct written Chinese character. Tones can have a significant effect on meaning. For example, *ma* pronounced with a high tone means 'mother', with a rising tone 'hemp', with a falling-rising tone 'horse', and with a falling tone 'to curse' or 'to shout at'. It can be very difficult for non-natives who have just arrived in the country even to hear these tones, let alone reproduce them – hence the phonetic transliteration system used here has been simplified, and excludes tonal markers.

Written Chinese is based on the pictographs that have told the story of China for thousands of years. In the interests of greater literacy, the government has simplified many of the traditional characters, but not enough to make it easy for foreigners, especially those who are only visiting for a short period. There is also a well-established and universal system for romanising Chinese words: the *pinyin* (literally 'phonetic sound') system is the reason 'Peking' is now written 'Beijing'.

Pronouncing *pinyin* has its own nuances and complications. Among the biggest stumbling blocks for foreigners are the following consonants (accompanied by approximate English equivalents).

c like ts in the word 'i**ts**'

Hello **Ni hao**
How are you? **Ni hao ma?**
Thank you **Xiexie**
Goodbye **Zai jian**
My name is... **Wo jiao...**
All right **Hao**
Not all right **Bu hao**
Can you speak English? **Nin hui shuo Yingyu ma?**
I do not understand **Wo bu dong**
Do you understand? **Nin dong ma?**
Please speak a little more slowly **Qing nin shuo man yidianr**
Please **Qing**
Sorry **Duibuqi**

g hard g as in '**g**ive'
h like ch in Scottish 'lo**ch**'
j like j in '**j**eer'
q halfway between ch in '**cheer**' and ts in the word 'its'
x like the letters h and s said together, 'hs'
z like ds in 'ki**ds**'
zh like j in '**j**ug'

The great majority of Chinese people know only a few standard phrases of English, although they may be able to read much more, as schools focus more on the written word. Conversations can become painfully stilted. Hotel and airline employees and others who deal with foreigners have usually learnt enough English to cope with everyday problems. Tour guides are trained to specialise in one or more foreign languages, but not all of them have a firm grasp of English. To make yourself understood, you might need to speak slowly, clearly and simply.

LAUNDRY AND DRY CLEANING

Hotels process laundry, dry cleaning and ironing quickly and efficiently; same-day or express service is common, though prices may be steep. There are laundries and dry cleaners *(ganxi)* outside hotels, but they are inconvenient for most foreigners to use.

LGBTQ TRAVELLERS

A few clubs, including one with the odd drag show modelled after Beijing Opera, welcome the LGBTQ community in Beijing. There is no palpable 'gay scene' per se. Travellers of any sexual persuasion will receive borderline hostile stares from locals for excessive displays of affection in public.

LOST PROPERTY

If you lose something valuable, file a police report and tell your hotel desk and tour guide. It's unlikely, but not unheard of, that valuables are returned to their owners.

M

MAPS

Hotels and tourist offices often issue free English-language tourist maps of major cities such as Beijing, Shanghai and Guangzhou. Maps can also be bought from hawkers outside railway stations, at bookshops, newspaper kiosks and tourist sights. Local maps are occasionally folded into English-language magazines. Some on the streets and in the stores are available in English and Chinese, though most in Chinese only. China's foremost mapmakers are the provincial cartography bureaux. China's chief news agency and book publisher, Xinhua, does maps as well, including online versions made in conjunction with Google.

MEDIA

Newspapers and magazines. Some foreign publications are sold at the news kiosks of major hotels, most commonly the *International Herald Tribune*, the *Asian Wall Street Journal*, the *South China Morning Post* (from Hong Kong) and one or two major dailies from Europe. International weekly news magazines and even some fashion and sports magazines are sometimes available, although in smaller or more remote places you might find nothing in a foreign language at any newsstand.

The Chinese English-language newspaper *China Daily*, and sometimes its weekly publication, *Beijing Weekend*, can be found in hotels, at newsstands and often in flight. The *Shanghai Daily*, found in its namesake city, is also available for English readers. These publications cover Chinese and foreign news, tourist features, sports and stock-market reports. Do not expect to read about internal dissent, political agitation abroad or other news that makes the Chinese government nervous.

Beijing, Guangzhou and Shanghai have a growing list of magazines aimed at expats, which are a useful source of local information and events listings. Such official government periodicals as *Beijing Review* and *Beijing This Month* are published in English.

Travellers with Internet access can access a few overseas English-language news websites; the censorship row with Google has brought more restrictions on Internet use, and even more websites are liable to be blocked during sensitive political periods.

Television and radio. Whether or not you understand Chinese, you will probably have a chance to catch a glimpse of the state-run television system. Features include the Chinese equivalent of soap operas, news bulletins, Chinese Operas, films, sports events and relentless advertising. Virtually all hotel rooms come with TVs (usually with CCTV9, the English-language channel), while many hotels also offer closed-circuit broadcasts of foreign-language films, news from overseas and satellite TV.

Some English-language programmes of interest to tourists, including news and weather reports, are broadcast on Chinese radio for the benefit of expatriates and locals seeking to practise English. In most parts of the country, a shortwave radio can pick up the BBC World Service, Voice of America and Radio Australia.

MONEY

Currency. The standard currency in China, called *renminbi* ('people's money', abbreviated as RMB), is based on the *yuan* (colloquially *kuai*), which is divided into 100 *fen*. Ten *fen* make a *jiao* (colloquially *mao*). For the most part, you will be using *yuan* notes, which come in denominations of 1, 2, 5, 10, 20, 50 and 100. One-*yuan* coins are increasingly common.

Banks and currency exchange. Foreign currency can be exchanged for RMB at international airports, hotels and – for the best rates – branches of the Bank of China. You'll have to show your passport.

Credit cards and traveller's cheques. Credit cards are accepted more and more in tourist areas. ATMs machines with international access have appeared in large cities, making cash withdrawals possible, but don't count on finding such machines. Bank fees for withdrawals may be steep. Most major hotels accept credit cards to pay all bills. Traveller's cheques are recognised at money-exchange counters in hotels, banks and some shops. China is still largely a cash society, and most transactions outside the big hotels will require a wallet full of *yuan* bills. For example, most transport costs – domestic bus and train tickets – are paid in cash, although air tickets can often be bought with a credit card.

Traveller's cheque **Luxing zhipiao**
Credit card **Xinyongka**
Foreign currency **Waihuiquan**

O

OPENING HOURS

Shops. Department stores are usually open from 9am to as late as 9pm, seven days a week, including public holidays. Local shops sometimes stay open later, especially in crowded commercial districts frequented by younger shoppers.

Banks, museums and temples are open daily 9am–5pm. In large hotels, foreign-exchange facilities and desks are routinely open 24 hours, seven days a week, but be sure to enquire about exact hours when you check in.

Restaurants are typically open 8am–10am for breakfast (if at all), 11.30am– 2pm for lunch, and 5–9.30pm for dinner, but these hours can vary greatly. In large towns and cities, especially as Chinese people get richer and eat out more often, restaurants tend to stay open later.

P

POLICE

Armed police, often referred to as military police, wear green uniforms and peaked caps displaying the national insignia. They are the only people in China who regularly carry firearms in public. They appear most often in Beijing's embassy district, where they look after diplomatic property, outside the Zhongnanhai leadership compound and wherever national leaders may be travelling. Tourists commonly confuse the armed police with members of the air force, who wear an identical uniform except for the red star on the cap. Common cops, who patrol streets and pursue everyday criminals, wear dark-blue uniforms. Young men standing outside stores in grey or light-green uniforms are security guards with no police power. The emergency telephone number for police assistance is 110.

POST OFFICES

Most neighbourhoods and office buildings have branch post offices or postal service desks. Some are open seven days a week. They sell stamps, paper, packaging boxes and postcards, and process mail for overseas delivery. Chinese envelopes are generally made without glue, as are some stamps, so a gluepot is provided. Street-side mailboxes in China are red or green cubes or tubes emblazoned with the English words 'China Post'. Airmail letters and postcards take seven to 10 days to reach overseas destinations; surface mail travels very slowly.

If you expect to receive mail while in China, ask correspondents to address letters to the hotels where you'll be staying. Courier services are also available in major cities.

Airmail **Hangkong xin**
Postage stamp **Youpiao**
Post office **Youju**

PUBLIC HOLIDAYS

Public holidays in China are declared yearly, around twenty days prior to New Year's Day. In general, offices and factories close nationwide on only seven public holidays:

New Year's Day 1 January
Spring Festival Mid-Jan to Mid-Feb, varies year to year
Tomb-Sweeping Day 4 April or 5 April, varies year to year

International Labour Day 1 May
Dragon Boat Festival Varies year to year (usually in June)
Mid-Autumn Festival Varies year to year (in September or October)
National Day 1 October
Other holidays, of modern origin, have little effect on daily life:
Women's Day 8 March
Youth Day 4 May
Children's Day 1 June
Communist Party Founding Day 1 July
Army Day 1 August
Lunar New Year, or the Spring Festival, starts in late January or early to mid-February. Exact dates shift according to the lunar calendar. It lasts for two weeks (the government allows workers seven days off work) through the Lantern Festival and is primarily a family holiday. National Day is the second week-long holiday. The holiday, beginning 1 May, is three days long.

T

TELEPHONE, EMAIL AND INTERNET

Telephone. The country code for China is **86**. To dial China directly from abroad, you must first dial the international access code, then 86, then the city code of your destination in China (for example, Beijing's code is 10; Shanghai's is 21), then the local Chinese number.

To make a long-distance call within China (for example, from Beijing to Shanghai), dial 0 plus the city code, then the local number. Domestic long-distance calls are cheap, but direct-dial international calls are expensive. To make an international direct-dial call from China, dial 00 plus the country code, then the area code and the number. Convenience stores and news kiosks sell stored-value cards for discounted long-distance calls. Follow the instructions in English on the backs of cards. Basically, you call toll-free, enter your card number followed by a password printed on the card and then dial the number you wish to call.

Local calls from your hotel may be free (check this before phoning) and are typically very cheap from card-operated public phones and kiosks.

If you have a mobile phone with international roaming, you will be able to use it in China. Although the rules are always changing, most of the time travellers can find prepaid SIM cards in airports or at China Mobile service counters in any business district.

Email and the Internet. Most hotels will have computers available in their business centres, for which they charge varying hourly rates. Travellers with laptops can use broadband connections in the rooms of more modern hotels. Check rates before signing on and use only PCs with updated virus-protection software. Internet connections in China range in speed, depending on who provides the service and how your building is wired. Internet cafés operate in most Chinese cities, with higher concentrations in the university districts, and usually charge two to four *yuan* per hour. Many coffee shops, bars and cafés now offer free wireless Internet in the bigger cities such as Beijing and Shanghai.

Telephone **Dianhua**
Long-distance call **Changtu dianhua**
International call **Guoji dianhua**

TIME ZONES

Although China extends across the longitudes, there is only one time zone in the whole country. China does not change the clocks for summer time. Standard time is GMT +8. The following chart shows time differences in winter:

Los Angeles	New York	London	**Beijing**	Sydney
4am	7am	noon	**8pm**	11pm

TOILETS

Public toilets throughout China, especially in towns and villages, are truly ghastly. Toilet facilities at tourist sights may be better, but prepare for overpowering smells and medieval standards of hygiene. Expect a squat toilet and always carry a supply of tissues with you. Travellers can identify toilets by the telltale alphabet letters 'WC'. Caricatures of men and women indicate which gender goes where.

Toilet **Cesuo**

TOURIST INFORMATION

Travellers keen to plan ahead can find routes and booking assistance from China International Travel Service (CITS; www.cits.net; info@cits.com.cn). CITS is geared towards foreigners, so its website contains elaborate English-language descriptions of tours. Staff members speak English, among other languages commonly used by inbound tourists. The China National Tourist Office (www.cnto.org) may have additional tips.

As China opens its tourism industry to private and foreign vendors, newer agencies such as www.ctrip.com and www.chinatour.com have edged in on the one-time government monopoly with new tours. Travellers starting in Hong Kong may consult China Travel Service at www.ctshk.com/english.

China lacks a coordinated, nationwide chain of tourist offices. That gap leaves travellers on their own to track down regional tourist offices or, more likely, privately run travel desks. Those usually turn up in hotels, airports, railway stations and airline ticketing offices. Many desk agents are friendly English-speakers who know the local scene.

Beijing Tourist Information Centre: 27 Sanlitun Beilu; tel: 10-6417-6627.

Shanghai Tourist Information Centre: 561 Nanjing Donglu; tel: 21-5353-1117.

Branches of **China National Tourist Office** abroad include:

Australia: China National Tourist Office, 11th floor, 234 George Street, Sydney, NSW2000; tel: (02) 9252 9838; fax: (02) 9252 2728.

Canada: China National Tourist Office, 480 University Avenue, Suite 806, Toronto, Ontario, M5G 1V2; tel: (416) 599-6636; fax: (416) 599-6382.

UK: China National Tourist Office, 71 Warwick Road, Earl's Court, London, SW5 9HB; tel: (020) 7373 0888; fax: (020) 7370 9989.

USA: China National Tourist Office, 370 Lexington Ave, Suite 912, New York, NY 10017, tel (toll-free): (212)-760 8218; fax: (212) 760 8809.

TRANSPORT

Domestic flights. Air service inside China is handled by domestic airlines. The air fleet is rapidly expanding and airports are being built and expanded throughout China, but delays are still common as capacity runs slightly behind demand, especially during peak travel seasons. On-board service on domestic flights varies greatly; refreshments, including full meals, are usually served.

Trains. The national railway serves all the major cities and tourist centres. Although train trips can take a very long time, a journey on a Chinese train can be an enjoyable and enlightening experience.

Express trains, such as the sleek high-speed services between Beijing and Shanghai, are more expensive than regular services, and sleeping berths attract an additional charge. Berths and seating are divided into the categories 'soft' and 'hard'. The hard seats are usually quite crowded as they are cheapest. The hard bunks are stacked in columns of three in open train carriages; the soft ones number four per private room. Tickets cost just a few dozen *yuan* for hard-seat trips of an hour or two to several hundred *yuan* for overnight journeys. Reserve a few days ahead in case the route you want sells out.

Passengers travelling first class (both Chinese and foreigners) have access to a separate waiting room at some provincial railway stations.

Trains between most major east coast and southern cities run at least once a day, usually more often. Some, such as from Beijing to Shanghai or Beijing to Xi'an, start at night and arrive after dawn, taking the place of an overnight hotel stay. Beijing, Tianjin and a few other cities have multiple railway stations, so ask the ticket-seller to be clear about which one you need. Check schedules online for major cities at www.cnvol.com.

Boats. Travelling through China by boat has its delights: the scenery, the comfort and the relaxed pace. However, the number of boats and routes has dwindled in recent years as an increasing number of people fly and travel by car and train.

Taxis. Almost everywhere in China, taxis can be hailed on the street. There are no taxi ranks, but you will find clusters near hotels, shopping malls, transit hubs, bar districts and convention centres. A restaurant can help call a taxi, but if you're out on your own sightseeing for a couple of hours, it might be more convenient to take a cab company's phone number to call for a pickup. In Beijing, to call a taxi, dial 96103. In Shanghai, where taxis can run short during commute hours, call the biggest company, Da Zhong Taxi (tel: 96822). For short trips, insist on using the meter *(dabiao)*; receipts are issued on demand. Meters usually charge 1.6 to 3 *yuan* per kilometre, with a per-trip minimum of 8 to 11 *yuan*. It may be cheaper to haggle for a flat price if a trip exceeds one hour.

Metro. China's first underground railway, the Beijing metro (www.bjsubway.com/en, tel: 96165, carries more than 9.2 million passengers a day quickly and cheaply. Trains run every two to three minutes on an ever-expanding network of lines, underground and above. Shanghai's sprawling metro lines (www.shmetro.com; tel: 6437-0000) are growing at top speed, too, as over 8 million people travel per day between any of 393 stations. There are also metro systems in Chongqing, Guangzhou, Nanjing, Shenyang, Shenzhen and Tianjin, among others. Tickets usually cost 3 to 10 *yuan* per ride, and stored-value cards are available on some lines. Station signs are written in *pinyin* as well as Chinese characters.

Bus **Gong gong qi che**
Taxi **Chu zu qi che**

V

VISA AND ENTRY REQUIREMENTS

Citizens of Brunei, Japan and Singapore can visit China for 15 days without a visa. Just about everyone else must apply ahead of time, usually well in advance of travel, at a Chinese Consulate or Embassy abroad. Some Chinese offices overseas allow tourists to process visas by mail. If your area lacks a Chinese government office that can issue visas, ask a travel agent to arrange it in a third country. Processing takes from two days (in Hong Kong) to 10 days (most other places), more if travel agents get involved. More information is available at www.china-embassy.org/eng.

W

WEBSITES

For up-to-date information on China, from daily news to travel hints, try these websites:

asiaXPAT (property information for relocation or temporary accommodation): http://shanghai.asiaxpat.com
China Blog List (what anyone who's anyone thinks about China): www.chinabloglist.org
China Daily newspaper online: www.chinadaily.com.cn
China.org.cn (news aggregator): www.china.org.cn
TravelChinaGuide: www.travelchinaguide.com
City of Beijing: www.ebeijing.gov.cn
Ministry of Foreign Affairs: www.fmprc.gov.cn/mfa_eng/
People's Daily newspaper online: http://en.people.cn

Y

YOUTH HOSTELS

China has a fast-evolving network of 316 youth hostels. Visitors may check specifics online (www.yhachina.com), call the Youth Hostels Association of China (tel: 20-8751 3731) or visit the association's Guangzhou headquarters at 103 Tiyuxi Road, Victory Plaza, Tower A, Room 3606.

Top on the association's list are the Peking Youth Hostel (113-2 Nan Luo Gu Xiang, Dong Cheng District; tel: 10-6401-3961, www.hostelworld.com), Shanghai Captain Youth Hostel (37 Fuzhou Road; tel: 21-6323-5053), Guangzhou Riverside Youth Hostel (15 Changdi Street, Luju Road; tel: 020-2239-2500), Mingtown Suzhou International Youth Hostel (28 Pingjiang Road, Suzhou; tel: 512-6581-6869) and Chongqing Perfect Time Youth Hostel (2 Zheng Street, Ciqikou Ancient Town; tel: 023-6547-7008).

DICTIONARY

ENGLISH–MANDARIN CHINESE

adj adjective **adv** adverb **BE** British English **n** noun **prep** preposition **v** verb

A

a.m. 上午 shàng wǔ
abbey 修道院 xiū dào yuàn
accept *v* 接受 jiē shòu
access 进入 jìn rù
accident 事故 shì gù
accommodation 住宿 zhù sù
account *n* 账户 zhàng hù
acupuncture 针灸 zhēn jiǔ
adapter 变压器 biàn yā qì
address 地址 dì zhǐ
admission 入场 rù chǎng
after 以后 yǐ hòu
afternoon 下午 xià wǔ
aftershave 须后水 xū hòu shuǐ
age 年龄 nián líng
agency 代办处 dài bàn chù
AIDS 爱滋病 ài zī bìng
air conditioning 空调 kōng tiáo
air pump 气筒 qì tǒng
airline 航空公司 háng kōng gōng sī
airmail 航空信 háng kōng xìn
airplane 飞机 fēi jī
airport 飞机场 fēi jī chǎng
aisle 过道 guò dào
aisle seat 靠过道的位子 kào guò dào de wèi zi
allergic 过敏 guò mǐn
allergic reaction 过敏反应 guò mǐn fǎn yìng
allow *v* 允许 yǔn xǔ
alone 单独 dān dú
alter *v* **(clothing)** 改 gǎi
alternate route 变更路线 biàn gēng lù xiàn
aluminum foil 厨房锡纸 chú fáng xī zhǐ
amazing 令人惊奇的 lìng rén jīng qí de
ambulance 救护车 jiù hù chē
American 美国人 měi guó rén
amusement park 游乐园 yóu lè yuán
anemic 贫血 pín xuè
anesthesia 麻醉 má zuì
animal 动物 dòng wù
ankle 脚腕 jiǎo wàn
antibiotic 抗生素 kàng shēng sù
antiques store 古董店 gǔ dǒng diàn
antiseptic cream 消毒药膏 xiāo dú yào gāo
anything 任何东西 rèn hé dōng xī
apartment 公寓 gōng yù
appendix (body part) 盲肠 máng cháng
appetizer 开胃菜 kāi wèi cài
appointment 约会 yuē huì
arcade 拱廊儿童游戏场 gǒng láng ér tóng yóu xì chǎng
area code 区号 qū hà
arm 胳膊 gē bo
aromatherapy 芳香疗法 fāng xiāng liáo fǎ
around (the corner) 拐角处 guǎi jiǎo chù
arrivals (airport) 抵达 dǐ dá
arrive *v* 到达 dào dá
artery 动脉 dòng mài
arthritis 关节炎 guān jié yán
Asian (restaurant) 亚洲 yà zhōu
aspirin 阿斯匹林 ā sī pǐ lín
asthmatic 气喘 qì chuǎn
ATM 自动取款机 zì dòng qǔ kuǎn jī
ATM card 自动取款卡 zì dòng qǔ kuǎn kǎ
attack (on person) 攻击 gōng jī
attend *v* 出席 chū xí
attraction (place) 游览胜地 yóu lǎn shèng dì
attractive 有吸引力的 yǒu xī yǐn lì de
Australian 澳大利亚人 ào dà lì yà rén
automatic 自动 zì dòng
automatic car 自动汽车 zì dòng qì chē

B

baby 婴儿 yīng ér
baby bottle 奶瓶 nǎi píng
baby wipe 婴儿纸巾 yīng ér zhǐ jīn
babysitter 保姆 bǎo mǔ
back (body part) 背部 bèi bù
backpack 背包 bēi bāo
bag 袋子 dài zi
baggage *[BE]* 行李 xíng li
baggage claim 行李认领 xíng li rèn lǐng
baggage ticket 行李票 xíng li piào
bakery 面包店 miàn bāo diàn
ballet 芭蕾 bā léi
bandage 绷带 bēng dài
bank 银行 yín háng
bar (place) 酒吧 jiǔ bā
barbecue 烤肉 kǎo ròu
barber 理发师 lǐ fà shī
baseball 棒球 bàng qiú
basket (grocery store) 购物篮子 gòu wù lán zi
basketball 篮球 lán qiú
bathroom 浴室 yù shì
battery 电池 diàn chí
battleground 战场 zhàn chǎng

be *v* 是 shì
beach 海滩 hǎi tān
beautiful 美丽 měi lì
bed 床 chuáng
bed and breakfast 带早餐的旅店 dài zǎo cān de lǚ diàn
begin *v* 开始 kāi shǐ
before 以前 yǐ qián
beginner (skill level) 初学者 chū xué zhě
behind (direction) 后面 hòu mian
beige 米黄色 mǐ huáng sè
belt 皮带 pí dài
berth 铺位 pùwèi
best 最好 zuì hǎo
better 更好 gèng hǎo
bicycle 自行车 zì xíng chē
big 大 dà
bigger 更大 gèng dà
bike route 自行车路线 zì xíng chē lù xiàn
bikini 比基尼泳装 bǐ jī ní yǒng zhuāng
bill *v* **(charge)** 开付款单 kāi fù kuǎn dān; ~ *n* **(money)** 纸币 zhǐ bì; ~ *n* **(of sale)** 账单 zhàng dān
bird 鸟 niǎo
birthday 生日 shēng rì
black 黑色 hēi sè
bladder 膀胱 páng guāng
bland 无味 wú wèi
blanket 毯子 tǎn zi
bleed *v* 流血 liú xuè
blood 血液 xuè yè
blood pressure 血压 xuè yā
blouse 女衬衫 nǚ chèn shān
blue 蓝色 lán sè
board *v* 登机 dēng jī
boarding pass 登机牌 dēng jī pái
boat 小船 xiǎo chuán
bone 骨头 gǔ tou
book 书 shū
bookstore 书店 shū diàn
boots 靴子 xuē zi
boring 无聊的 wú liáo de
botanical garden 植物园 zhí wù yuán
bother *v* 打扰 dǎ rǎo
bottle 瓶 píng
bottle opener 瓶启子 píng qǐ zi
bowl 碗 wǎn
box 箱子 xiāng zi
boxing match 拳击比赛 quán jī bǐ sài
boy 男孩 nán hái
boyfriend 男朋友 nán péng you
bra 胸罩 xiōng zhào
bracelet 手镯 shǒu zhuó
brakes (car) 闸 zhá
break *v* **(tooth)** 断 duàn
break-in (burglary) 闯入 chuǎng rù
breakdown 出故障 chū gù zhàng
breakfast 早餐 zǎo cān
breast 乳房 rǔ fáng
breastfeed 母乳喂养 mǔ rǔ wèi yǎng
breathe *v* 呼吸 hū xī
bridge 桥梁 qiáo liáng
briefs (clothing) 男内裤 nán nèi kù
bring *v* 带来 dài lái
British 英国人 yīng guó rén
broken 破了 pò le
brooch 别针 bié zhēn
broom 笤帚 tiáo zhou
brother 兄弟 xiōng dì
brown 褐色 hè sè
bug 虫子 chóng zi
building 大厦 dà shà
burn *v* 烧 shāo
bus 公共汽车 gōng gòng qì chē
bus station 公共汽车站 gōng gòng qì chē zhàn
bus stop 公共汽车站 gōng gòng qì chē zhàn
bus ticket 公共汽车票 gōng gòng qì chē piào
bus tour 公共汽车游览 gōng gòng qì chē yóu lǎn
business 商务 shāng wù
business card 名片 míng piàn
business center 商业中心 shāng yè zhōng xīn
business class 商务舱 shāng wù cāng
business hours 营业时间 yíng yè shí jiān
butcher 屠户 tú hù
buttocks 屁股 pì gu
buy *v* 买 mǎi
bye 再见 zài jiàn

C

cabin 客舱 kè cāng
cable car 缆车 lǎn chē
café 小餐馆 xiǎo cān guǎn
call *v* 打电话 dǎ diàn huà; ~ *n* 电话 diàn huà
calligraphy supplies 书法用品 shū fǎ yòng pǐn
calories 卡路里 kǎ lù lǐ
camera 照相机 zhào xiàng jī
camera case 照相机套 zhào xiàng jī tào
camera store 照相器材商店 zhào xiàng qì cái shāng diàn
camp *v* 露营 lù yíng
camping stove 露营炉 lù yíng lú
campsite 露营地 lù yíng dì
can opener 开罐器 kāi guàn qì
Canada 加拿大 jiā ná dà
Canadian 加拿大人 jiā ná dà rén
cancel *v* 取消 qǔ xiāo
candy 糖果 táng guǒ
canned good 罐装食品 guàn zhuāng shí pǐn
canyon 峡谷 xiá gǔ
car 汽车 qì chē
car hire *[BE]* 租车 zū chē
car park *[BE]* 停车场 tíng chē chǎng
car rental 租车 chū zū qì chē
car seat (儿童)车座 (ér tóng)chē zuò
carafe 玻璃调料瓶 bō li tiáo liào píng
card 卡 kǎ
carry-on 手提行李 shǒu tí xíng li
cart (grocery store) 手推车 shǒu tuī chē; ~ **(luggage)** 行李推车 xíng li tuī chē
carton 条 tiáo
case (amount) 件 jiàn
cash *v* 兑现金 duì xiàn jīn; ~ *n* 现金 xiàn jīn
cash advance 预支现金 yù zhī xiàn jīn
cashier 出纳员 chū nà yuán

casino 赌博娱乐场 dǔ bó yú lè chǎng
castle 城堡 chéng bǎo
cathedral 大教堂 dà jiào táng
cave 洞 dòng
CD CD CD
cell phone 手机 shǒu jī
Celsius 摄氏 shè shì
centimeter 厘米 lí mǐ
ceramic spoon 汤勺 tāng sháo
certificate 证明 zhèng míng
chair 椅子 yǐ zi
chair lift 升降椅 shēng jiàng yǐ
change *v* **(buses)** 换车 huàn chē; ~ *v* **(money)** 换钱 huàn qián; ~ *v* **(baby)** 换尿布 huàn niào bù; ~ *n* **(money)** 零钱 líng qián
charcoal 木炭 mù tàn
charge *v* **(credit card)** 用信用卡付款 yòng xìn yòng kǎ fù kuǎn; *n* **(cost)** 收费 shōu fèi
cheap 便宜 pián yi
cheaper 更便宜 gèng pián yi
check *v* **(something)** 检查 jiǎn chá; ~ *v* **(luggage)** 托运 tuō yùn; ~ *n* **(payment)** 支票 zhī piào
check-in (hotel) 办入住 bàn rù zhù; ~ **(airport)** 办理登机手续 bàn lǐ dēng jī shǒu xù
checking account 支票账户 zhī piào zhàng hù
check-out (hotel) *n* 退房 tuì fáng
chemical toilet 简易厕所 jiǎn yì cè suǒ
chemist *[BE]* 药剂师 yào jì shī
cheque *[BE]* 支票 zhī piào
chest (body part) 胸口 xiōng kǒu
chest pain 胸口痛 xiōng kǒu tòng
chewing gum 口香糖 kǒu xiāng táng
child 孩子 hái zi
child's seat 儿童座椅 ér tóng zuò yǐ
children's menu 儿童菜单 ér tóng cài dān
children's portion 儿童饭量 ér tóng fàn liàng
china 瓷器 cí qì
China 中国 zhōng guó
Chinese 中文 zhōng wén
Chinese painting 中国画 zhōng guó huà
chopsticks 筷子 kuài zi
church 教堂 jiào táng
cigar 雪茄 xuě jiā
cigarette 香烟 xiāng yān
class 等级 děng jí
clay pot 砂锅 shā guō
cloisonné 景泰蓝 jǐng tài lán
classical music 古典音乐 gǔ diǎn yīn yuè
clean *v* 清洗 qīng xǐ; ~ **adv** 干净 gān jìng
cleaning product 清洁产品 qīng jié chǎn pǐn
cleaning supplies 清洁产品供应 qīng jié chǎn pǐn gōng yìng
clear *v* **(on an ATM)** 清除 qīng chú
cliff 峭壁 qiào bì
cling film *[BE]* 保鲜膜 bǎo xiān mó
close *v* **(a shop)** 关门 guān mén; ~ *adj* 近 jìn
closed 关闭 guān bì
clothing 衣物 yī wù
clothing store 服装店 fú zhuāng diàn
club 俱乐部 jù lè bù
coat 外套 wài tào
coffee shop 咖啡店 kā fēi diàn
coin 硬币 yìng bì
cold (sickness) 感冒 gǎn mào; ~ **(temperature)** 冷 lěng
colleague 同事 tóng shì
cologne 科隆香水 kē lóng xiāng shuǐ
color 颜色 yán sè
comb 梳子 shū zi
come *v* 来 lái
complaint 怨言 yuàn yán
computer 计算机 jì suàn jī
concert 音乐会 yīn yuè huì
concert hall 音乐厅 yīn yuè tīng
condition (medical) 症状 zhèng zhuàng
conditioner 护发素 hù fà sù
condom 避孕套 bì yùn tào
conference 会议 huì yì
confirm *v* 证实 zhèng shí
congestion 充血 chōng xuè
connect *v* **(internet)** 连接 lián jiē
connection (internet) 连接 lián jiē; ~ **(flight)** 转机 zhuǎn jī
constipated 便秘 biàn mì
consulate 领事馆 lǐng shì guǎn
consultant 顾问 gù wèn
contact *v* 联系 lián xì
contact lens 隐形眼镜 yǐn xíng yǎn jìng
contact lens solution 隐形眼镜液 yǐn xíng yǎn jìng yè
contagious 传染的 chuán rǎn de
convention hall 会议厅 huì yì tīng
conveyor belt 传送带 chuán sòng dài
cook *v* 烹调 pēng tiáo
cooking gas 烹调煤气 pēng tiáo méi qì
cool (temperature) 凉 liáng
copper 铜 tóng
corkscrew 开塞钻 kāi sāi zuàn
cost *v* 花费 huā fèi
cot 轻便小床 qīng biàn xiǎo chuáng
cotton 棉花 mián hua
cough 咳嗽 ké sou
country code 国家代号 guó jiā dài hào
cover charge 附加费 fù jiā fèi
crash *v* **(car)** 撞 zhuàng
cream (ointment) 药膏 yào gāo
credit card 信用卡 xìn yòng kǎ
crew neck 圆领 yuán lǐng
crib 摇篮 yáo lán
crystal 水晶 shuǐ jīng
cup 杯子 bēi zi
currency 货币 huò bì
currency exchange 货币兑换 huò bì duì huàn
currency exchange office 货币兑换局 huò bì duì huàn jú

current account *[BE]* 支票账户 zhī piào zhàng hù
customs 海关 hăi guān
cut *v* **(hair)** 剪 jiăn; ~ *n* **(injury)** 伤口 shāng kǒu
cute 逗人喜爱 dòu rén xĭ ài
cycling 騎自行車 qí zì xíng chē

D

damage *v* 损伤 sŭn shāng
damaged 坏了 huài le
dance *v* 跳舞 tiào wǔ
dance club 舞蹈俱乐部 wŭ dăo jù lè bù
dancing 跳舞 tiào wǔ
dangerous 危险 wēi xiăn
dark 黑暗 hēi àn
date (calendar) 日期 rì qī
day 天 tiān
deaf 聋 lóng
debit card 借记卡 jiè jì kă
deck chair 轻便折叠躺椅 qīng biàn zhé dié tăng yĭ
declare *v* 申报 shēn bào
decline *v* **(credit card)** 拒绝 jù jué
deeply 深深地 shēn shēn de
degrees (temperature) 度 dù
delay *v* 晚点 wăn diăn
delete *v* 删除 shān chú
delicatessen 熟食 shú shí
delicious 可口 kĕ kǒu
denim 斜紋粗棉布 xié wén cū mián bù
dentist 牙医 yá yī
denture 假牙 jiă yá
deodorant 止汗露 zhĭ hàn lù
department store 百货商店 băi huò shāng diàn
departure 离开 lí kāi
deposit *v* 存钱 cún qián; ~ *n* **(bank)** 储蓄 chŭ xù
desert 沙漠 shā mò
detergent 洗涤剂 xĭ dí jì
diabetic 糖尿病 táng niào bìng
dial *v* 拨号 bō hào
diamond 钻石 zuàn shí
diaper 尿布 niào bù
diarrhea 腹泻 fù xiè
diesel 柴油 chái yóu
difficult 困难 kùn nan
digital 数码 shù mă
digital camera 数码相机 shù mă xiàng jī
digital photo 数码相片 shù mă xiàng piàn
digital print 数码印刷品 shù mă yìn shuā pĭn
dining room 餐厅 cān tīng
dinner 晚餐 wăn cān
direction 方向 fāng xiàng
dirty 肮脏 āng zāng
disabled 残疾 cán jí
disabled accessible *[BE]* 残疾人通道 cán jí rén tōng dào
disconnect (computer) 断开 duàn kāi
discount 折扣 zhé kòu
dish (kitchen) 碟子 dié zi
dishwasher 洗碗机 xĭ wăn jī
dishwashing liquid 洗碗液 xĭ wăn yè
display 显示 xiăn shì
display case 陈列橱 chén liè chú
disposable 一次性 yí cì xìng
disposable razor 一次性剃刀 yí cì xìng tì dāo
dive *v* 潜水 qián shuĭ
diving equipment 潜水用具 qián shuĭ yòng jù
divorce *v* 离婚 lí hūn
dizzy 头昏眼花 tóu hūn yăn huā
doctor 医生 yī shēng
doll 玩具娃娃 wán jù wá wá
dollar (U.S.) 美元 mĕi yuán
domestic 国内 guó nèi
domestic flight 国内航班 guó nèi háng bān
dormitory 宿舍 sù shè
double bed 双人床 shuāng rén chuáng
downtown 市中心 shì zhōng xīn
dozen 十二 shí èr
drag lift 牵引缆车 qiān yĭn lăn chē
dress (piece of clothing) 連衣裙 lián yī qún
dress code 着装要求 zhuó zhuāng yāo qiú
drink *v* 喝 hē; ~ *n* 饮料 yĭn liào
drink menu 饮料单 yĭn liào dān
drinking water 饮用水 yĭn yòng shuĭ
drive *v* 开车 kāi chē
driver's license number 司机驾照号 sī jī jià zhào hào
drop (medicine) 滴 dī
drowsiness 睡意 shuì yì
dry cleaner 干洗店 gān xĭ diàn
during 期间 qī jiān
duty (tax) 关税 guān shuì
duty-free 免税 miăn shuì
DVD DVD DVD

E

ear 耳朵 ĕr duo
earache 耳朵疼 ĕr duo téng
early 早 zăo
earrings 耳环 ĕr huán
east 东部 dōng bù
easy 容易 róng yì
eat *v* 吃 chī
economy class 经济舱 jīng jì cāng
elbow 肘 zhǒu
electric outlet 电插座 diàn chā zuò
elevator 电梯 diàn tī
e-mail *v* 发电邮 fā diàn yóu; ~ *n* 电子邮件 diàn zĭ yóu jiàn
e-mail address 电邮地址 diàn yóu dì zhĭ
emergency 紧急状态 jĭn jí zhuàng tài
emergency exit 紧急出口 jĭn jí chū kǒu
empty *v* 倒空 dào kōng
enamel (jewelry) 珐琅 fà láng
end *v* 结束 jié shù
English 英语 yīng yŭ
engrave *v* 雕刻 diāo kè
enjoy *v* 享用 xiăng yòng
enter *v* 进入 jìn rù
entertainment 娱乐 yú lè

entrance 入口 rù kǒu
envelope 信封 xìn fēng
epileptic 癫痫 diān xián
equipment 设备 shè bèi
escalator 自动扶梯 zì dòng fú tī
e-ticket 电子票 diàn zǐ piào
evening 晚上 wǎn shang
excess 超过 chāo guò
exchange *v* **(money)** 兑换 duì huàn; ~ *v* **(goods)** 交换 jiāo huàn; ~ *n* **(place)** 换地方 huàn dì fāng
exchange rate 兑换率 duì huàn lǜ
excursion 游览 yóu lǎn
excuse *v* 原谅 yuán liàng
exhausted 用尽 yòng jìn
exit *v* 出去 chū qù; ~ *n* 出口 chū kǒu
expensive 昂贵 ang guì
expert (skill level) 专家 zhuān jiā
exposure (film) 曝光 bào guāng
express 快 kuài
extension (phone) 分机 fēn jī
extra 额外 é wài
extra large 特大号 tè dà hào
extract *v* **(tooth)** 拔 bá
eye 眼睛 yǎn jīng

F

face 面孔 miàn kǒng
facial 面部 miàn bù
family 家庭 jiā tíng
fan (appliance) 电扇 diàn shàn
far 远 yuǎn
far-sighted 远视 yuǎn shì
farm 农场 nóng chǎng
fast 快速 kuài sù
fast food 快餐 kuài cān
fat free 无脂肪 wú zhī fáng
father 父亲 fù qīn
fax *v* 发传真 fā chuán zhēn; ~ *n* 传真 chuán zhēn
fax number 传真号 chuán zhēn hào
fee 费用 fèi yòng
feed *v* 喂 wèi
ferry 轮渡 lún dù
fever 发烧 fā shāo
field (sports) 运动场 yùn dòng chǎng
fill up *v* **(food)** 加满 jiā mǎn
fill out *v* **(form)** 填写 tián xiě
filling (tooth) 填充物 tián chōng wù
film (camera) 胶卷 jiāo juǎn
fine (fee) 罚款 fá kuǎn
finger 手指 shǒu zhǐ
fingernail 指甲 zhi jia
fire 火 huǒ
fire department 消防队 xiāo fáng duì
fire door 防火门 fáng huǒ mén
first class 头等舱 tóu děng cāng
fit (clothing) 适合 shì hé
fitting room 试衣间 shì yī jiān
fix *v* **(repair)** 修理 xiū lǐ
fixed-price menu 价格固定的菜单 jià gé gù dìng de cài dān
flashlight 手电 shǒu diàn
flight 航班 háng bān
floor 地板 dì bǎn
florist 卖花人 mài huā rén
flower 花 huā
folk music 民间音乐 mín jiān yīn yuè
food 食物 shí wù
foot 脚 jiǎo
football game *[BE]* 足球赛 zú qiú sài
for 为 wéi
forecast 预报 yù bào
forest 森林 sēn lín
fork 叉子 chā zi
form (fill-in) 表格 biǎo gé
formula (baby) 奶粉 nǎi fěn
fort 要塞 yào sài
fountain 喷泉 pēn quán
free 免费 miǎn fèi
freezer 冷冻机 lěng dòng jī
fresh 新鲜 xīn xiān
friend 朋友 péng you
frying pan 煎锅 jiān guō
full-service 全面服务 quán miàn fú wù

G

game 游戏 yóu xì
garage 车库 chē kù
garbage bag 垃圾袋 lā jī dài
gas 汽油 qì yóu
gas station 加油站 jiā yóu zhàn
gate (airport) 登机门 dēng jī mén
gay 男同性恋 nán tóng xìng liàn
gay bar 男同性恋酒吧 nán tóng xìng liàn jiǔ bā
gay club 男同性恋俱乐部 nán tóng xìng liàn jù lè bù
gel (hair) 发胶 fà jiāo
get to 到 dào
get off (a train/bus/subway) 下车 xià chē
gift 礼物 lǐ wù
gift shop 礼品店 lǐ pǐn diàn
girl 女孩 nǚ hái
girlfriend 女朋友 nǚ péng you
give *v* 给 gěi
glass (drinking) 玻璃杯 bō li bēi; ~ **(material)** 玻璃 bō li
glasses 眼镜 yǎn jìng
go *v* **(somewhere)** 去 qù
gold 金子 jīn zi
golf course 高尔夫球场 gāo ěr fū qiú chǎng
golf tournament 高尔夫球比赛 gāo ěr fū qiú bǐ sài
good 好 hǎo
good afternoon 下午好 xià wu hǎo
good evening 晚上好 wǎn shang hǎo
good morning 早晨好 zǎo chen hǎo
goodbye 再见 zài jiàn
goods 物品 wù pǐn
gram 克 kè
grandchild 孙子 sūn zi
grandparent 祖父/母 zǔ fù/mǔ
gray 灰色 huī sè
Great Hall of the People 人民大会堂 rén mín dà huì táng
green 绿色 lǜ sè
grocery store 杂货店 zá huò diàn
ground floor 一楼 yī lóu
group 小组 xiǎo zǔ
guide *n* 指南 zhǐ nán
guide book 指南书 zhǐ nán shū

guide dog 导盲犬 dǎo máng quǎn
gym 体操 tǐ cāo
gynecologist 妇产科医师 fù chǎn kē yī shī

H

hair 头发 tóu fà
hair dryer 吹风机 chuī fēng jī
hair salon 发廊 fà láng
hairbrush 梳子 shū zi
haircut 理发 lǐ fà
hairspray 喷发剂 pēn fā jì
hairstyle 发型 fà xíng
hairstylist 发型师 fà xíng shī
halal 清真食品 qīng zhēn shí pǐn
half 半 bàn
half hour 半小时 bàn xiǎo shí
half-kilo 半公斤 bàn gōng jīn
hammer 锤子 chuí zi
hand 手 shǒu
hand luggage *[BE]* 手提行李 shǒu tí xíng li
handbag *[BE]* 提包 tí bāo
handicapped 残疾 cán ji
handicapped-accessible 残疾人通道 cán ji rén tōng dào
hangover 宿醉 sù zuì
happy 愉快 yú kuài
hat 帽子 mào zi
have *v* 有 yǒu
hay fever 花粉症 huā fěn zhèng
head (body part) 头 tóu
headache 头疼 tóu téng
headphones 耳机 ěr jī
health 健康 jiàn kāng
health food store 健康食品商店 jiàn kāng shí pǐn shāng diàn
hearing impaired 听力障碍 tīng lì zhàng ài
heart 心脏 xīn zàng
heart condition 心脏病 xīn zàng bìng
heat 暖气 nuán qì
heater 加热器 jiā rè qì
heating *[BE]* 暖气 nuán qì
hello 你好 nǐ hǎo
helmet 头盔 tóu kuī
help 帮助 bāng zhù
here 这里 zhè lǐ
hi 你好 nǐ hǎo
high 高 gāo
highchair 高脚椅 gāo jiǎo yǐ
highway 高速公路 gāo sù gōng lù
hill 小山 xiǎo shān
hire *v [BE]* 雇用 gù yòng
hire car *[BE]* 租用汽车 zū yòng qì chē
hitchhike *v* 搭车 dā chē
hockey 曲棍球 qū gùn qiú
holiday *[BE]* 假日 jià rì
horse track 跑马场 pǎo mǎ chǎng
hospital 医院 yī yuàn
hostel 旅舍 lǚ shè
hot (temperature) 热 rè; **~ (spicy)** 辣 là
hot spring 温泉 wēn quán
hot water 热水 rè shuǐ
hotel 旅馆 lǚ guǎn
hour 小时 xiǎo shí
house 房子 fáng zi
household good 家用物品 jiā yòng
housekeeping services 客房清洁服务 kè fáng qīng jié fú wù
how 怎么 zěn me
how much 多少 duō shǎo
hug *v* 拥抱 yōng bào
hungry 饥饿 jī è
hurt 疼 téng
husband 丈夫 zhàng fu

I

ibuprofen 布洛芬 bù luò fēn
ice 冰 bīng
ice hockey 冰球 bīng qiú
icy 冰冷 bīng lěng
identification 证件 zhèng jiàn
ill 病 bìng
in 在 zài
include *v* 包括 bāo kuò
indoor pool 室内游泳池 shì nèi yóu yǒng chí
inexpensive 不贵 bú guì
infected 传染 chuán rǎn
information (phone) 留言 liú yán
information desk 问讯处 wèn xùn chù
insect bite 虫咬 chóng yǎo
insect repellent 杀虫剂 shā chóng jì
insert *v* **(on an ATM)** 插入 chā rù
insomnia 失眠 shī mián
instant message 即时讯息 jí shí xùn xī
insulin 胰岛素 yí dǎo sù
insurance 保险 bǎo xiǎn
insurance card 保险卡 bǎo xiǎn kǎ
insurance company 保险公司 bǎo xiǎn gōng sī
interesting 有趣 yǒu qù
international (airport area) 国际 guó jì
international flight 国际航班 guó jì háng bān
international student card 国际学生证 guó jì xué shēng zhèng
internet 互联网 hù lián wǎng
internet café 网吧 wǎng bā
internet service 互联网服务 hù lián wǎng fú wù
interpreter 口译员 kǒu yì yuán
intersection 十字路口 shí zì lù kǒu
intestine 肠子 cháng zi
introduce *v* 介绍 jiè shào
invoice 发货票 fā huò piào
Ireland 爱尔兰 ài ěr lán
Irish 爱尔兰人 ài ěr lán rén
iron *v* 熨衣服 yùn yī fu; ~ *n* 熨斗 yùn dǒu

J

jacket 夹克 jiá kè
jade 翡翠 fěi cuì
Japanese (restaurant) 日本 rì běn
jar 罐子 guàn zi
jaw 下颌 xià hé
jazz 爵士乐 jué shì yuè
jazz club 爵士乐俱乐部 jué shì yuè jù lè bù
jeans 牛仔裤 niú zǎi kù
jeweler 珠宝商 zhū bǎo shāng
jewelry 首饰 shǒu shì
join *v* 加入 jiā rù
joint (body part) 关节 guān jié

K

key 钥匙 yào shi
key card 钥匙卡 yào shi kǎ
key ring 钥匙圈 yào shi quān
kiddie pool 儿童游泳池 ér tóng yóu yǒng chí
kidney (body part) 肾脏 shèn zàng
kilogram 公斤 gōng jīn
kilometer 公里 gōng lǐ
kiss *v* 亲吻 qīn wěn
kitchen 厨房 chú fáng
kitchen foil *[BE]* 厨房锡纸 chú fáng xī zhǐ
knee 膝盖 xī gài
knife 刀子 dāo zi
kosher 犹太食品 yóu tài shí pǐn

L

lace 鞋带 xié dài
lacquerware 漆器 qī qì
lactose intolerant 乳糖过敏 rǔ táng guò mǐn
lake 湖 hú
large 大 dà
last 最后 zuì hòu
late (time) 晚了 wǎn le
later 以后 yǐ hòu
launderette *[BE]* 洗衣店 xǐ yī diàn
laundromat 洗衣店 xǐ yī diàn
laundry 要洗的衣物 yào xǐ de yī wù
laundry facility 洗衣店设施 xǐ yī diàn shè shī
laundry service 洗衣服务 xǐ yī fú wù
lawyer 律师 lǜ shī
leather 皮革 pí gé
leave *v* 起飞 qǐ fēi
left (direction) 左边 zuǒ bian
leg 腿 tuǐ
lens 镜片 jìng piàn
less 较少 jiào shǎo
lesson 课程 kè chéng
letter 信件 xìn jiàn
library 图书馆 tú shū guǎn
life jacket 救生衣 jiù shēng yī
lifeguard 救生员 jiù shēng yuán
lift 搭车 dā chē; ~ *[BE]* 电梯 diàn tī
lift pass 缆车票 lǎn chē piào
light (overhead) 灯 dēng; ~ **(cigarette)** 点 diǎn
lightbulb 电灯泡 diàn dēng pào
lighter 打火机 dǎ huǒ jī
like *v* 喜欢 xǐ huan
line (train) 线 xiàn
linen 亚麻布 yà má bù
lip 嘴唇 zuǐ chún
liquor store 酒店 jiǔ diàn
liter 公升 gōng shēng
little 少许 shǎo xǔ
live *v* 居住 jū zhù
live music 现场音乐 xiàn chǎng yīn yuè
liver (body part) 肝脏 gān zàng
loafers 游荡者 yóu dàng zhě
local 当地 dāng dì
lock up 锁 suǒ
lock *n* 锁 suǒ
locker 衣物柜 yī wù guì
log on 登录 dēng lù
log off 退出 tuì chū
long 长 cháng
long sleeves 长袖子 cháng xiù zi
long-sighted *[BE]* 远视 yuǎn shì
look *v* 看 kàn
lose *v* **(something)** 丢失 diū shī
lost 失去 shī qù
lost and found 失物招领处 shī wù zhāo lǐng chù
lotion 化妆乳液 huà zhuāng rǔ yè
louder 大声 dà shēng
love 爱 ài
low 低 dī
luggage 行李 xíng li
luggage cart 行李推车 xíng li tuī chē
luggage locker 行李暂存箱 xíng li zàn cún xiāng
luggage ticket 行李票 xíng li piào
lunch 午餐 wǔ cān
lung 肺 fèi

M

magazine 杂志 zá zhì
magnificent 壮观 zhuàng guān
mail *v* 邮寄 yóu jì; ~ *n* 邮件 yóu jiàn
mailbox 邮箱 yóu xiāng
main attraction 主要景点 zhǔ yào jǐng diǎn
main course 主菜 zhǔ cài
make up *v [BE]* **(a prescription)** 配药方 pèi yào fāng
mall 购物中心 gòu wù zhōng xīn
man 男人 nán rén
manager 经理 jīng lǐ
manicure 修手指甲 xiū shǒu zhi jia
manual car 手动汽车 shǒu dòng qì chē
map *n* 地图 dì tú
market 市场 shì chǎng
married 结婚 jié hūn
marry *v* 结婚 jié hūn
mass (church service) 礼拜 lǐ bài
massage 按摩 àn mó
match *n* 火柴 huǒ chái
meal 饭 fàn
measure *v* **(someone)** 测量 cè liáng
measuring cup 量杯 liáng bēi
measuring spoon 量匙 liáng chí
mechanic 技工 jì gōng
medicine 医药 yī yào
medium (size) 中等 zhōng děng
meet *v* **(someone)** 见面 jiàn miàn
meeting 会议 huì yì
meeting room 会议室 huì yì shì
membership card 会员证 huì yuán zhèng
memorial (place) 纪念馆 jì niàn guǎn
memory card 存储卡 cún chǔ kǎ
mend *v* 修理 xiū lǐ
menstrual cramp 经期腹痛 jīng qī fù tòng
menu 菜单 cài dān
message 信息 xìn xī
meter (parking) 计时器 jì shí qì
microwave 微波炉 wēi bō lú
midday *[BE]* 午间 wǔ jiān
midnight 午夜 wǔ yè
mileage 里程(数) lǐ chéng shù
mini-bar 小酒吧 xiǎo jiǔ bā

minute 分钟 fēn zhōng
missing 错过 cuò guò
mistake 差错 chā cuò
mobile phone *[BE]* 手机 shǒu jī
mobility 流动性 liú dòng xìng
monastery 修道院 xiū dào yuàn
money 钱 qián
month 月 yuè
mop 擦 cā
moped 电动自行车 diàn dòng zì xíng chē
more 更多 gèng duō
morning 早晨 zǎo chén
mosque 清真寺 qīng zhēn sì
mother 母亲 mǔ qīn
motion sickness 晕动病 yùn dòng bìng
motor boat 汽船 qì chuán
motorcycle 摩托车 mó tuō chē
motorway *[BE]* 高速公路 gāo sù gōng lù
mountain 山 shān
mountain bike 山地车 shān dì chē
mousse (hair) 摩丝 mó sī
mouth 嘴 zuǐ
movie 电影 diàn yǐng
movie theater 电影院 diàn yǐng yuàn
mug *v* 抢 qiǎng
multiple-trip (ticket) 不限使用次数的 bú xiàn shǐ yòng cì shù de
muscle 肌肉 jī ròu
museum 博物馆 bó wù guǎn
music 音乐 yīn yuè
music store 音乐商店 yīn yuè shāng diàn

N

nail file 指甲锉 zhī jia cuò
nail salon 美甲沙龙 měi jiǎ shā lóng
name 名字 míng zì
napkin 餐巾 cān jīn
nappy *[BE]* 尿布 niào bù
nationality 国籍 guó jí
nature preserve 自然保护区 zì rán bǎo hù qū
nauseous 恶心 ě xin
near (在. . . 的)附近 (zài... de) fù jìn
near-sighted 近视 jìn shì
nearby 附近 fù jìn
neck 脖子 bó zǐ
necklace 项链 xiàng liàn
need *v* 需要 xū yào
newspaper 报纸 bào zhǐ
newsstand 报摊 bào tān
next 下一个 xià yí gè
nice 好 hǎo
night 夜 yè
nightclub 夜总会 yè zǒng huì
no 不 bú/bù
non-alcoholic 无酒精 wú jiǔ jīng
non-smoking 禁烟 jìn yān
noon 中午 zhōng wǔ
north 北部 běi bù
nose 鼻子 bí zi
notes *[BE]* 笔记 bǐ jì
nothing 没什么 méi shén me
notify *v* 通知 tōng zhī
novice (skill level) 新手 xīn shǒu
now 现在 xiàn zài
number 数字 shù zì
nurse 护士 hù shi

O

office 办公室 bàn gōng shì
office hours 办公时间 bàn gōng shí jiān
off-licence *[BE]* 酒店 jiǔ diàn
oil 油 yóu
OK 好 hǎo
old 老 lǎo
on the corner 在拐角处 zài guǎi jiǎo chù
once 一次 yí cì
one 一 yī
one-way (ticket) 单程 dān chéng
one-way street 单行道 dān xíng dào
only 只 zhǐ
open *v* 打开 dǎ kāi; ~ *adj* 开着 kāi zhe
opera 歌剧 gē jù
opera house 歌剧院 gē jù yuàn
opposite 相反 xiāng fǎn
optician 验光师 yàn guāng shī
orange (colour) 桔色 jú sè
orchestra 乐队 yuè duì
order *v* 点菜 diǎn cài
outdoor pool 室外游泳池 shì wài yóu yǒng chí
outside 外面 wài miàn
over the counter (medication) 非处方药 feī chǔ fāng yào
overdone 过熟 guò shú
overlook (scenic place) 俯视 fǔ shì
overnight 隔夜 gé yè
oxygen treatment 氧气治疗 yǎng qì zhì liáo

P

p.m. 下午 xià wǔ
pacifier 橡皮奶嘴 xiàng pí nǎi zuǐ
pack *v* 打包 dǎ bāo
package 包裹 bāo guǒ
paddling pool *[BE]* 儿童游泳池 ér tóng yóu yǒng chí
pad *[BE]* 垫 diàn
pain 痛 tòng
pajamas 睡衣 shuì yī
palace 宫殿 gōng diàn
pants 裤子 kù zi
pantyhose 裤袜 kù wà
paper 纸 zhǐ
paper towel 纸巾 zhǐ jīn
paracetamol *[BE]* 泰诺 tài nuò
park *v* 停车 tíng chē; ~ *n* 公园 gōng yuán
parking garage 车库 chē kù
parking lot 停车场 tíng chē chǎng
parking meter 停车计时器 tíng chē jì shí qì
part (for car) 部件 bù jiàn
part-time 兼职 jiān zhí
passenger 乘客 chéng kè
passport 护照 hù zhào
passport control 护照管制 hù zhào guǎn zhì
password 密码 mì mǎ
pastry shop 点心店 diǎn xīn diàn
path 道路 dào lù
pay *v* 支付 zhī fù
pay phone 公用电话 gōng yòng diàn huà

peak (of a mountain) 山顶 shān dǐng
pearl 珍珠 zhēn zhū
pedestrian 行人 xíng rén
pediatrician 儿科医生 ér kē yī shēng
pedicure 修脚趾甲 xiū jiǎo zhǐ jiǎ
pen 笔 bǐ
penicillin 青霉素 qīng méi sù
penis 阴茎 yīn jìng
per 每 měi
per day 每天 měi tiān
per hour 每小时 měi xiǎo shí
per night 每晚 měi wǎn
per week 每星期 měi xīng qī
perfume 香水 xiāng shuǐ
period (menstrual) 月经 yuè jīng; **~(of time)** 期间 qī jiān
permit *v* 允许 yǔn xǔ
petite 娇小 jiāo xiāo
petrol *[BE]* 汽油 qì yóu
petrol station *[BE]* 加油站 jiā yóu zhàn
pharmacy 药房 yào fáng
phone *v* 打电话 dǎ diàn huà; *~ n* 电话 diàn huà
phone call 电话 diàn huà
phone card 电话卡 dǎ diàn kǎ
phone number 电话号码 diàn huà hào mǎ
photo 相片 xiàng piàn
photocopy 复印件 fù yìn jiàn
photography 摄影 shè yǐng
pick up (something) 取 qǔ
picnic area 野餐区 yě cān qū
piece 片 piàn
pill (birth control) 计划生育药片 jì huà shēng yù yào piàn
pillow 枕头 zhěn tou
personal identification number (PIN) 个人密码 gè rén mì mǎ
pink 粉红色 fěn hóng sè
piste *[BE]* 小道 xiǎo dào
piste map *[BE]* 小道路线图 xiǎo dào lù xiàn tú
pizzeria 比萨店 bǐ sà diàn
place *v* **(a bet)** 下 xià
plane 飞机 fēi jī
plastic wrap 塑料包装 sù liào bāo zhuāng
plate 盘子 pán zi
platform 站台 zhàn tái
platinum 铂金 bó jīn
play *v* 玩 wán; *~ n* **(theatre)** 戏剧 xì jù
playground 操场 cāo chǎng
playpen 游戏围栏 yóu xì wéi lán
please 请 qǐng
pleasure 乐趣 lè qù
plunger 下水道疏通器 xià shuǐ dào shū tōng qì
plus size 加大号 jiā dà hào
pocket 口袋 kǒu dài
poison 毒药 dú yào
poles (skiing) 滑雪杆 huá xuě gan
police 警察 jǐng chá
police report 警察报告 jǐng chá bào gào
police station 警察局 jǐng chá jú
pond 池塘 chí táng
pool 水池 shuǐ chí
pop music 流行音乐 liú xíng yīn yuè
portion 部分 bù fen
post *[BE]* 邮件 yóu jiàn
post office 邮局 yóu jú
postbox *[BE]* 邮箱 yóu xiāng
postcard 明信片 míng xìn piàn
pot 罐 guàn
pottery 陶器 táo qì
pound (weight) 磅 bàng; **~ (British sterling)** 英镑 yīng bàng
pregnant 怀孕 huái yùn
prescribe *v* 开处方 kāi chǔ fāng
prescription 处方药 chǔ fāng yào
press *v* **(clothing)** 熨 yùn
price 价格 jià gé
print *v* 打印 dǎ yìn
problem 问题 wèn tí
produce 农产品 nóng chǎn pǐn
produce store 农产品商店 nóng chǎn pǐn shāng diàn
prohibit *v* 禁止 jìn zhǐ
pronounce *v* 发音 fā yīn
public 公共 gōng gòng
pull *v* 拉 lā
purple 紫色 zǐ sè
purse 提包 tí bāo
push *v* 按 àn
pushchair *[BE]* 婴儿车 yīng ér chē

Q

quality 质量 zhì liàng
question 问题 wèn tí
quiet 安静 ān jìng

R

racetrack 跑马场 pǎo mǎ chǎng
racket (sports) 球拍 qiú pāi
railway station *[BE]* 火车 huǒ chē
rain *n* 雨 yǔ
raincoat 雨衣 yǔ yī
rainforest 雨林 yǔ lín
rainy 多雨 duō yǔ
rap (music) 说唱乐 shuō chàng yuè
rape 强奸 qiáng jiān
rare (object) 罕见 hǎn jiàn
rash 皮疹 pí zhěn
ravine 峡谷 xiá gǔ
razor blade 剃须刀 tì xū dāo
reach *v* 够 gòu
ready 准备好 zhǔn bèi hǎo
real 真正 zhēn zhèng
receipt 收据 shōu jù
receive *v* 接受 jiē shòu
reception 招待会 zhāo dài huì
recharge *v* 充电 chōng diàn
recommend *v* 推荐 tuī jiàn
recommendation 推荐 tuī jiàn
recycling 回收 huí shōu
red 红色 hóng sè
refrigerator 冰箱 bīng xiāng
region 区域 qū yù
registered mail 挂号信 guà hào xìn
regular 普通 pǔ tōng
relationship 关系 guān xì
Ren Min Bi 人民币 rén mín bì
rent *v* 租 zū
rental car 出租车 chū zū chē
repair *v* 修理 xiū lǐ

repeat *v* 重复 chóng fù
reservation 预定 yù dìng
reservation desk 服务台 fú wù tái
reserve *v* 预定 yù dìng
restaurant 餐馆 cān guǎn
restroom (formal/informal) 洗手间/厕所 xǐ shǒu jiān/cè suǒ
retired 退休 tuì xiū
return *v* 归还 guī huán; ~ *n [BE]* 返还 fǎn huán
reverse *v* **(the charges)** *[BE]* 对方付费电话 duì fāng fù fèi diàn huà
rib (body part) 肋骨 lèi gǔ
rice cooker 电饭锅 diàn fàn guō
right of way 路权 lù quán
ring 戒指 jiè zhi
river 河 hé
road map 路线图 lù xiàn tú
roast *v* 烤 kǎo
rob *v* 抢夺 qiǎng duó
robbed 被抢了 bèi qiǎng le
romantic 浪漫 làng màn
room 房间 fáng jiān
room key 房间钥匙 fáng jiān yào shi
room service 客房送餐服务 kè fáng sòng cān fú wù
round-trip 双程 shuāng chéng
route 路线 lù xiàn
rowboat 划艇 huá tǐng
rubbish *[BE]* 垃圾 lā jī
rubbish bag *[BE]* 垃圾袋 lā jī dài
ruins 废墟 fèi xū
rush 赶时间 gǎn shí jiān

S

sad 伤心 shāng xīn
safe (thing) 保险柜 bǎo xiǎn guì; ~ **(protected)** 安全 ān quán
sales tax 销售税 xiāo shòu shuì
sandals 凉鞋 liáng xié
sanitary napkin 卫生棉 wèi shēng mián
saucepan 平底锅 píng dǐ guō
sauna 蒸汽浴 zhēng qì yù
save *v* **(on a computer)** 保存 bǎo cún
savings (account) 储蓄 chǔ xù
scanner 扫描器 sǎo miáo qì
scarf 围巾 wéi jīn
schedule *v* 预定日程 yù dìng rì chéng; ~ *n* 日程表 rì chéng biǎo
school 学校 xué xiào
science 科学 kē xué
scissors 剪刀 jiǎn dāo
sea 海 hǎi
seat 座位 zuò wèi
security 安检 ān jiǎn
see *v* 看见 kàn jiàn
self-service 自助 zì zhù
sell *v* 卖 mài
seminar 研讨会 yán tǎo huì
send *v* 送 sòng
senior citizen 老年人 lǎo nián rén
separated (marriage) 分居 fēn jū
serious 严肃 yán sù
service (in a restaurant) 服务 fú wù
sexually transmitted disease (STD) 性传播疾病 xìng chuán bō jí bìng
shampoo 香波 xiāng bō
sharp 锋利 fēng lì
shaving cream 剃须膏 tì xū gāo
sheet 床单 chuáng dān
ship *v* **(mail)** 邮寄 yóu jì
shirt 衬衫 chèn shān
shoe store 鞋店 xié diàn
shoes 鞋子 xié zi
shop *v* 购物 gòu wù
shopping 购物 gòu wù
shopping area 购物区 gòu wù qū
shopping centre *[BE]* 购物中心 gòu wù zhōng xīn
shopping mall 商城 shāng chéng
short 短小 duǎn xiǎo
short sleeves 短袖 duǎn xiù
shorts 短裤 duǎn kù
short-sighted *[BE]* 近视 jìn shì
shoulder 肩膀 jiān bǎng
show *v* 显示 xiǎn shì
shower 淋浴 lín yù
shrine 寺庙 sì miào
sick 病了 bìng le
side dish 配菜 pèi cài
side effect 副作用 fù zuò yòng
sightseeing 观光 guān guāng
sightseeing tour 观光旅游 guān guāng lǚ yóu
sign *v* 签字 qiān zì
silk 丝绸 sī chóu
silver 银 yín
single (unmarried) 单身 dān shēn
single bed 单人床 dān rén chuáng
single room 单人房间 dān rén fáng jiān
sink 水槽 shuǐ cáo
sister 姐妹 jiě mèi
sit *v* 坐下 zuò xià
size 尺寸 chǐ cùn
skin 皮肤 pí fū
skirt 裙子 qún zi
ski 滑雪 huá xuě
ski lift 滑雪缆车 huá xuě lǎn chē
sleep *v* 睡觉 shuì jiào
sleeper car 卧铺车 wò pù chē
sleeping bag 睡袋 shuì dài
sleeping car *[BE]* 卧铺车 wò pù chē
slice (of something) 切片 qiē piàn
slippers 拖鞋 tuō xié
slower 更慢 gèng màn
slowly 慢慢地 màn màn de
small 小 xiǎo
smaller 更小 gèng xiǎo
smoke *v* 吸烟 xī yān
smoking (area) 吸烟区 xī yān qū
snack bar 小吃店 xiǎo chī diàn
sneaker 运动鞋 yùn dòng xié
snorkeling equipment 水下呼吸设备 shuǐ xià hū xī shè bèi
snowboard 滑雪板 huá xuě bǎn
snowshoe 雪靴 xuě xuē
snowy 多雪 duō xuě
soap 肥皂 féi zào
soccer 足球 zú qiú

sock 袜子 wà zi
soother *[BE]* 橡皮奶嘴 xiàng pí nǎi zuǐ
sore throat 喉咙痛 hóu lóng tòng
sorry 抱歉 bào qiàn
south 南 nán
souvenir 纪念品 jì niàn pǐn
souvenir store 纪念品商店 jì niàn pǐn shāng diàn
spa 温泉 wēn quán
spatula 小铲子 xiǎo chǎn zi
speak *v* 讲话 jiǎng huà
specialist (doctor) 专家 zhuān jiā
specimen 标本 biāo běn
speeding 超速开车 chāo sù kāi chē
spell *v* 拼写 pīn xiě
spicy 辣 là
spine (body part) 脊椎 jǐ zhuī
spoon 勺子 sháo zi
sports 体育 tǐ yù
sporting goods store 体育用品商店 tǐ yù yòng pǐn shāng diàn
sports massage 体育按摩 tǐ yù àn mó
sprain 扭伤 niǔ shāng
stadium 体育场 tǐ yù chǎng
stairs 台阶 tái jiē
stamp *v* **(a ticket)** 盖印 gài yìn; ~ *n* **(postage)** 邮票 yóu piào
start *v* 开始 kāi shǐ
starter *[BE]* 开胃菜 kāi wèi cài
station 站 zhàn
statue 雕像 diāo xiàng
stay *v* 住在 zhù zài
steal *v* 偷 tōu
steamer 蒸锅 zhēng guō
steep 陡峭 dǒu qiào
sterling silver 纯银 chún yín
sting *n* 蜇 zhē
stolen 被偷了 bèi tōu le
stomach 胃 wèi
stomachache 胃疼 wèi téng
stop v 住手 zhù shǒu; ~ *n* 站 zhàn
store directory 商店目录 shāng diàn mù lù
storey *[BE]* 楼层 lóu céng
stove 炉子 lú zi
straight 直 zhí
strange 奇怪 qí guài
stream 小溪 xiǎo xī
stroller 婴儿推车 yīng ér tuī chē
student 学生 xué shēng
study *v* 学习 xué xí
stunning 震惊 zhèn jīng
subtitle 副标题 fù biāo tí
subway 地铁 dì tiě
subway station 地铁站 dì tiě zhàn
suit 西服套装 xī fú tào zhuāng
suitcase 手提箱 shǒu tí xiāng
sun 太阳 tài yáng
sunblock 防晒霜 fáng shài shuāng
sunburn 晒伤 shài shāng
sunglasses 太阳镜 tài yáng jìng
sunny 晴朗 qíng lǎng
sunscreen 防晒霜 fáng shài shuāng
sunstroke 中暑 zhòng shǔ
super (fuel) 超级 chāo jí
supermarket 超级市场 chāo jí shì chǎng
supervision 监督 jiān dū
surfboard 冲浪板 chōng làng bǎn
swallow *v* 吞下 tūn xià
sweater 毛衣 máo yī
sweatshirt 运动衫 yùn dòng shān
sweet (taste) 甜 tián
sweets *[BE]* 甜点 tián diǎn
swelling 肿胀 zhǒng zhàng
swim *v* 游泳 yóu yǒng
swimsuit 游泳衣 yóu yǒng yī
symbol (keyboard) 标志 biāo zhì
synagogue 犹太教堂 yóu tài jiào táng

T

table 桌子 zhuō zi
tablet (medicine) 片剂 piàn jì
take *v* 吃药 chī yào
take away *[BE]* 拿走 ná zǒu
tampon 月经栓 yuè jīng shuān
taste *v* 尝尝 cháng chang
taxi 出租车 chū zū chē
team 队 duì
teahouse 茶馆 chá guǎn
teaspoon 茶匙 chá chí
telephone 电话 diàn huà
temple (religious) 寺庙 sì miào
temporary 临时 lín shí
tennis 网球 wǎng qiú
tent 帐篷 zhàng péng
tent peg 帐篷桩 zhàng péng zhuāng
tent pole 帐篷杆 zhàng péng gǎn
terminal (airport) 候机厅 hòu jī tīng
terracotta 赤土陶 chì tǔ táo
terrible 可怕 kě pà
text *v* **(send a message)** 发短信 fā duǎn xìn; ~ *n* **(message)** 文字 wén zì
thank *v* 感谢 gǎn xiè
thank you 谢谢 xiè xie
that 那 nà
theater 剧院 jù yuàn
theft 偷窃 tōu qiè
there 那里 nà li
thief 小偷 xiǎo tōu
thigh 大腿 dà tuǐ
thirsty 渴 kě
this 这 zhè
throat 喉咙 hóu lóng
thunderstorm 雷雨 léi yǔ
ticket 票 piào
ticket office 售票处 shòu piào chù
tie (clothing) 领带 lǐng dài
tights *[BE]* 裤袜 kù wà
time 时间 shí jiān
timetable *[BE]* 时间表 shí jiān biǎo
tire 轮胎 lún tāi
tired 累了 lèi le
tissue 面巾纸 miàn jīn zhǐ
to go 拿走 ná zǒu
tobacconist 烟草零售商 yān cǎo líng shòu shāng
today 今天 jīn tiān
toe 脚趾 jiǎo zhǐ
toenail 脚趾甲 jiǎo zhǐ jia
toilet *[BE]* **(formal/informal)** 洗手间/厕所 xǐ shǒu jiān/cè suǒ
toilet paper 卫生纸 wèi shēng zhǐ

tomorrow 明天 míng tiān
tongue 舌头 shé tou
tonight 今晚 jīn wǎn
too 太 tài
tooth 牙 yá
toothpaste 牙膏 yá gāo
total (amount) 共计 gòng jì
tough (food) 硬 yìng
tourist 游人 yóu rén
tourist information office 旅游信息办公室 lǚ yóu xìn xī bàn gōng shì
tour 游览 yóu lǎn
tow truck 拖车 tuō chē
towel 毛巾 máo jīn
tower 塔 tǎ
town 镇 zhèn
town hall 市政厅 shì zhèng tīng
town map 市区地图 shì qū dì tú
town square 市中心广场 shì zhōng xīn guǎng chǎng
toy 玩具 wán jù
toy store 玩具店 wán jù diàn
track (train) 铁轨 tiě guǐ
traditional 传统 chuán tǒng
traffic light 红绿灯 hóng lǜ dēng
trail 山路小径 shān lù xiǎo jìng
trail map 山路图 shān lù tú
train 火车 huǒ chē
train station 火车站 huǒ chē zhàn
transfer *v* **(change trains/flights)** 转 zhuǎn; ~ *v* **(money)** 转账 zhuǎn zhàng
translate *v* 翻译 fān yì
trash 垃圾 lā jī
travel agency 旅行社 lǚ xíng shè
travel sickness 晕动病 yūn dòng bìng
traveler's check 旅行支票 lǚ xíng zhī piào
traveller's cheque *[BE]* 旅行支票 lǚ xíng zhī piào
tree 树 shù
trim (hair cut) 剪 jiǎn
trip 旅程 lǚ chéng
trolley *[BE]* 电车 diàn chē
trousers *[BE]* 长裤 cháng kù
T-shirt T恤衫 T xù shān
turn off (lights) 关 guān
turn on (lights) 开 kāi
TV 电视 diàn shì
type *v* 打字 dǎ zì
tyre *[BE]* 轮胎 lún tāi

U

United Kingdom (U.K.) 英国 yīng guó
United States (U.S.) 美国 měi guó
ugly 难看 nán kàn
umbrella 伞 sǎn
unattended 无人看管 wú rén kān guǎn
unconscious 没有知觉 méi yǒu zhī jué
underground *[BE]* 地下 dì xià
underground station *[BE]* 地铁站 dì tiě zhàn
underpants *[BE]* 内裤 nèi kù
understand *v* 理解 lǐ jiě
underwear 内衣 nèi yī
unemployed 失业者 shī yè zhě
university 大学 dà xué
unleaded (gas) 无铅 wú qiān
upper 上部 shàng bù
upset stomach 肠胃不适 cháng wèi bú shì
urgent 迫切 pò qiè
urine 尿 niào
use *v* 使用 shǐ yòng
username 用户名 yòng hù míng
utensil 器皿 qì mǐn

V

vacancy 有空房 yǒu kōng fáng
vacation 休假 xiū jià
vaccination 接种 jiē zhòng
vacuum cleaner 吸尘器 xī chén qì
vagina 阴道 yīn dào
vaginal infection 阴道传染 yīn dào chuán rǎn
valid 合法 hé fǎ
valley 河谷 hé gǔ
valuable 贵重的 guì zhòng de
value 价值 jià zhí
vegetarian 素食者 sù shí zhě
vehicle registration 车辆注册 chē liàng zhù cè
viewpoint *[BE]* 观点 guān diǎn
village 村庄 cūn zhuāng
vineyard 葡萄园 pú táo yuán
visa 签证 qiān zhèng
visit *v* 参观 cān guān
visiting hours 探病时间 tàn bìng shí jiān
visually impaired 弱视者 ruò shì zhě
vitamin 维生素 wéi shēng sù
V-neck V领 V lǐng
volleyball game 排球赛 pái qiú sài
vomit *v* 呕吐 ǒu tù

W

wait *v* 等待 děng dài; ~ *n* 等候时间 děng hòu shí jiān
waiter 服务员 fú wù yuán
waiting room 候诊室 hòu zhěn shì
waitress 女服务员 nǚ fú wù yuán
wake *v* 醒 xǐng
wake-up call 叫醒服务 jiào xǐng fú wù
walk *v* 走 zǒu; ~ *n* 步行 bù xíng
walking route 步行路线 bù xíng lù xiàn
wall clock 挂钟 guà zhōng
wallet 钱包 qián bāo
war memorial 战争纪念馆 zhàn zhēng jì niàn guǎn
warm *v* **(something)** 温暖 wēn nuǎn; **~ adj (temperature)** 暖和 nuǎn huo
washing machine 洗衣机 xǐ yī jī
watch 手表 shǒu biǎo
water skis 滑水板 huá shuǐ bǎn
waterfall 瀑布 pù bù
weather 天气 tiān qì
week 星期 xīng qī
weekend 周末 zhōu mò
weekly 每周 měi zhōu
welcome *v* 欢迎 huān yíng
well-rested 休息得很好 xiū xī dé hěn hǎo

west 西部 xī bù
what 什么 shén me
wheelchair 轮椅 lún yǐ
wheelchair ramp 轮椅道 lún yǐ dào
when 什么时候 shén me shí hòu
where 哪里 nǎ li
white 白色 bái sè
who 谁 shuí/shéi
widowed 寡居 guǎ jū
wife 妻子 qī zi
window 窗 chuāng
window case 橱窗 chú chuāng
wine list 酒类表 jiǔ lèi biǎo
wireless internet 无线互联网 wú xiàn hù lián wǎng
wireless internet service 无线互联网服务 wú xiàn hù lián wǎng fú wù
wireless phone 手机 shǒu jī
with 跟 gēn
withdraw *v* 退出 tuì chū
withdrawal (bank) 取钱 qǔ qián
without 没有 méi yǒu
wok 炒锅 chǎo guō
woman 妇女 fù nǚ
wool 羊毛 yáng máo
work *v* 工作 gōng zuò
wrap *v* **(a package)** 包 bāo
wrist 手腕 shǒu wàn
write *v* 写 xiě

Y

year 年 nián
yellow 黄色 huáng sè
yes 是 shì
yesterday 昨天 zuó tiān
young 年轻 nián qīng
you're welcome 没关系 méi guān xi
youth hostel 青年旅舍 qīng nián lǚ shè
yuan 元 yuán

Z

zoo 动物园 dòng wù yuán

MANDARIN CHINESE–ENGLISH

A

ā sī pǐ lín 阿斯匹林 aspirin
ài 爱 love
ài ěr lán 爱尔兰 Ireland
ài ěr lán rén 爱尔兰人 Irish
ài zī bìng 爱滋病 AIDS
ān jiǎn 安检 security
ān jìng 安静 quiet
ān quán 安全 safe (protected)
àn 按 *v* push
àn mó 按摩 massage
āng zāng 肮脏 dirty
áng guì 昂贵 expensive
ào dà lì yà rén 澳大利亚人 Australian

B

bā léi 芭蕾 ballet
bá 拔 *v* extract (tooth)
bái sè 白色 white
bǎi huò shāng diàn 百货商店 department store
bàn 半 half
bàn gōng jīn 半公斤 half-kilo
bàn gōng shì 办公室 office
bàn gōng shí jiān 办公时间 office hours
bàn lǐ dēng jī shǒu xù 办理登机手续 check-in (airport)
bàn rù zhù 办入住 check-in (hotel)
bàn xiǎo shí 半小时 half hour
bāng zhù 帮助 help
bàng 磅 pound (weight)
bàng qiú 棒球 baseball
bāo 包 *v* wrap (a package)
bāo guǒ 包裹 package
bāo kuò 包括 *v* include
bǎo xiān mó 保鲜膜 plastic wrap [cling film BE]
bǎo xiǎn 保险 insurance
bǎo xiǎn gōng sī 保险公司 insurance company
bǎo xiǎn guì 保险柜 safe (thing)
bǎo xiǎn kǎ 保险卡 insurance card
bǎo cún 保存 *v* save (on a computer)
bǎo mǔ 保姆 babysitter
bào guāng 曝光 exposure (film)
bào qiàn 抱歉 sorry
bào tān 报摊 newsstand
bào zhǐ 报纸 newspaper
bēi bāo 背包 backpack
bēi zi 子 cup
běi bù 北部 north
bèi bù 背部 back (body part)
bèi qiǎng le 被抢了 robbed
bèi tōu le 被偷了 stolen
bēng dài 绷带 bandage
bí zi 鼻子 nose
bǐ 笔 pen
bǐ jī ní yǒng zhuāng 比基尼泳装 bikini
bǐ jì 笔记 bill [note BE]
bǐ sà diàn 比萨店 pizzeria
bì yùn tào 避孕套 condom
biàn gēng lù xiàn 变更路线 alternate route
biàn mì 便秘 constipated
biàn yā qì 变压器 adapter
biāo běn 标本 specimen
biāo zhì 标志 symbol (keyboard)
biǎo gé 表格 form (fill-in)
bié zhēn 别针 brooch
bīng 冰 ice
bīng lěng 冰冷 icy
bīng qiú 冰球 ice hockey
bīng xiāng 冰箱 refrigerator
bìng 病 sick [ill BE]
bō hào 拨号 *v* dial
bō li 玻璃 glass (material)
bō li bēi 玻璃 glass

(drinking)
bō li tiáo liào píng 玻璃调料瓶 carafe
bó jīn 铂金 platinum
bó wù guǎn 博物馆 museum
bó zi 脖子 neck
bú / bù 不 no
bú guì 不贵 inexpensive
bú xiàn shǐ yòng cì shù de 不限使用次数的 multiple-trip (ticket)
bǔ yǎng 哺养 *v* feed
bù fen 部分 portion
bù jiàn 部件 part (for car)
bù luò fēn 布洛芬 ibuprofen
bù xíng 步行 *n* walk
bù xíng lù xiàn 步行路线 walking route

C

cā 擦 mop
cài dān 菜单 menu
cān guān 参观 *v* visit
cān guǎn 餐馆 restaurant
cān jīn 餐巾 napkin
cán jí 残疾 handicapped [disabled BE]
cán ji rén tōng dào 残疾人通道 handi-capped- [disabled- BE] accessible
cāng 舱 cabin
cāo chǎng 操场 playground
CD CD CD
cè liáng 测量 *v* measure (someone)
chā cuò 差错 mistake
chā rù 插入 *v* insert (on an ATM)
chā zi 叉子 fork
chá chí 茶匙 teaspoon
chá guǎn 茶馆 teahouse
chái yóu 柴油 diesel
cháng 长 long
cháng chang 尝尝 *v* taste
cháng kù 长裤 pants [trousers BE]
cháng wèi bú shì 肠胃不适 upset stomach
cháng xiù zi 长袖子 long sleeves
cháng zi 肠子 intestine
chāo guò 超过 excess
chāo jí 超级 super (fuel)
chāo jí shì chǎng 超级市场 supermarket
chāo sù kāi chē 超速开车 speeding
chǎo guō 炒锅 wok
chē kù 车库 garage
chē liàng zhù cè 车辆注册 vehicle registration
chén liè chú 陈列橱 display case
chèn shān 衬衫 shirt
chéng bǎo 城堡 castle
chéng kè 乘客 passenger
chī 吃 *v* eat
chī yào 吃药 *v* take medicine
chí táng 池塘 pond
chǐ cùn 尺寸 size
chì tǔ táo 赤土陶 terracotta
chōng diàn 充电 *v* recharge
chōng làng bǎn 冲浪板 surfboard
chōng xuè 充血 congestion
chóng fù 重复 *v* repeat
chóng yǎo 虫咬 insect bite
chóng zi 虫子 bug
chū gù zhàng 出故障 breakdown
chū kǒu 出口 *n* exit
chū nà yuán 出纳员 cashier
chū qù 出去 *v* exit
chū xí 出席 *v* attend
chū xué zhě 初学者 beginner (skill level)
chū zū chē 出租车 rental car, taxi
chū zū qì chē 出租汽车 car rental [hire BE]
chú chuāng 橱窗 window case
chú fáng 厨房 kitchen
chú fáng xī zhǐ 厨房锡纸 aluminum [kitchen BE] foil
chǔ fāng yào 处方药 prescription
chǔ xù 储蓄 savings (account)
chuán rǎn 传染 infected
chuán rǎn de 传染的 contagious
chuán sòng dài 传送带 conveyor belt
chuán tǒng 传统 traditional
chuán zhēn 传真 *n* fax
chuán zhēn hào 传真号 fax number
chuāng 窗 window
chuáng 床 bed
chuáng dān 床单 sheet
chuǎng rù 闯入 break-in (burglary)
chuī fēng jī 吹风机 hair dryer
chuí zi 锤子 hammer
chún yín 纯银 sterling silver
cí qì 瓷器 china
cūn zhuāng 村庄 village
cún chǔ kǎ 存储卡 memory card
cún qián 存钱 *v* deposit
cuò guò 错过 missing

D

dā chē 搭车 *v* hitchhike
dǎ diàn hào mǎ 电话号码 phone number
dǎ bāo 打包 *v* pack
dǎ diàn huà 打电话 *v* call
dǎ huǒ jī 打火机 lighter
dǎ kāi 打开 *v* open
dǎ rǎo 打扰 *v* bother
dǎ yìn 打印 *v* print
dǎ zì 打字 *v* type
dà 大 big
dà jiào táng 大教堂 cathedral
dà shà 大厦 building
dà tuǐ 大腿 thigh
dà xué 大学 university
dài bàn chù 代办处 agency
dài lái 带来 *v* bring
dài zǎo cān de lǚ diàn 带早餐的旅店 bed and breakfast
dài zi 袋子 bag
dān chéng 单程 one-way (ticket)
dān dú 单独 alone
dān rén chuáng 单人床 single bed
dān rén fáng jiān 单人房间 single room
dān shēn 单身 single (unmarried)
dān xíng dào 单行道 one-way street
dāng dì 当地 local
dāo zi 刀子 knife
dǎo máng quǎn 导盲犬 guide dog
dào dá 到达 *v* arrive

dào kōng 倒空 *v* empty
dào lù 道路 path
dēng 灯 light (overhead)
dēng jī 登机 *v* board
dēng jī mén 登机门 gate (airport)
dēng jī pái 登机牌 boarding pass
dēng lù 登录 log on
děng dài 等待 *v* wait
děng hòu shí jiān 等候时间 *n* wait
dī 滴 drop (medicine)
dī 低 low
dǐ dá 抵达 arrivals (airport)
dì bǎn 地板 floor
dì tiě 地铁 subway [underground BE]
dì tiě zhàn 地铁站 subway [underground BE] station
dì tú 地图 *n* map
dì zhǐ 地址 address
dié zi 碟子 dish (kitchen)
diān xián 癫痫 epileptic
diǎn 点 light (cigarette)
diǎn cài 点菜 *v* order
diǎn xīn diàn 点心店 pastry shop
diàn 垫 sanitary napkin [pad BE]
diàn chā zuò 电插座 electric outlet
diàn chē 电车 trolley
diàn chí 电池 battery
diàn dēng pào 电灯泡 lightbulb
diàn dòng zì xíng chē 电动自行车 moped
diàn fàn guō 电饭锅 rice cooker
diàn huà 电话 telephone, phone call
diàn huà hào mǎ 电话号码 phone
diàn huà kǎ 电话卡 phone card
diàn shàn 电扇 fan (appliance)
diàn shì 电视 TV
diàn tī 电梯 elevator [lift BE]
diàn yǐng 电影 movie
diàn yǐng yuàn 电影院 movie theater
diàn yóu dì zhǐ 电邮地址 e-mail address
diàn zǐ piào 电子票 e-ticket
diàn zǐ yóu jiàn 电子邮件 *n* e-mail
diāo kè 雕刻 *v* engrave
diāo xiàng 雕像 statue
diū shī 丢失 *v* lose (something)
dōng bù 东部 east
dòng 洞 cave
dòng mài 动脉 artery
dòng wù 动物 animal
dòng wù yuán 动物园 zoo
dǒu qiào 陡峭 steep
dòu rén xǐ ài 逗人喜爱 cute
dú yào 毒药 poison
dǔ bó yú lè chǎng 赌博娱乐场 casino
dù 度 degrees (temperature)
duǎn kù 短裤 shorts
duǎn xiǎo 短小 short
duǎn xiù 短袖 short sleeves
duàn 断 *v* break (tooth)
duàn kāi 断开 disconnect (computer)
duì 队 team
duì fāng fù fèi diàn huà 对方付费电话 *v* call collect [reverse the charges] BE]
duì huàn 兑换 *v* exchange (money)
duì huàn lǜ 兑换率 exchange rate
duì xiàn jīn 兑现金 *v* cash
dùn 炖 stewed
duō shǎo 多少 how much
duō xuě 多雪 snowy
duō yǔ 多雨 rainy
DVD DVD DVD

E

é wài 额外 extra
ě xin 恶心 nauseous
ér kē yī shēng 儿科医生 pediatrician
ér tóng cài dān 儿童菜单 children's menu
ér tóng fàn liàng 儿童饭量 children's portion
ér tóng yóu yǒng chí 儿童游泳池 kiddie [paddling BE] pool
ér tóng zuò yǐ 儿童座椅 child's seat
ěr duo 耳朵 ear
ěr duo téng 耳朵疼 earache
ěr huán 耳环 earrings
ěr jī 耳机 headphones

F

fā chuán zhēn 发传真 *v* fax
fā diàn yóu 发电邮 *v* e-mail
fā duǎn xìn 发短信 *v* text (send a message)
fā huò piào 发货票 invoice
fā shāo 发烧 fever
fā yīn 发音 *v* pronounce
fá kuǎn 罚款 fine (fee)
fà jiāo 发胶 gel (hair)
fà láng 珐琅 enamel (jewelry)
fà láng 发廊 hair salon
fà xíng 发型 hairstyle
fà xíng shī 发型师 hairstylist
fān yì 翻译 *v* translate
fǎn huán 返还 round-trip [return BE]
fàn 饭 meal
fàn tīng 饭厅 dining room
fāng xiàng 方向 direction
fāng xiāng liáo fǎ 芳香疗法 aromatherapy
fáng huǒ mén 防火门 fire door
fáng jiān 房间 room
fáng jiān yào shi 房间钥匙 room key
fáng shài shuāng 防晒霜 sunblock
fáng zi 房子 house
fēi chǔ fāng yào 非处方药 over the counter [unbranded BE] (medication)
fēi jī 飞机 airplane
fēi jī chǎng 飞机场 airport
féi zào 肥皂 soap
fěi cuì 翡翠 jade
fèi 肺 lung
fèi xū 废墟 ruins
fèi yòng 费用 fee
fēn jī 分机 extension (phone)
fēn jū 分居 separated (marriage)
fēn zhōng 分钟 minute
fěn hóng sè 粉红色 pink
fēng lì 锋利 sharp
fú wù 服务 service (in a

restaurant)
fú wù tái 服务台 reservation desk
fú wù yuán 服务员 waiter
fú zhuāng diàn 服装店 clothing store
fǔ shì 俯视 overlook (scenic place)
fù biāo tí 副标题 subtitle
fù chǎn kē yī shī 妇产科医师 gynecologist
fù jiā fèi 附加费 cover charge
fù jìn 附近 near
fù nǚ 妇女 woman
fù qīn 父亲 father
fù xiè 腹泻 diarrhea
fù yìn jiàn 复印件 photocopy
fù zuò yòng 副作用 side effect

G

gǎi 改 *v* alter (clothing)
gài yìn 盖印 *v* stamp (a ticket)
gān jìng 干净 *adj* clean
gān xǐ diàn 干洗店 dry cleaner
gān zàng 肝脏 liver (body part)
gǎn mào 感冒 cold (sickness)
gǎn shí jiān 赶时间 rush
gǎn xiè 感谢 *v* thank
gāo 高 high
gāo ěr fū qiú bǐ sài 高尔夫球比赛 golf tournament
gāo ěr fū qiú chǎng 高尔夫球场 golf course
gāo jiǎo yǐ 高脚椅 highchair
gāo sù gōng lù 高速公路 highway [motorway BE]
gē bo 胳膊 arm
gē jù 歌剧 opera
gē jù yuàn 歌剧院 opera house
gé yè 隔夜 overnight
gè rén mì mǎ 个人密码 personal identification number (PIN)
gěi 给 *v* give
gēn 跟 with
gèng dī 更低 lower
gèng duō 更多 more
gèng hǎo 更好 better
gèng kuài 更快 faster
gèng màn 更慢 slower
gèng pián yi 更便宜 cheaper
gèng xiǎo 更小 smaller
gèng zǎo 更早 earlier
gōng diàn 宫殿 palace
gōng gòng 公共 public
gōng gòng qì chē 公共汽车 bus
gōng gòng qì chē piào 公共汽车票 bus ticket
gōng gòng qì chē yóu lǎn 公共汽车游览 bus tour
gōng gòng qì chē zhàn 公共汽车站 bus station, bus stop
gōng jī 攻击 attack (on person)
gōng jīn 公斤 kilo(gram)
gōng lǐ 公里 kilometer
gōng shēng 公升 liter
gōng yòng diàn huà 公用电话 pay phone
gōng yù 公寓 apartment
gōng yuán 公园 *n* park
gōng zuò 工作 *v* work
gǒng láng ér tóng yóu xì chǎng 拱廊儿童游戏场 arcade
gòng jì 共计 total (amount)
gòu 够 *v* reach
gòu wù 购物 shop
gòu wù lán zǐ 购物篮子 basket (grocery store)
gòu wù qū 购物区 shopping area
gòu wù zhōng xīn 购物中心 shopping mall [centre BE]
gǔ diǎn yīn yuè 古典音乐 classical music
gǔ dǒng diàn 古店 antiques store
gǔ tou 骨头 bone
gù dìng jià gé cài dān 价格固定的菜单 fixed-price menu
gù wèn 顾问 consultant
gù yòng 雇用 *v* rent [hire BE]
guǎ jū 寡居 widowed
guà hào xìn 挂号信 registered mail
guà zhōng 挂钟 wall clock
guǎi jiǎo chù 拐角处 around (the corner)
guān 关 turn off (lights)
guān bì 关闭 closed
guān diǎn 观点 overlook [viewpoint BE]
guān guāng 观光 sightseeing
guān guāng lǚ yóu 观光旅游 sightseeing tour
guān jié 关节 joint (body part)
guān jié yán 关节炎 arthritis
guān mén 关门 *v* close (a shop)
guān shuì 关税 duty (tax)
guān xì 关系 relationship
guàn 罐 pot
guàn zhuāng shí pǐn 罐装食品 canned good
guàn zi 罐子 jar
guī huán 归还 *v* return
guì zhòng de 贵重的 valuable
guó jí 国籍 nationality
guó jì 国际 international (airport area)
guó jì háng bān 国际航班 international flight
guó jì xué shēng zhèng 国际学生证 international student card
guó jiā dài hào 国家代号 country code
guó nèi 国内 domestic
guó nèi háng bān 国内航班 domestic flight
guò dào 过道 aisle
guò mǐn 过敏 allergic
guò mǐn fǎn yìng 过敏反应 allergic reaction
guò shú 过熟 overdone

H

hǎi 海 sea
hǎi guān 海关 customs
hǎi tān 海滩 beach
hái zi 孩子 child
hǎn jiàn 罕见 rare (object)
háng bān 航班 flight
háng kōng gōng sī 航空公司 airline
háng kōng xìn 航空信 airmail
hǎo 好 good, nice, OK
hē 喝 *v* drink
hé 河 river
hé fǎ 合法 valid

hé gǔ 河谷 valley
hè sè 褐色 brown
hēi àn 黑暗 dark
hēi sè 黑色 black
hóng lǜ dēng 红绿灯 traffic light
hóng sè 红色 red
hóu lóng 喉咙 throat
hóu lóng tòng 喉咙痛 sore throat
hòu jī tīng 候机厅 terminal (airport)
hòu mian 后面 behind (direction)
hòu zhěn shì 候诊室 waiting room
hū xī 呼吸 *v* breathe
hú 湖 lake
hù fà sù 护发素 conditioner
hù lián wǎng 互联网 internet
hù lián wǎng fú wù 互联网服务 internet service
hù shi 护士 nurse
hù zhào 护照 passport
hù zhào guǎn zhì 护照管制 passport control
huā 花 flower
huā fèi 花费 *v* cost
huā fěn zhèng 花粉症 hay fever
huá shuǐ bǎn 滑水板 water skis
huá tǐng 划艇 rowboat
huá xuě 滑雪 ski
huá xuě bǎn 滑雪板 snowboard
huá xuě gǎn 滑雪杆 poles (skiing)
huá xuě lǎn chē 滑雪缆车 ski lift
huà zhuāng rǔ yè 化妆乳液 lotion
huái yùn 怀孕 pregnant
huài le 坏了 damaged
huān yíng 欢 *v* welcome
huàn chē 换车 *v* change (buses)
huàn dì fang 换地方 *n* exchange (place)
huàn niào bù 换尿布 *n* change (baby)
huàn qián 换钱 *v* change (money)
huáng sè 黄色 yellow
huī sè 灰色 gray
huí shōu 回收 recycling
huì yì 会议 conference, meeting
huì yì shì 会议室 meeting room
huì yì tīng 会议厅 convention hall
huì yuán zhèng 会员证 membership card
huǒ 火 fire
huǒ chái 火柴 *n* match (sports)
huǒ chē zhàn 火车站 train [railway BE] station
huǒ chē 火车 train
huò bì 货币 currency
huò bì duì huàn 货币兑换 currency exchange
huò bì duì huàn jú 货币兑换局 currency exchange office

J

jī è 饥饿 hungry
jī ròu 肌肉 muscle
jǐ zhuī 脊椎 spine (body part)
jì gōng 技工 mechanic
jì huà shēng yù yào piàn 计划生育药片 Pill (birth control)
jì niàn guǎn 纪念馆 memorial (place)
jì niàn pǐn 纪念品 souvenir
jì niàn pǐn shāng diàn 纪念品商店 souvenir store
jì shí qì 计时器 meter (parking)
jí shí xùn xī 即时讯息 instant message
jì suàn jī 计算机 computer
jiā dà hào 加大号 plus size
jià gé 价格 price
jiá kè 夹克 jacket
jiā ná dà 加拿大 Canada
jiā ná dà rén 加拿大人 Canadian
jiā rè 加热 heat
jiā rè qì 加热器 heater
jià rì 假日 vacation [holiday BE]
jiā rù 加入 *v* join
jiā tíng 家庭 family
jiā yòng wù pǐn 家用物品 household good
jiā yóu zhàn 加油站 gas [petrol BE] station
jiǎ yá 假牙 denture
jià zhí 价值 value
jiān bǎng 肩膀 shoulder
jiān dū 监督 supervision
jiān guō 煎锅 frying pan
jiān zhí 兼职 part-time
jiǎn 剪 *v* cut (hair)
jiǎn chá 检查 *v* check (something)
jiǎn dāo 剪刀 scissors
jiàn 件 case (amount)
jiàn kāng 健康 health
jiàn kāng shí pǐn shāng diàn 健康食品商店 health food store
jiàn miàn 见面 *v* meet (someone)
jiǎng huà 讲话 *v* speak
jiāo huàn 交换 *v* exchange (goods)
jiāo juǎn 胶卷 film (camera)
jiāo xiǎo 娇小 petite
jiǎo 脚 foot
jiǎo wàn 脚腕 ankle
jiǎo zhǐ 脚趾 toe
jiào shǎo 较少 less
jiào táng 教堂 church
jiào xǐng fú wù 叫醒服务 wake-up call
jiē shòu 接受 *v* receive
jiē zhòng 接种 vaccination
jié hūn 结婚 *v* marry
jié shù 结束 *v* end
jiě mèi 姐妹 sister
jiè jì kǎ 借记卡 debit card
jiè shào 介绍 *v* introduce
jiè zhi 戒指 ring
jīn tiān 今天 today
jīn wǎn 今晚 tonight
jīn zi 金子 gold
jǐn jí chū kǒu 紧急出口 emergency exit
jǐn jí zhuàng tài 紧急状态 emergency
jìn 近 close
jìn rù 进入 *v* enter, access
jìn yān 禁烟 non-smoking
jìn zhǐ 禁止 *v* prohibit
jīng jì cāng 经济舱 economy class
jīng lǐ 理 manager
jīng qī fù tòng 经期腹痛 menstrual cramp
jǐng chá 警察 police
jǐng chá jú 警察局 police station
jǐng chá bào gào 警察报告 police report
jǐng tài lán 景泰蓝 cloisonné
jìng piàn 镜片 lens

jiǔ bā 酒吧 bar (place)
jiǔ diàn 酒店 liquor store [off-licence BE]
jiù hù chē 救护车 ambulance
jiǔ lèi biǎo 酒类表 wine list
jiù shēng yī 救生衣 life jacket
jiù shēng yuán 救生员 lifeguard
jū zhù 居住 *v* live
jú sè 桔色 orange (color)
jù jué 拒绝 *v* decline (credit card)
jù lè bù 俱乐部 club
jù yuàn 剧院 theater
jué shì yuè 爵士乐 jazz
jué shì yuè jù lè bù 爵士乐俱乐部 jazz club

K

kā fēi diàn 咖啡店 coffee shop
kǎ 卡 card
kǎ lù lǐ 卡路里 calorie
kāi 开 turn on (lights)
kāi chē 开车 *v* drive
kāi chǔ fāng 开处方 *v* prescribe
kāi fù kuǎn dān 开付款单 *v* bill (charge)
kāi guàn qì 开罐器 can opener
kāi sāi zuàn 开塞钻 corkscrew
kāi shǐ 开始 *v* begin
kāi shǐ 开始 *v* start
kāi wèi cài 开胃菜 appetizer [starter BE]
kāi zhe 开着 *adj* open
kàn 看 *v* look
kàn jiàn 看见 *v* see
kàng shēng sù 抗生素 antibiotic
kǎo ròu 烤肉 barbecue
kào guò dào de wèi zi 靠过道的位子 aisle seat
kē lóng xiāng shuǐ 科隆香水 cologne
kē xué 科学 science
ké sou 咳嗽 cough
kě kǒu 可口 delicious
kě pà 可怕 terrible
kě 渴 thirsty
kè 克 gram
kè cāng 客舱 cabin
kè chéng 课程 lesson
kè fáng qīng jié fú wù 客房清洁服务 housekeeping services
kè fáng sòng cān fú wù 客房送餐服务 room service
kōng tiáo 空调 air conditioning
kǒu dài 口袋 pocket
kǒu xiāng táng 口香糖 chewing gum
kǒu yì yuán 口译员 interpreter
kù wà 裤袜 pantyhose [tights BE]
kuài 快 express
kuài cān 快餐 fast food
kuài sù 快速 fast
kuài zi 筷子 chopsticks
kùn nan 困难 difficult

L

lā *v* pull
lā jī 垃圾 trash [rubbish BE]
lā jī dài 垃圾袋 garbage [rubbish BE] bag
là 辣 hot (spicy)
lái 来 *v* come
lán sè 蓝色 blue
lán qiú 篮球 basketball
lǎn chē 缆车 cable car
lǎn chē piào 缆车票 lift pass
làng màn 浪漫 romantic
lǎo 老 old
lǎo nián rén 老年人 senior citizen
lè qù 乐趣 pleasure
léi yǔ 雷雨 thunderstorm
lèi gǔ 肋骨 rib (body part)
lèi le 累了 tired
lěng 冷 cold (temperature)
lěng dòng jī 冷冻机 freezer
lí hūn 离婚 *v* divorce
lí kāi 离开 departures
lí mǐ 厘米 centimeter
lǐ bài 礼拜 mass (church service)
lǐ chéng shù 里程数 mileage
lǐ fà 理发 haircut
lǐ fà shī 理发师 barber
lǐ jiě 理解 *v* understand
lǐ pǐn diàn 礼品店 gift shop
lǐ wù 礼物 gift
lián jiē 连接 *v* connect (internet)
lián xì 联系 *v* contact
lián yi qún 连衣裙 dress (piece of clothing)
liáng 凉 cool (temperature)
liáng bēi 量 measuring cup
liáng chí 量匙 measuring spoon
liáng xié 凉鞋 sandals
lín shí 临时 temporary
lín yù 淋浴 shower
líng qián 零钱 *v* change (money)
lǐng dài 领带 tie (clothing)
lǐng shì guǎn 领事馆 consulate
lìng rén jīng qí de 令人惊奇的 amazing
liú dòng xìng 流动性 mobility
liú xíng yīn yuè 流行音乐 pop music
liú xuè 流血 *v* bleed
lóng 聋 deaf
lóu céng 楼层 floor [storey BE]
lú zi 炉子 stove
lù quán 路权 right of way
lù xiàn 路线 route
lù xiàn tú 路线图 road map
lù yíng 露营 *v* camp
lù yíng dì 露营地 campsite
lù yíng lú 露营炉 camping stove
lún dù 轮渡 ferry
lún tāi 轮胎 tire [tyre BE]
lún yǐ 轮椅 wheelchair
lún yǐ dào 轮椅道 wheelchair ramp
lǚ chéng 旅程 trip
lǚ guǎn 旅馆 hotel
lǚ xíng shè 旅行社 travel agency
lǚ xíng zhī piào 旅行支票 travelers check [cheque BE]
lǚ yóu xìn xī bàn gōng shì 旅游信息办公室 tourist information office
lǚ shè 旅舍 hostel
lǜ sè 绿色 green
lǜ shī 律师 lawyer

M

má zuì 麻醉 anesthesia
mǎi 买 *v* buy
mài 卖 *v* sell

mài huā rén 卖花人 florist
màn màn de 慢慢地 slowly
máng cháng 盲肠 appendix (body part)
máo jīn 毛巾 towel
máo yī 毛衣 sweater
mào zi 帽子 hat
méi guān xi 没关系 you're welcome
méi shén me 没什么 nothing
méi yǒu 没有 without
méi yǒu zhī jué 没有知觉 unconscious
měi 每 every
měi tiān 每天 per day
měi wǎn 每晚 per night
měi xiǎo shí 每小时 per hour
měi xīng qī 每星期 per week
měi zhōu 每周 weekly
měi guó 美国 United States (U.S.)
měi guó rén 美国人 American
měi jiǎ shā lóng 美甲沙龙 nail salon
měi lì 美丽 beautiful
měi yuán 美元 dollar (U.S.)
mǐ huáng sè 米黄色 beige
mì mǎ 密码 password
mián hua 棉花 cotton
miǎn fèi 免费 free
miǎn shuì 免税 duty-free
miàn bāo diàn 面包店 bakery
miàn bù 面部 facial
miàn jīn zhǐ 面巾纸 tissue
miàn kǒng 面孔 face
mín jiān yīn yuè 民间音乐 folk music
míng piàn 名片 business card
míng tiān 明天 tomorrow
míng xìn piàn 明信片 postcard
míng zì 名字 name
mó sī 摩丝 mousse (hair)
mó tuō chē 摩托车 motorcycle
mǔ qīn 母亲 mother
mǔ rǔ wèi yǎng 母乳喂养 breastfeed
mù tàn 木炭 charcoal

N

ná zǒu 拿走 to go [take away BE]
nǎ lǐ 哪里 where
nà 那 that
nà lǐ 那里 there
nǎi fěn 奶粉 formula (baby)
nǎi píng 奶瓶 baby bottle
nán 南 south
nán hái 男孩 boy
nán kàn 难看 ugly
nán nèi kù 男内裤 briefs (clothing)
nán péng you 男朋友 boyfriend
nán rén 男人 man
nán tóng xìng liàn 男同性恋 gay
nán tóng xìng liàn jiǔ bā 男同性恋酒吧 gay bar
nán tóng xìng liàn jù lè bù 男同性恋俱乐部 gay club
nèi kù 内裤 underwear [underpants BE]
nǐ hǎo 你好 hello
nián 年 year
nián líng 年龄 age
nián qīng 年轻 young
niǎo 鸟 bird
niào 尿 urine
niào bù 尿布 diaper [nappy BE]
niú zǎi kù 牛仔裤 jeans
niǔ shāng 扭伤 sprain
nóng chǎn pǐn 农产品 produce
nóng chǎn pǐn shāng diàn 农产品商店 produce store
nóng chǎng 农场 farm
nuǎn huo 暖和 *adj* warm (temperature)
nuǎn qì 暖气 heat [heating BE]
nǚ chèn shān 女衬衫 blouse
nǚ fú wù yuán 女服务员 waitress
nǚ hái 女孩 girl
nǚ péng you 女朋友 girlfriend

O

ǒu tù 呕吐 *v* vomit

P

pái qiú sài 排球赛 volleyball game
pán zi 盘子 plate
páng guāng 膀胱 bladder
pǎo mǎ chǎng 跑马场 racetrack
pèi cài 配菜 side dish
pèi yào fāng 配药方 *v* fill [make up BE] (a prescription)
pēn fà jì 喷发剂 hairspray
pēn quán 喷泉 fountain
pēng tiáo 烹调 *v* cook
pēng tiáo méi qì 烹调煤气 cooking gas
péng you 朋友 friend
pí dài 皮带 belt
pí fū 皮肤 skin
pí gé 皮革 leather
pí zhěn 皮疹 rash
pì gu 屁股 buttocks
pián yi 便宜 cheap
piàn 片 piece
piàn jì 片剂 tablet (medicine)
piào 票 ticket
pīn xiě 拼写 *v* spell
pín xuè 贫血 anemic
píng 瓶 bottle
píng dǐ guō 平底锅 saucepan
píng qǐ zi 瓶启子 bottle opener
pò le 破了 broken
pò qiè 迫切 urgent
pú táo yuán 葡萄园 vineyard
pǔ tóng 普通 regular
pù bù 瀑布 waterfall
pù wèi 铺位 berth

Q

qī zi 妻子 wife
qī jiān 期间 period (of time)
qī qì 漆器 lacquerware
qí guài 奇怪 strange
qǐ fēi 起飞 *v* leave
qì tǒng 气筒 air pump
qì chuǎn 气喘 asthmatic
qì chē 汽车 car
qì chē zhàn 汽车站 bus station
qì chē zuò wèi 汽车座位 car seat
qì chuán 汽船 motor boat
qì mǐn 器皿 utensil
qiān yǐn lǎn chē 牵引缆车 drag lift

qiān zhèng 签证 visa
qiān zì 签字 *v* sign
qián 钱 money
qián bāo 钱包 purse, wallet
qián shuǐ 潜水 *v* dive
qián shuǐ yòng jù 潜水用具 diving equipment
qiáng jiān 强奸 rape
qiǎng 抢 *v* mug
qiǎng duó 抢夺 *v* rob
qiáo liáng 桥梁 bridge
qiào bì 峭壁 cliff
qiē piàn 切片 slice (of something)
qīn wěn 亲吻 *v* kiss
qīng biàn xiǎo chuáng 轻便小床 cot
qīng biàn zhé dié tǎng yǐ 轻便折叠躺椅 deck chair
qīng chú 清除 *v* clear (on an ATM)
qīng jié chǎn pǐn 清洁产品 cleaning product
qīng jié chǎn pǐn gōng yìng 清洁产品供应 cleaning supplies
qīng méi sù 青霉素 penicillin
qīng nián lǚ shè 青年旅舍 youth hostel
qīng xǐ 清洗 *v* clean
qīng zhēn shí pǐn 清真食品 halal
qīng zhēn sì 清真寺 mosque
qíng lǎng 晴朗 sunny
qǐng 请 please
qiú pāi 球拍 racket (sports)
qū gùn qiú 曲棍球 hockey
qū hà 区号 area code
qū yù 区域 region
qǔ 取 pick up (something)
qǔ qián 取钱 withdrawal (bank)
qǔ xiāo 取消 *v* cancel
qù 去 *v* go (somewhere)
quán miàn fú wù 全面服务 full service
quán jī bǐ sài 击比赛 boxing match
qún zi 裙子 skirt

R

rè 热 hot (temperature)
rè shuǐ 热水 hot water
rén mín bì 人民币 Ren Min Bi
rén min dà huì táng 人民大会堂 Great Hall of the People
rèn hé dōng xī 任何东西 anything
rì běn 日本 Japanese (restaurant)
rì chéng biǎo 日程表 *n* schedule
rì qī 日期 date (calendar)
róng yì 容易 easy
rǔ fáng 乳房 breast
rǔ táng guò mǐn 乳糖过敏 lactose intolerant
rù chǎng 入场 admission
rù kǒu 入口 entrance
ruò shì zhě 弱视者 visually impaired

S

sǎn 伞 umbrella
sǎo miáo qì 扫描器 scanner
sēn lín 森林 forest
shā chóng jì 杀虫剂 insect repellent
shā guō 砂锅 clay pot
shā mò 沙漠 desert
shài shāng 晒伤 sunburn
shān 山 mountain
shān dì chē 山地车 mountain bike
shān dǐng 山顶 peak (of a mountain)
shān lù tú 山路图 trail map
shān lù xiǎo jìng 山路小径 trail
shān chú 删除 *v* delete
shāng kǒu 伤口 *n* cut (injury)
shāng xīn 伤心 sad
shāng diàn mù lù 商店目录 store directory
shāng wù 商务 business
shāng wù cāng 商务舱 business class
shāng yè zhōng xīn 商业中心 business center
shàng bù 上部 upper
shàng wǔ 上午 a.m.
shāo 烧 *v* burn
sháo zǐ 勺子 spoon
shǎo xǔ 少许 little
shè bèi 设备 equipment
shè shì 摄氏 Celsius
shè yǐng 摄影 photography
shēn bào 申报 *v* declare
shēn shēn de 深深地 deeply
shén me 什么 what
shén me shí hòu 什么时候 when
shèn zàng 肾脏 kidney (body part)
shēng jiàng yǐ 升降椅 chair lift
shēng rì 生日 birthday
shī mián 失眠 insomnia
shī qù 失去 lost
shī wù zhāo lǐng chù 失物招领处 lost and found
shī yè zhě 失业者 unemployed
shí èr 十二 dozen
shí zì lù kǒu 十字路口 intersection
shí jiān 时间 time
shí jiān biǎo 时间表 schedule [timetable BE]
shí wù 食物 food
shǐ yòng 使用 *v* use
shì chǎng 市场 market
shì qū dì tú 市区地图 town map
shì zhèng tīng 市政厅 town hall
shì zhōng xīn 市中心 downtown
shì zhōng xīn guǎng chǎng 市中心广场 town square
shì hé 适合 fit (clothing)
shì gù 事故 accident
shì yī jiān 试衣间 fitting room
shì 是 yes
shì 是 *v* be
shì nèi yóu yǒng chí 室内游泳池 indoor pool
shì wài yóu yǒng chí 室外游泳池 outdoor pool
shōu fèi 收费 *n* charge (cost)
shōu jù 收据 receipt
shǒu 手 hand
shǒu biǎo 手表 watch
shǒu diàn 手电 flashlight
shǒu dòng qì chē 手动汽车 manual car
shǒu jī 手机 cell [mobile BE] phone
shǒu tí xiāng 手提箱 suitcase

shǒu tí xíng li 手提行李 carry-on [hand luggage BE]
shǒu tuī chē 手推车 cart (grocery store)
shǒu wàn 手腕 wrist
shǒu zhǐ 手指 finger
shǒu zhuó 手镯 bracelet
shǒu shì 首饰 jewelry
shòu piào chù 售票处 ticket office
shū 书 book
shū diàn 书店 bookstore
shū fǎ yòng pǐn 书法用品 calligraphy supplies
shū zi 梳子 comb, hairbrush
shú shí 熟食 delicatessen
shù 树 tree
shù mǎ 数码 digital
shù mǎ xiàng jī 数码相机 digital camera
shù mǎ xiàng piàn 数码相片 digital photos
shù zì 数字 number
shuāng chéng 双程 round-trip
shuāng rén chuáng 双人床 double bed
shuí/shéi who
shuǐ cáo 水槽 sink
shuǐ chí 水池 pool
shuǐ jīng 水晶 crystal
shuì dài 睡袋 sleeping bag
shuì jiào 睡觉 *v* sleep
shuì yī 睡衣 pajamas
shuì yì 睡意 drowsiness
shuō chàng yuè 说唱乐 rap (music)
sī chóu 丝绸 silk
sī jī jià zhào hào 司机驾照号 driver's license number
sì miào 寺庙 shrine, temple (religious)
sòng 送 *v* send
sù liào bāo zhuāng 塑料包装 plastic wrap [cling film BE]
sù shè 宿舍 dormitory
sù shí zhě 素食者 vegetarian
sù zuì 宿醉 hangover
sūn zi 孙子 grandchild
sǔn shāng 损伤 *v* damage
suǒ 锁 *n* lock

T

T xù shān T恤衫 T-shirt
tǎ 塔 tower
tái jiē 台阶 stairs
tài 太 too
tài yáng 太阳 sun
tài yáng jìng 太阳镜 sunglasses
tài nuò 泰诺 acetaminophen [paracetamol BE]
tǎn zi 毯子 blanket
tàn bìng shí jiān 探病时间 visiting hours
táng guǒ 糖果 candy
táng niào bìng 糖尿病 diabetic
táo qì 陶器 pottery
tè dà hào 特大号 extra large
téng 疼 hurt, pain
tí bāo 提包 purse [handbag BE]
tǐ cāo 体操 gym
tǐ yù 体育 sports
tǐ yù àn mó 体育按摩 sports massage
tǐ yù chǎng 体育场 stadium
tǐ yù yòng pǐn shāng diàn 体育用品商店 sporting goods store
tì xū dāo 剃须刀 razor blade
tì xū gāo 剃须膏 shaving cream
tiān 天 day
tiān qì 天气 weather
tián 甜 sweet (taste)
tián diǎn 甜点 candy [sweets BE]
tián chōng wù 填充物 filling (tooth)
tián xiě 填写 fill out (form)
tiáo 条 carton
tiáo zhou 笤帚 broom
tiào wǔ 跳舞 *v* dance
tiě guǐ 铁轨 track (train)
tīng lì zhàng ài 听力障碍 hearing impaired
tíng chē 停车 *v* park
tíng chē chǎng 停车场 parking lot [car park BE]
tíng chē jì shí qì 停车计时器 parking meter
tōng zhī 通知 *v* notify
tóng 铜 copper
tóng shì 同事 colleague
tòng 痛 pain
tōu 偷 *v* steal
tōu qiè 偷窃 theft
tóu 头 head (body part)
tóu děng cāng 头等舱 first class
tóu fà 头发 hair
tóu hūn yǎn huā 头昏眼花 dizzy
tóu kuī 头盔 helmet
tóu téng 头疼 headache
tú hù 屠户 butcher
tú shū guǎn 图书馆 library
tuī jiàn 推荐 *v* recommend; ~ *n* recommendation
tuǐ 腿 leg
tuì chū 退出 log off, withdraw
tuì fáng 退房 check-out (hotel)
tuì xiū 退休 retired
tūn xià 吞下 *v* swallow
tuō chē 拖车 tow truck
tuō xié 拖鞋 slippers
tuō yùn 托运 *v* check (luggage)

V

V lǐng V领 V-neck

W

wà zi 袜子 sock
wài miàn 外面 outside
wài tào 外套 coat
wán 玩 *v* play
wán jù 玩具 toy
wán jù diàn 玩具店 toy store
wán jù wá wá 玩具娃娃 doll
wǎn 碗 bowl
wǎn cān 晚餐 dinner
wǎn diǎn 晚点 *v* delay
wǎn le 晚了 late (time)
wǎn shang 晚上 evening
wǎn shang hǎo 晚上好 good evening
wǎng bā 网吧 internet cafe
wǎng qiú 网球 tennis
wēi bō lú 微波炉 microwave
wēi xiǎn 危险 dangerous
wéi 为 for
wéi jīn 围巾 scarf
wéi shēng sù 维生素 vitamin
wèi shēng zhǐ 卫生纸 toilet paper
wèi 喂 *v* feed
wèi 胃 stomach
wèi téng 胃疼 stomachache
wēn nuǎn 温暖 *v* warm

(something)
wēn quán 温泉 hot spring, spa
wén zì 文字 *n* text (message)
wèn tí 问题 problem, question
wèn xùn chù 问讯处 information desk
wò pù chē 卧铺车 sleeper car
wú jiǔ jīng 无酒精 non-alcoholic
wú liáo de 无聊的 boring
wú rén kān guǎn 无人看管 unattended
wú wèi 无味 bland
wú xiàn hù lián wǎng 无线互联网 wireless internet
wú xiàn hù lián wǎng fú wù 无线互联网服务 wireless internet service
wǔ cān 午餐 lunch
wǔ dǎo jù lè bù 舞蹈俱乐部 dance club
wǔ jiān 午间 noon [midday BE]
wǔ yè 午夜 midnight
wù pǐn 物品 goods

X

xī bù 西部 west
xī chén qì 吸尘器 vacuum cleaner
xī fú tào zhuāng 西服套装 suit
xī gài 膝盖 knee
xī yān 吸烟 *v* smoke
xī yān qū 吸烟区 smoking (area)
xǐ dí jì 洗涤剂 detergent
xǐ huan 喜欢 *v* like
xǐ shǒu jiān 洗手间 restroom [toilet BE]
xǐ wǎn jī 洗碗机 dishwasher
xǐ wǎn yè 洗碗液 dishwashing liquid
xǐ yī diàn 洗衣店 laundromat [launderette BE]
xǐ yī diàn shè shī 洗衣店设施 laundry facility
xǐ yī fú wù 洗衣服务 laundry service
xǐ yī jī 洗衣机 washing machine
xì jù 戏剧 *n* play (theatre)
xiá gǔ 峡谷 canyon
xiá gǔ 峡谷 ravine
xià 下 *v* place (a bet)
xià chē 下车 get off (a train/bus/subway)
xià hé 下颌 jaw
xià shuǐ dào shū tōng qì 下水道疏通器 plunger
xià wǔ 下午 afternoon
xià wǔ 下午 p.m.
xià wǔ hǎo 下午好 good afternoon
xià yí gè 下一个 next
xiàn 线 line (train)
xiàn chǎng yīn yuè 现场音乐 live music
xiǎn shì 显示 display
xiǎn shì 显示 *v* show
xiàn jīn 现金 *n* cash
xiàn zài 现在 now
xiāng bō 香波 shampoo
xiāng fǎn 相反 opposite
xiāng shuǐ 香水 perfume
xiāng yān 香烟 cigarette
xiāng zi 箱子 box
xiǎng yòng 享用 *v* enjoy
xiàng liàn 项链 necklace
xiàng pí nǎi zuǐ 橡皮奶嘴 pacifier [soother BE]
xiàng piàn 相片 photo
xiāo dú yào gāo 消毒药膏 antiseptic cream
xiāo fáng duì 消防队 fire department
xiāo shòu shuì 销售税 sales tax
xiǎo 小 small
xiǎo cān guǎn 小餐馆 cafe
xiǎo chǎn zi 小铲子 spatula
xiǎo chī diàn 小吃店 snack bar
xiǎo chuán 小船 boat
xiǎo dào 小道 trail [piste BE]
xiǎo dào lù xiàn tú 小道路线图 trail [piste BE] map
xiǎo jiǔ bā 小酒吧 mini-bar
xiǎo shān 小山 hill
xiǎo shí 小时 hour
xiǎo tōu 小偷 thief
xiǎo xī 小溪 stream
xiǎo xíng kè chē 小型客车 station wagon
xiǎo zǔ 小组 group
xié dài 鞋带 lace
xié diàn 鞋店 shoe store
xié zi 鞋子 shoes
xié wén cū mián bù 斜纹粗棉布 denim
xiě 写 *v* write
xiè xiè 谢谢 thank you
xīn zàng 心脏 heart
xīn zàng bìng 心脏病 heart condition
xīn xiān 新鲜 fresh
xìn fēng 信封 envelope
xìn jiàn 信件 letter
xìn xī 信息 information (phone); ~ 信息 message
xìn yòng kǎ 信用卡 credit card
xīng qī 星期 week
xíng rén 行人 pedestrian
xíng li 行李 luggage [baggage BE]
xíng li piào 行李票 luggage ticket
xíng li rèn lǐng 行李认领 baggage claim
xíng li tuī chē 行李推车 cart (luggage)
xíng li zàn cún xiāng 行李暂存箱 luggage locker
xìng chuán bō jí bìng 性传播疾病 sexually transmitted disease (STD)
xiōng dì 兄弟 brother
xiōng kǒu 胸口 chest (body part)
xiōng kǒu tòng 胸口痛 chest pain
xiōng zhào 胸罩 bra
xiū dào yuàn 修道院 abbey, monastery
xiū jià 休假 vacation
xiū jiǎo zhī jia 修脚趾甲 pedicure
xiū lǐ 修理 *v* fix (repair), mend
xiū shǒu zhīī jia 修手指甲 manicure
xū hòu shuǐ 须后水 aftershave
xū yào 需要 *v* need
xuē zi 靴子 boots
xué shēng 学生 student
xué xí 学习 study
xué xiào 学校 school
xuě jiā 雪茄 cigar
xuě xuē 雪靴 snowshoe
xuè yā 血压 blood pressure
xuè yè 血液 blood

xún huán 环 cycling

Y

yá 牙 tooth
yá gāo 牙膏 toothpaste
yá yī 牙医 dentist
yà má bù 亚麻布 linen
yà zhōu 亚洲 Asian (restaurant)
yān cǎo líng shòu shāng 烟草零售商 tobacconist
yán sè 颜色 color
yán sù 严肃 serious
yán tǎo huì 研讨会 seminar
yǎn jīng 眼睛 eye
yǎn jìng 眼镜 glasses
yàn guāng shī 验光师 optician
yáng máo 羊毛 wool
yǎng qì zhì liáo 氧气治疗 oxygen treatment
yáo lán 摇篮 crib
yào 药 medication
yào fáng 药房 pharmacy [chemist BE]
yào gāo 药膏 cream (ointment)
yào sài 要塞 fort
yào shi 钥匙 key
yào shi kǎ 钥匙卡 key card
yào shi quān 钥匙圈 key ring
yào xǐ de yī wù 要洗的衣物 laundry
yě cān qū 野餐区 picnic area
yè 夜 night
yè zǒng huì 夜总会 nightclub
yī lóu 一楼 ground floor
yī wù 衣物 clothing
yī wù guì 衣物柜 locker
yī shēng 医生 doctor
yī yào 医药 medicine
yī yuàn 医院 hospital
yí cì 一次 once
yí cì xìng 一次性 disposable
yí cì xìng tì dāo 一次性剃刀 disposable razor
yí dǎo sù 胰岛素 insulin
yí dòng diàn huà 移动电话 cell [mobile BE] phone
yǐ hòu 以后 after, later
yǐ qián 以前 before
yǐ zi 椅子 chair
yì shù 艺术 arts
yì tiān 一天 one day
yīn yuè 音乐 music
yīn yuè huì 音乐会 concert
yīn yuè shāng diàn 音乐商店 music store
yīn yuè tīng 音乐厅 concert hall
yīn dào 阴道 vagina
yīn dào chuán rǎn 阴道传染 vaginal infection
yīn jìng 阴茎 penis
yín 银 silver
yín háng 银行 bank
yǐn liào 饮料 *n* drink
yǐn liào dān 饮料单 drink menu
yǐn yòng shuǐ 饮用水 drinking water
yǐn xíng yǎn jìng 隐形眼镜 contact lens
yǐn xíng yǎn jìng yè 隐形眼镜液 contact lens solution
yīng bàng 英镑 pounds (British sterling)
yīng guó 英国 United Kingdom (U.K.)
yīng guó rén 英国人 British
yīng yǔ 英语 English
yīng ér 婴儿 baby
yīng ér chē 婴儿车 stroller [pushchair BE]
yīng ér zhǐ jīn 婴儿纸巾 baby wipe
yíng yè shí jiān 营业时间 business hours
yìng bì 硬币 coin
yōng bào 拥抱 *v* hug
yòng hù míng 用户名 username
yòng jìn 用尽 exhausted
yòng xìn yòng kǎ fù kuǎn 用信用卡付款 *v* charge (credit card)
yóu 油 oil
yóu jì 邮寄 *v* mail
yóu jiàn 邮件 *n* mail [post BE]
yóu jú 邮局 post office
yóu piào 邮票 *n* stamp (postage)
yóu xiāng 邮箱 mailbox [postbox BE]
yóu tài jiào táng 犹太教堂 synagogue
yóu lǎn 游览 excursion, tour
yóu lǎn shèng dì 游览胜地 attraction (place)
yóu lè yuán 游乐园 amusement park
yóu rén 游人 tourist
yóu xì 游戏 game
yóu xì wéi lán 游戏围栏 playpen
yóu yǒng 游泳 *v* swim
yóu yǒng yī 游泳衣 swimsuit
yǒu kōng fáng 有空房 vacancy
yǒu 有 have
yǒu qù 有趣 interesting
yǒu xī yǐn lì de 有吸引力的 attractive
yú kuài 愉快 happy
yú lè 娱乐 entertainment
yǔ 雨 *n* rain
yǔ lín 雨林 rainforest
yǔ yī 雨衣 raincoat
yù bào 预报 forecast
yù dìng 预定 *v* reserve ; ~ *n* reservation
yù dìng rì chéng 预定日程 *v* schedule
yù zhī xiàn jīn 预支现金 cash
yù shì 浴室 bathroom [toilet BE]
yuán 元 yuan (currency)
yuán liàng 谅 *v* excuse
yuǎn 远 far
yuàn yán 怨言 complaint
yuē huì 约会 appointment
yuè 月 month
yuè jīng 月经 period (menstrual)
yuè jīng shuān 月经栓 tampon
yuè duì 乐队 orchestra
yūn dòng bìng 晕动病 motion sickness
yūn dòng bìng 晕动病 travel sickness
yǔn xǔ 允许 *v* allow, permit
yùn dòng chǎng 运动场 field (sports)
yùn dòng xié 运动鞋 sneaker
yùn sòng 运送 *v* ship (mail)
yùn 熨 *v* press (clothing)
yùn dǒu 熨斗 *n* iron
yùn yī fu 熨衣服 *v* iron

Z

zá huò diàn 杂货店 grocery store
zá zhì 杂志 magazine

zài 在 in; on; at
zài guǎi jiǎo chù 在拐角处 on the corner
zài jiàn 再见 goodbye
zǎo 早 early
zǎo cān 早餐 breakfast
zǎo chén 早晨 morning
zǎo chen hǎo 早晨好 good morning
zěn me 怎么 how
zhá 闸 brakes (car)
zhàn 站 station, stop
zhàn chǎng 战场 battleground
zhàn tái 站台 platform
zhàn zhēng jì niàn guǎn 战争纪念馆 war memorial
zhàng fu 丈夫 husband
zhàng dān 账单 *n* bill (of sale)
zhàng hù 账户 *n* account
zhàng péng 帐篷 tent
zhàng péng gān 帐篷杆 tent pole
zhàng péng zhuāng 帐篷桩 tent peg
zhāo dài huì 招待会 reception
zhào xiàng jī 照相机 camera
zhào xiàng jī tào 照相机套 camera case
zhào xiàng qì cái shāng diàn 照相器材商店 camera store
zhē 蜇 *v* sting
zhé kòu 折扣 discount
zhè 这 this
zhè lǐ 这里 here
zhēn jiǔ 针灸 acupuncture
zhēn zhū 珍珠 pearl
zhēn zhèng 真正 real
zhěn tóu 枕头 pillow
zhèn 镇 town
zhèn jīng 震惊 stunning
zhēng guō 蒸锅 steamer
zhēng qì yù 蒸汽浴 sauna
zhèng jiàn 证件 identification
zhèng míng 证明 certificate
zhèng shí 证实 *v* confirm
zhèng zhuàng 症状 condition (medical)
zhī fù 支付 *v* pay
zhī piào 支票 *n* check [cheque BE] (payment)
zhī piào zhàng hù 支票账户 checking [current BE] account
zhí 直 straight
zhí wù yuán 植物园 botanical garden
zhǐ hàn lù 止汗露 deodorant
zhǐ 只 only
zhǐ 纸 paper
zhǐ bì 纸币 *n* bill [note BE] (money)
zhǐ jīn 纸巾 paper towel
zhī jia 指甲 fingernail
zhīī jia cuò 指甲锉 nail file
zhǐ nán 指南 *n* guide
zhǐ nán shū 指南书 guide book
zhǐ jiǎ 趾甲 toenail
zhì liàng 质量 quality
zhōng děng 中等 medium (size)
zhōng guó 中国 China
zhōng guó huà 中国 Chinese painting
zhōng wén 中文 Chinese
zhōng wǔ 中午 noon
zhǒng zhàng 肿胀 swelling
zhòng shǔ 中暑 sunstroke
zhōu mò 周末 weekend
zhǔ cài 主菜 main course
zhù sù 住宿 accommodation
zhù shǒu 住手 *v* stop
zhǔ yào jǐng diǎn 主要景点 main attraction
zhù zài 住在 *v* stay
zhuān jiā 专家 specialist (doctor)
zhuǎn 转 *v* transfer (change trains/flights)
zhuǎn jī 转机 connection (flight)
zhuǎn zhàng 转账 *v* transfer (money)
zhuàng guān 壮观 magnificent
zhuàng 撞 *v* crash (car)
zhǔn bèi hǎo 准备好 ready
zhuō zi 桌子 table
zhuó zhuāng yāo qiú 着装要求 dress code
zǐ sè 紫色 purple
zì dòng 自动 automatic
zì dòng fú tī 自动扶梯 escalator
zì dòng qì chē 自动汽车 automatic car
zì dòng qǔ kuǎn jī 自动取款机 ATM
zì rán bǎo hù qū 自然保护区 nature preserve
zì xíng chē 自行车 bicycle
zì xíng chē lù xiàn 自行车路线 bike route
zì zhù 自助 self-service
zǒu 走 *v* walk
zū 租 *v* rent
zū chē 租车 car rental [hire BE]
zū yòng qì chē 租用汽车 rental [hire BE] car
zú qiú sài 足球赛 soccer [football BE]
zǔ fù/mǔ 祖父/母 grandparent
zuàn shí 钻石 diamond
zuǐ 嘴 mouth
zuǐ chún 嘴唇 lip
zuì hǎo 最好 best
zuì hòu 最后 last
zuó tiān 昨天 yesterday
zuǒ bian 左边 left (direction)
zuò xià 坐下 *v* sit

INDEX

Ancient Lute Terrace, Wuhan 145
Ancient Observatory, Beijing 61
Aquarium, Beijing 62
Astana Cemetery 197

Badaling (Great Wall) 67
Bamboo Temple, Kunming 182
Banpo 106
Beihai Park, Beijing 58, 63
Beijing 15, 34, 35, 49
Bell Tower Xi'an 103
Big Bell Temple, Beijing 61
Big Wild Goose Pagoda 106
Black Horse Mountain, Xi'an 109
Bright Summit, Huangshan 141
Bund, Shanghai 115

Catch-Cloud Pavilion, Guilin 164
Chairman Mao Zedong Memorial Hall, Beijing 54
Changsha 154
Chen Family Temple, Guangzhou 151
Chengde 71
Chengdu 170
China Central Television Headquarters, Beijing 53
China National Grand Theatre 54
China National Grand Theatre, Beijing 53
China National Silk Museum, Hangzhou 134
Chongqing 175
Confucius 26, 61, 90
Crescent Moon Lake 193
Crouching Tiger Temple 174

Dai Temple Taishan 88
Dali 184
Dalian 74
Daoli Old Town, Harbin 77
Dark Green Temple, Leshan 174
Datong 83
Daxu 167
Dazu Caves 180
Diecaishan, Guilin 164
District of the Two Lakes, Guilin 165
Divine Light Monastery, Chengdu 171
Dongyuemiao, Xi'an 104
Dragon Gate Village 166
Dragon Pavilion Park, Kaifeng 95
Dragon Well, Hangzhou 134
Drum Tower, Beijing 63, 138
Drum Tower, Nanjing 137
Dunhuang 191

Eastern Qing Tombs 70
East Lake, Wuhan 144
Emin Minaret, Turpan 196
Erdaoqiao Bazaar, Urumqi 199
Erquan Spring, Wuxi 130

Fenghuang 157
Five Pagoda Temple, Beijing 61
Five Springs Hill Park, Lanzhou 190
Flaming Mountains, Turpan 197
Flower Pagoda, Guangzhou 151
Forbidden City, Beijing 55
Forest of Lions Garden 125
Forest of Steles Museum, Xi'an 105
Fuzhou 161

Gansu Provincial Museum 190
Gaochang 197
Gaoling, Jingdezhen 158
Garden of the Master of the Nets 126
Gate of Heavenly Peace, Beijing 55
Gegentala, Hohhot 81
Genghis Khan Mausoleum 82
Giant Panda Breeding Research Base, Chengdu 170
Grand Canal 29, 124, 127, 129, 132
Grand Theatre, Shanghai 122
Grand View Park, Kunming 182
Grand Xiangguo Monastery, Kaifeng 95
Great Buddha, Leshan 174

Great Hall of the People, Beijing 54
Great Mosque, Hohhot 80
Great Mosque, Xi'an 103
Great Wall 28, 34, 67, 71
Guangzhou 145
Guangzhou Museum 149
Guilin 161
Gui Yuan Temple, Wuhan 144
Guizhou province 169
Gulangyu, Xiamen 160

Haikou, Hainan 154
Hainan Island 153
Hall of Great Harmony, Beijing 57
Hall of Middle Harmony, Beijing 57
Hall of Prayer for Good Harvest Beijing 59
Hall of Ten Thousand Flowers, Shanghai 117
Hangzhou 131
Hangzhou Silk Printing and Dyeing Complex 134
Harbin 75
Heavenly Capital Peak, Huangshan 141
Heavenly Lake, Urumqi 200
Hebei Provincial Museum, Shijiazhuang 85
Henan Provincial Museum, Zhengzhou 96
Hohhot 79
Huaisheng Mosque, Guangzhou 151
Huangguoshu Falls 169
Huangshan 140
Huaqing Hot Springs, Xi'an 108
Huayan Monastery, Datong 84
Hubei Provincial Museum 144
Huli Mountain, Xiamen 159
Humble Administrator's Garden, Suzhou 124
Hunan Provincial Museum 155
Huxinting Teahouse, Shanghai 117

Imperial Flower Garden, Beijing 58
Imperial Way, Kaifeng 95
Inner Mongolia Museum, Hohhot 80
Iron Pagoda, Kaifeng 94

Jade Buddha Temple, Shanghai 121
Jiaohe 196
Jiayuguan, Gansu Province 194
Jichang Garden, Wuxi 129
Jinan 87
Jinci, Taiyuan 86
Jingdezhen 158
Jingshan Park, Beijing 58
Jin Mao Tower, Shanghai 121

Kaifeng 94
Kashgar 201
Kunming 180

Labrang Monastery, Lanzhou 190
Lake Dian, Kunming 182
Lake Tai, Wuxi 130
Lama Temple, Beijing 61
Lama Temple, Xi'an 104
Lanzhou 189
Laoshan, Qingdao 93
Laoshan,Qingdao 225
Leshan 173
Lhasa, Tibet 202
LGBTQ travellers 240
Li Garden, Wuxi 129
Lijiang 186
Lingering Garden, Suzhou 125
Lingshan Dafo, Lake Tai 131
Lingyin Temple, Hangzhou 133
Li River 164, 166
Liulichang, Beijing 65
Longhua Temple, Shanghai 122
Longmen Caves, Luoyang 97
Loquat Hill, Chongqing 178
Lotus Flower Peak, Huangshan 141
Loyalty to Country Temple, Leshan 174
Luohan Temple, Chongqing 177
Luoyang 97
Lushan Temple, Changsha 155

Maijishan Caves, Lanzhou 191
Marble Boat, Beijing 66
Mausoleum of Dr Sun Yat-sen, Nanjing 139
Meiling Palace, Nanjing 140
Meridian Gate 55
Ming Tombs 69
Mogao Caves, Dunhuang 192
Moon Hill, Yangshuo 169
Mt Emei, Leshan 173, 174
Mt Lushan National Park 158

Mt Sumeru Longevity and Happiness Temple, Chengde 73
Museum of Chinese History, Beijing 55
Museum of Suzhou Embroidery, Suzhou 127
Museum of the Chinese Revolution, Beijing 55
Mutianyu (Great Wall) 68

Nancheng Ancient Mosque, Kunming 182
Nanjing 34, 135
Nanputuo Temple, Xiamen 159
Nanyue Museum, Guangzhou 150
National Aquatics Centre, Beijing 66
National Museum of China 55
National Stadium, Beijing 53
National Stadium, Beijing, 66
Naxia Dongbei Cultural Museum, Lijiang 186
Nine Dragon Wall, Datong 83
Ningbo 135

Ohel Moshe Synagogue, Shanghai 115
Old Summer Palace, Beijing 66
Olympics 2008, Beijing 46, 53, 66
Orange Island, Changsha 154
Orient Pearl Tower, Shanghai 121

Palace of Harmony and Peace, Beijing 60
Panjiayuan, Beijing 65
Panmen Gate, Suzhou 127
Pavilion of Ten Thousand Springs, Beijing 58
Peace Hotel, Shanghai 115
Pearl River, Guangzhou 147
People's Park, Shanghai 116
Pingyao 86
Potala Palace, Lhasa 202
Prince Gong's Palace, Beijing 63
Pudong, Shanghai 120
Puning Temple, Chengde 74
Purity and Truth Synagogue, Kaifeng 96
Puxian Pagoda, Guilin 164

Qianhai Pier, Qingdao 92
Qianling Tombs, Xi'an 109
Qingdao 91
Qingming Park 95
Qingping, Guangzhou 152
Qingyanggong, Chengdu 171
Qufu 26, 90

Reed Flute Cave, Guilin 165
Refuse Pit Prison, Chongqing 178
Resonant Sand Gorge, Hohhot 82

Sacred Way (Ming Tombs) 69
Sacred Way (Purple Hills) 140
Santa Sophia Church, Harbin 77
Seven Star Cave, Guilin 166
Shaanxi History Museum, Xi'an 105
Shamian Island, Guangzhou 151
Shanghai 110
Shanghai Centre Theatre 121
Shanghai Museum 116
Shanghai Museum of Arts and Crafts 119
Shanghai World Financial Center 121
Shangri-la 187
Shanhaiguan 71
Shanhua Monastery, Datong 84
Shaolin Monastery 97
Shaoshan 156
Shaoxing 225
Shaping, Dali 185
Shenyang 75
Shenzhen 152
Shijiazhuang 85
Shuzhuang, Xiamen 160
Siberian Tiger Park, Harbin 77
Sichuan Opera 172
Simatai (Great Wall) 68
Small Potala Temple, Chengde 74
Songhua River, Harbin 77
Songqingling Guju, Beijing 63
Songshan Mountains 100
Southern Heng Mountain 156
Stalin Park 77
Stone Forest, Yunnan 183
Summer Palace 66
Sun Island, Harbin 77
Sun Yat-sen Memorial

Hall, Guangzhou 151
Suzhou 123
Suzhou History Museum 127
Taishan 88
Taiyuan 86
Temple of Bliss, Harbin 77
Temple of Confucius and Imperial Academy, Beijing 61
Temple of Heaven Park, Beijing 59
Temple of Marquis Wu, Chengdu 170
Temple of Mystery, Suzhou 127
Temple of the Eight Immortals, Xi'an 104
Temple of the Six Banyan Trees, Guangzhou 151
Temple of the Three Pagodas, Dali 185
Temple of the White Pagoda, Beijing 61
Temple Suspended over the Void, Datong 84
Temple to the Town Gods, Shanghai 118
terracotta warriors, Xi'an, 106
Thousand Buddha Temple and Caves, Lanzhou 190
Three Gorges 176, 179
Three Hills Island, Wuxi 130
Tiananmen Square 44, 52
Tianjin 71
Tiger Hill, Suzhou 127
Tiger Leaping Gorge, Lijiang 187
Tomb of Princess Zhaojun, Hohhot 80
Turtle Head Island, Wuxi 130

Urumqi 198

Wangfujing, Beijing 64
Wenshu Temple, Chengdu 171
West Garden 126
West Lake, Hangzhou 131, 132
White Clouds Daoist Temple, Beijing 61
White Dagoba, Beijing 59
White Horse Temple, Luoyang 97
White Pagoda Hill Park, Lanzhou 190
Wolong Nature Reserve 173
Wolongsi, Xi'an 104
Wudang Lama Temple, Hohhot 82
Wuhan 142
Wuxi 127

Xiamen 158
Xi'an 25, 100, 225
Xiangguo Monastery, Kaifeng 95
Xiaqinggong, Laoshan 93
Xilamuren, Hohhot 81
Xiletuzhao Temple, Hohhot 80
Xinhua Square, Hohhot 79
Xinjiang Museum, Urumqi 199
Xintiandi, Shanghai 119
Xishuangbanna 188

Yan'an 110
Yangshuo, Li River 168
Yangzi River Bridge, Nanjing 136
Yangzi River Bridge, Wuhan 142
Yangzi River cruise 179
Yantai 93, 225
Yellow Crane Tower, Wuhan 145
Yuelu Hill, Changsha 154
Yuexiu Park, Guangzhou 149
Yungang Caves, Datong 84
Yunnan Nationalities Village, Kunming 182
Yunnan Provincial Museum, Kunming 181
Yuyuan Garden, Shanghai 116

Zhangjiajie (Wulingyuan), Hunan 156
Zhejiang Provincial Museum, Hangzhou 133
Zhengzhou 96
Zhoukoudian, Beijing 50
Zoo, Beijing 61

Berlitz pocket guide

CHINA

Tenth Edition 2019

Editor: Aimee White
Author: Ken Bernstein
Head of Production: Rebeka Davies
Managing Editor: Carine Tracanelli
Picture Editor: Tom Smyth
Cartography Update: Carte
Update Production: Apa Digital
Photography Credits: Alex Havret/Apa Publications 31, 156; AWL Images 90, 192; Brice Minnigh/Apa Publications 4MC, 883, 85, 87, 97, 98, 100, 101, 104, 107, 108, 143, 144, 154, 176, 190; David Henley/Apa Publications 15, 155, 159, 163, 164, 165, 167, 169, 170, 173, 175, 179, 181, 183, 184, 187; David Shen-Kai/Apa Publications 5M, 13, 20, 25, 124, 129, 133, 134, 139, 207, 213; Fotolia 130; Getty Images 4TL, 5MC, 10, 18, 32, 34, 44, 48, 71, 72, 89, 93, 150, 161, 188, 201; iStock 1, 4ML, 5TC, 5MC, 5M, 6L, 6R, 7R, 16, 27, 58, 62, 69, 76, 141, 149, 195, 197, 199, 202, 204; Lee Hin Mun/Apa Publications 4TC, 68, 208, 223, 225; Ming Tang-Evans/Apa Publications 38, 41, 51, 60, 64, 65, 66, 210, 211, 218; Nowitz Photography/Apa Publications 43, 70; Public domain 37; Pubuhan 148; Ryan Pyle/Apa Publications 23, 111, 114, 117, 119, 120, 122, 219, 221; Shutterstock 5T, 7L, 52, 54, 75, 79, 81, 86, 95, 112, 126, 137, 153, 215, 216, The Art Archive 28
Cover Picture: Getty Images

Distribution
UK, Ireland and Europe: Apa Publications (UK) Ltd; sales@insightguides.com
United States and Canada: Ingram Publisher Services; ips@ingramcontent.com
Australia and New Zealand: Woodslane; info@woodslane.com.au
Southeast Asia: Apa Publications (SN) Pte; singaporeoffice@insightguides.com
Hong Kong, Taiwan and China: Apa Publications (HK) Ltd; hongkongoffice@insightguides.com
Worldwide: Apa Publications (UK) Ltd; sales@insightguides.com

Special Sales, Content Licensing and CoPublishing
Insight Guides can be purchased in bulk quantities at discounted prices. We can create special editions, personalised jackets and corporate imprints tailored to your needs. sales@insightguides.com; www.insightguides.biz

Printed in China by CTPS

Contact us
Every effort has been made to provide accurate information in this publication, but changes are inevitable. The publisher cannot be responsible for any resulting loss, inconvenience or injury. We would appreciate it if readers would call our attention to any errors or outdated information. We also welcome your suggestions; please contact us at: berlitz@apaguide.co.uk www.insightguides.com/berlitz